CONCUBINES IN PUBLIC

Moving beyond familiar narratives of abolition, Xia Shi introduces the contentious public presence of concubines in Republican China. Drawing on a rich variety of historical sources, Shi highlights the shifting social and educational backgrounds of concubines, showing how some served as public companions of elite men in China and on the international stage from the late nineteenth to the mid twentieth century. Shi also demonstrates how concubines' membership in progressive women's institutions was fiercely contested by China's early feminists, keen to liberate women from oppression, but uneasy about associating with women with such degraded social status. Bringing the largely forgotten stories of these women's lives to light, Shi argues for recognition of the pioneering roles concubines played as social wives and their impact on the development of gender politics and on the changing relationship between the domestic and the public for women during a transformative period of modern Chinese history.

Xia Shi is Associate Professor of History and Marian Hoppin Chair of Asian Studies at New College of Florida.

CONCUBINES IN PUBLIC

The Rise of the Social Wife in Republican China

Xia Shi

Shaftesbury Road, Cambridge CB2 8EA, United Kingdom

One Liberty Plaza, 20th Floor, New York, NY 10006, USA

477 Williamstown Road, Port Melbourne, VIC 3207, Australia

314–321, 3rd Floor, Plot 3, Splendor Forum, Jasola District Centre, New Delhi – 110025, India

103 Penang Road, #05–06/07, Visioncrest Commercial, Singapore 238467

Cambridge University Press is part of Cambridge University Press & Assessment, a department of the University of Cambridge.

We share the University's mission to contribute to society through the pursuit of education, learning and research at the highest international levels of excellence.

www.cambridge.org
Information on this title: www.cambridge.org/9781009724296

DOI: 10.1017/9781009724319

© Xia Shi 2026

This publication is in copyright. Subject to statutory exception and to the provisions of relevant collective licensing agreements, no reproduction of any part may take place without the written permission of Cambridge University Press & Assessment.

When citing this work, please include a reference to the
DOI 10.1017/9781009724319

First published 2026

Cover Image: "Shirley T.C. Chow" (Chinese name: Zhou Shunqin, Zhou Ziqi's concubine), from Grace Gallatin Seton, *Chinese Lanterns* (New York: Dodd, Mead and Co., 1924), 208.

A catalogue record for this publication is available from the British Library

A Cataloging-in-Publication data record for this book is available from the Library of Congress

ISBN 978-1-009-72430-2 Hardback
ISBN 978-1-009-72429-6 Paperback

Cambridge University Press & Assessment has no responsibility for the persistence or accuracy of URLs for external or third-party internet websites referred to in this publication and does not guarantee that any content on such websites is, or will remain, accurate or appropriate.

For EU product safety concerns, contact us at Calle de José Abascal, 56, 1°, 28003 Madrid, Spain, or email eugpsr@cambridge.org

For Ruslan

Contents

Acknowledgments *page* ix

Introduction 1
1 The Emergence of the Social Wife in Late Qing Diplomacy..... 44
2 From Courtesan to Social Wife 70
3 From "Female Student" to Concubine 95
4 Excluding Concubines: The Politics of Virtue and
   Contamination 119
Epilogue 142

Notes 153
Glossary of Chinese Names and Terms 175
Works Cited 183
Index 205

Acknowledgments

The research and writing of this book coincided with a period when life had thrown its own surprises at me, with which I have been gradually learning to cope. Now that I look back, I am very grateful to those who helped me at various stages of this project. First, I'd like to thank the following funding sources for my research and writing: (1) The National Endowment for the Humanities Summer Stipend, which enabled me to make the most of my summer by working on this project; (2) the Fulbright US Scholar Research Grant to Taiwan (I'd like to thank Dr. Lien Lingling at Academia Sinica in Taipei for facilitating my affiliation as a visiting scholar; I'd also like to thank Dr. Sun Huimin for our stimulating conversations on various interesting topics); and (3) the Institute of International Education China–US Scholars Program Fellowship. Specifically, this fellowship drew funding from the Carnegie Corporation of New York, the Ford Foundation, the Harvard-Yenching Institute, the Henry Luce Foundation, and the Rockefeller Brothers Fund. During my fellowship in Shanghai, Professor Chen Yan of the History Department at Fudan University helped facilitate my affiliation as a visiting scholar. I thoroughly enjoyed our conversations about studying the history of Chinese women and gender. I would also like to express my sincere appreciation to Kenneth Pomeranz and Ann Waltner for taking the time to provide feedback on my grant proposals and writing letters in support of my applications. Ann Walthall, Ann Waltner, and David Rohrbacher also read early versions of the whole manuscript and offered helpful comments. Kate Merkel-Hess and Emily Baum generously shared tips on how to improve grant proposals.

I thank the fellow participants of the Henry Luce/American Council of Learned Societies (ACLS) Early Career Seminar for Postdoctoral

Fellows of the Luce/ACLS Program in China Studies for the feedback and brainstorming they provided. I also appreciate the helpful suggestions and comments from the participants and audience of a dozen or so conferences where I presented my research over the years. Dan Barish and David Schley read the draft chapters and gave encouraging feedback at the early stages. I am also very grateful to the anonymous reviewers of the book manuscript. Their comments and suggestions helped significantly improve the book.

Last but not least, I'd like to thank my friends and family who have been through life's challenges with me during the years I have been working on this book. Without their support, I would not have been able to do it. I'm glad I finally have a product in print to present to them.

An earlier version of Chapter 1 has appeared as: "The Gendered Politics of Socializing and the Emergence of the 'Public Wife' in Late Qing Diplomacy," *Research on Women in Modern Chinese History* 37 (June 2021): 139–94. Part of an earlier version of Chapter 2 has appeared as "Just Like a 'Modern' Wife? Concubines on the Public Stage in Early Republican China," *Social History* 43, no. 2 (February 2018): 211–33. I thank the publishers for allowing me to reproduce the materials.

Introduction

ON JANUARY 16, 1913, nearly a year after the founding of the Republic of China, *Shenbao* (*Shanghai News*), the era's most influential Chinese newspaper, reported an incident entitled: "A New Scandal among Women's Circles of Hubei Province." Yao Wenyu, a general secretary (*shuwu zhang*) at the newly established Hubei Women's School of Law and Politics (Hubei nüzi fazheng xuexiao), had been fired after "shamelessly" becoming the concubine of a wealthy man. A modern educated woman, active in the Women's Suffrage Alliance (Nüzi canzheng tongmenghui), Yao did not accept her dismissal without a fight. Instead, according to *Shenbao*, she gathered twenty to thirty "rogues," led them to the school, and proceeded to "make a scene" in what the reporter deemed a "barbaric" demonstration.

Yao put three questions to the school's president, who finally appeared after calling the police. First, why did another concubine, Li Benwei, retain her elevated public position at the school while Yao was dismissed? Was Li Benwei spared because she was the concubine of Li Yuanhong (1864–1928), Vice President of the Republic? Second, how could "distinguished men" who had concubines, thereby violating the principle of monogamy, continue to hold public office while women who became concubines were immediately fired? Finally, why should a concubine be looked down upon even though she was formally and properly "married"?[1] Yao's questions did not change the school president's mind; he believed she could no longer serve as a "role model" (*mofan*) for students. Later, the leaders of the Women's Suffrage Alliance, together with the school president, formally reported this personnel decision to the Ministry of Education.[2] By becoming a "backward" concubine, they

INTRODUCTION

suggested, Yao had compromised her moral worth and surrendered her right to act as a progressive "New Woman" in the public sphere.

This incident was one of many controversial instances involving the public presence of concubines during the Republican China period (1912–1949). Contrary to popular stereotypes of concubines as backward, unproductive, and parasitic women who remained at home, Yao's case represents the modern, educated, and progressive concubines who entered the public realm during this period. It also reveals the tensions created by some concubines' public activism and the divisions that arose within progressive women's organizations and institutions. In fact, many progressive women's organizations denied concubines' requests to become members, arguing that their presence would only tarnish the reputation of "good women" who were willing to work *on behalf of* concubines but not *with* them. The historiography of the concubine issue in Republican China has devoted most of its attention to the legal and social efforts of abolishing concubinage, largely overlooking the heterogeneous public experiences of the women themselves.

This book, therefore, examines the controversial presence of concubines in new public spaces and social functions in China during the late Qing and the Republican periods. Moving beyond familiar narratives about concubines' changing legal status, it investigates the overlooked public activities of some concubines and the tensions elicited when they stepped into the public realm during a period when protracted campaigns were carried out to legally and socially abolish concubinage. By showing that these women were far from being marginalized and outdated in Republican society, this book complicates the existing abolition-centered historiography and highlights innovations in the institution of concubinage, such as the changing social and educational backgrounds of concubines and their separate living arrangements in urban environments. It demonstrates how some concubines played pioneering roles as elite men's public companions in modern social occasions in China and on the international stage from the late nineteenth century to the mid twentieth century. Moreover, it shows issues around concubines being members of progressive women's institutions engendered contested gender politics. This study of concubines' public activities sheds new light on understudied important changes in this period, such as the emerging role of the modern "social wife," the new skills required of women in socialization and networking circles, and the conflicts within progressive women's groups and Chinese women's liberation movements.

AN OVERVIEW OF CONCUBINAGE IN CHINESE HISTORY

Historians of China have long noted important distinctions between principal wives and concubines, and Gail Hershatter has succinctly summarized the traditional logic behind choosing one or the other:

> Principal wives were usually acquired for a man by his family on the basis of matched backgrounds and with the aim of enhancing family assets and status, and a courtesan could not contribute much on any of these counts. Concubines, by contrast, were usually picked by the men themselves with an eye to sex, romantic attraction, and good conversation, as well as the production of male heirs.[3]

Laws in imperial China required that a man have only one wife (*qi*) at a time, but allowed him to have any number of concubines (*qie*).[4] The specific number of concubines was often connected to a man's rank and status, though this rule had gradually eroded by late imperial times, when it was no longer strictly enforced.[5] A concubine often had low-status origins (many were former courtesans, entertainers, maidservants, etc.), was purchased outright, and brought into the household with little formality.

Unlike Western historical narratives, in which concubines tend to evoke associations with sexuality and illegitimacy, the concubine in Chinese history primarily signaled status – both in relation to the man to whom she "belonged" and the main wife, to whom she was made to feel inferior. In every aspect of her domestic life, a concubine was supposed to remain subordinate to the principal wife. Even after the death of a man's principal wife, a concubine could not be elevated to the position of wife, though this restriction gradually lifted during the Ming dynasty (1368–1644). The children a concubine bore had to address the principal wife as their legal mother; that is, the principal wife exercised full legal parental rights, while the concubine was regarded merely as the birth mother. At different moments in China's history, as Kathryn Bernhart has pointed out, a concubine's motherhood and fidelity as a chaste widow could be rewarded with certain privileges and rights enjoyed by a main wife, such as varying degrees of control over property and succession.[6] From the Song dynasty (960–1279) to the Qing dynasty, as status boundaries loosened in the face of pervasive commercialization and increased social mobility, the concubine's legal status concurrently and gradually upgraded as well – from that of a maid and sexual servant to a minor wife.[7]

Jealousy was often the dominant emotion among the principal wife and the concubines, though a virtuous wife was expected not to display or to overcome such a disruptive and sometimes dangerous emotion. Jealousy was one of the seven grounds a man could divorce his wife during the imperial period.[8] Women were enjoined to welcome concubines their husbands took and moralizing tales abound about those who did not. A nonjealous wife could earn her husband's special respect if she took the initiative to bring concubines home for him to produce sons for the patrilineal family. However, in reality, a jealous main wife often punished the concubines at will, due to the authority she wielded in the household. This sometimes led to violence. Chinese texts recorded many instances of domestic violence perpetrated by women living in the same households serving the same husbands since the early imperial period.[9] However, wives' violence could be sanctioned if it emerged from the need to maintain the hierarchical order between wives and concubines instead of jealousy. Since the late imperial period, with the rise of the cult of *qing* (love, passion), wifely jealousy was celebrated as an expression of a deep, genuine emotion between the husband and the wife, but was criminalized when it threatened the production of male heirs for the patriarchal family.[10] In Chinese history and literature, many accounts recorded the dangers caused by jealous women living in polygynous households, warning against serious domestic disorder and the familial and social disruptions that jealousy could generate.[11]

The early Jesuits in Ming China were the first group of Western missionaries to insist that their elite Chinese converts adopt Western-modeled monogamous marriages. However, this clashed with the long-standing customs of the elite Chinese families. Seeing that their insistence was creating further obstacles to Chinese conversion, the Jesuits reluctantly made a compromise. Apart from the Western challenges, some Chinese intellectuals also voiced their opposition to concubinage. Critiques of polygamy existed before Western intrusion as early as the nineteenth century, according to Keith McMahon. However, the social and cultural impact of this critique was far weaker than the wave later initiated by Westerners.[12] The most prominent critique came from Yu Zhengxie (1775–1840) and Li Ruzhen (1763–1830) of the Qing dynasty. In an essay on the problem of a jealous wife against concubines, Yu emphasized the unfairness of concubinage. In his view, jealousy was not the fault of the wife but that of the husband who took the concubines. It is natural for the wife to be jealous in such circumstances unless she is indifferent, which destroys the way of the family.[13] Li expressed his view on concubinage in his novel *Flowers in the Mirror* (*Jinghua yuan*, completed in 1827) through the voice of the wife of a bandit chief, who beats her husband when he attempts to take a concubine. She scolds him for ignoring her feelings and questions whether he would be happy if she were to take a male concubine, which exposes the double standard of chastity.[14] Overall, the nature of the opposition is primarily focused on the gender inequality inherent in concubinage and the moral and social concerns caused by the internal strife within families due to jealousy and competition among wives and concubines, rather than whether it made China appear backward.

By the mid nineteenth century, as Qing China was defeated by Western powers and forced to open its borders to commercial trade, pressure to conform to Western models increased. Missionaries and other Westerners who came to China and witnessed this "evil" custom initiated a wave of critiques advocating for the replacement of concubinage by Western-style monogamy.[15] Facing a national crisis, reform-minded Chinese intellectuals during the late Qing dynasty, especially those with knowledge of the West, such as Wang Tao (1828–1897), Tan Sitong (1865–1898), and Liang Qichao (1873–1929), reflected critically on the harms caused by this traditional Chinese custom.[16] They spoke out about the unfair treatment of women and the domestic distrust incited by the existing system and praised Western nations' "superior" institution of monogamy. They began to take an anti-concubinage stance, even establishing a society to promote this principle. An increasing number of Chinese intellectuals, such as Cai Yuanpei (1868–1940), returned from their overseas studies ready to join the opposition to concubinage.[17]

Progressive overseas Chinese intellectuals during the last years of the Qing dynasty also criticized the Chinese custom of concubinage, often with more sensitivity. They were concerned about how concubinage could affect the public perceptions of overseas Chinese as backward and barbaric racial groups in the Western countries to which they immigrated. The sensitivity and sense of urgency on this issue among overseas Chinese communities could be seen from the fact that concubinage was singled out as the primary target of critique in the first novel written and published by a Chinese Australian around 1909–1910, titled *The Poison of Polygamy* (*Duo qi du*). Although the novel was set during the Australian Gold Rush era, its tone and themes reflected developments and events of the early twentieth century.[18] Its author, Wong Shee Ping (c. 1875–1948), immigrated from Guangdong Province to Melbourne as a young man and later became a progressive newspaper editor, political activist, and Christian preacher. He first published the novel in serial form in the *Chinese Times*, a pro-revolutionary newspaper he edited in Melbourne.[19] The novel tells the story of a Chinese man who immigrated from a village in Guangdong during the Qing dynasty in the 1850s to Australia during the Victorian gold rush. He left behind his wife, who endured much suffering and loneliness, eagerly waiting for him to come back one day. However, once his fortune turned in Australia, he quickly forgot his promises and acquired a beautiful concubine. The concubine turned out to be a seductive, unfaithful, and cunning villain and eventually poisoned his wife and strangled him.

The author claims that he aimed to recount the events truthfully "without resort to fictional means," except by making slight changes to names. He also clearly states in the opening of the book that "monogamy is the most perfect system," but China is "a country of polygamy," which often resulted in "the collapse of whole families." (Similarly, as early as 1904, another Chinese language newspaper in Australia, the *Tung Wah Times*, declare that monogamy was the norm for all modern civil societies and China could never modernize itself if it did not enforce the law of monogamy.[20]) Last but not least, the author expressed his hopes that the story can "hold a lens to society" and serve as "a clarion call" to "wake some from that sweet concubinary dream."[21] Since the novel was written in classical Chinese, the author's target audience was probably those literate Chinese who could afford concubines. Although it is likely only a very small number of Chinese male immigrants practiced concubinage, the author was concerned with the broader social impacts of this custom on perceptions of the overseas Chinese communities in white Australia. In these condemnations of concubinage, we can also sense the overseas Chinese's wish for a stronger China that could shed its traditional weaknesses, modernize itself, and protect overseas Chinese from being discriminated against. (In Chapter 2, we will see how this sensitivity on concubinage continued to play out among overseas Chinese students in 1920s America.)

As the iconoclastic New Culture Movement (circa 1915–1923) intensified its attacks on Chinese traditions, a growing number of Chinese social progressives believed that concubinage was the "shame" of a "degenerate" nation, reviled as a "barbaric" institution incompatible with modern civilization.[22] The detrimental impact of this custom was now believed to extend far beyond personal immorality; it was harmful to marriage, family, lineage, and race – the entirety of China. Progressive intellectuals and reformers argued that eliminating this oppressive practice was necessary to strengthen the nation and enable it to compete with Western powers on equal terms in health and confidence. Consequently, abolishing concubinage was incorporated into larger contemporary social reform agendas, such as the promotion of the conjugal nuclear family in place of the extended family, the shift from arranged to companionate marriage, and the call for women's liberation.[23]

Progressive intellectuals and social reformers identified at least three reasons for the continued prevalence of concubinage in the Republican era, beginning with the lingering "feudal" belief in the necessity of having male descendants to carry on family lines. As late as the 1930s, these voices were lamenting the continued widespread adherence to Mencius's teaching, which specified three unfilial acts, of which not having a male heir was the worst. Therefore, if a wife "failed" to produce male heirs, her husband was entitled to take concubines. Second, men who were unhappy in arranged marriages could not divorce for various reasons (from fear of challenging patriarchal authority to scorn levied out for leaving an arranged wife financially unsupported and socially stigmatized), so they resorted to taking concubines as a remedy.[24] The third reason for the custom's continued practice was believed to be economic: Certain wealthy men chose to show off their success and satisfy their "insatiable desires" by taking concubines. Meanwhile, some reformers acknowledged that "common" families also used concubines as an extra source of labor for domestic chores, which reminds us of the traditional function of concubines as maidservants.[25] Furthermore, some women from poor families had no alternative but to become the concubines of wealthy men in return for financial support.[26] Most reformers and progressive intellectuals seemed to believe that concubinage continued largely due to the initiatives of men, with women playing only passive roles.

Progressive reformers and public intellectuals were intensely critical of these three rationales. Some pointed out that the failure to produce children, or male heirs, was not necessarily due to women and that many men used this complaint as an excuse to take concubines. In addition, men were free to adopt children or choose not to have them.[27] As for unhappy, arranged marriages leading to concubinage, some conceded that this may have been a reasonable practice in earlier times. But by the 1930s, they argued, the ideal of free companionate marriages had been widespread for decades and a man who did not want an arranged marriage should resist it rather than acquire concubines to "sacrifice his wife and seek pleasure for himself." Divorce was now also a possible solution.[28] Finally, in addition to the government's legal ban on concubinage, social campaigns were needed to raise awareness of the institution's profound immorality, so that men who desired concubines would be persuaded by public opinion to do without.[29] Meanwhile, more women should be educated and – most importantly – should be encouraged to achieve economic independence. Some social reformers reasoned: "If she could make an independent living by herself, why would she be willing to become a concubine?"[30] These intellectuals and reformers now regarded taking concubines as "a major evil deed" regardless of the rationale.[31] However, as we will see, many of their proposed solutions were simplistic, failing to consider these long-standing arrangements in their full complexity.

The reality of concubines' economic and social vulnerability made any quick change to the system impossible. There were still many men with concubines who depended on them economically, not to mention the children born of these unions. The immediate expulsion of concubines from these households hardly seemed a responsible or feasible solution. During the entire Republican period, the question of how to discourage but not criminalize concubinage remained a central issue to Chinese lawmakers and court judges. At the same time, they sought ways to offer concubines certain protections, as Lisa Tran has pointed out.[32] In the early Republican period, the Daliyuan, the highest court until 1927, decided that China's laws must uphold the modern principle of monogamy. Unlike the Qing legal framework, the Daliyuan refused to acknowledge concubinage's semi-legitimate marriage status, establishing a regulation that concubinage could no longer be defined as a marriage of any kind. Since a concubine was legally no longer a wife, her relationship with her master should be interpreted as merely a contractual arrangement between a woman and a family head; as long as their contract remained valid, the concubine should be provided for as a member of the household, regardless of whether she resided with the master.[33]

After the Nationalist government established control over China in 1928, it made a further legal attempt to curtail concubinage by issuing a new civil code (1929–1930). In principle, the code continued to espouse monogamy and gender equality and refused to acknowledge concubinage as a form of marriage. However, it also continued to define concubines as household members, implicitly tolerating their existence and offering them certain legal protections. The newly adopted criteria for a concubine's household member status, as decided by the Supreme Court and Judicial Yuan, hinged on her residence in the household rather than the mere existence of her contract. To be provided for, in other words, she had to live in the same household with her master – a rule with ramifications for both the concubine and the household she entered.[34] Because concubinage was not defined as a marriage, men who practiced it could take any number of concubines without facing criminal liability or charges of bigamy. This regulation helps to explain the persistence and resilience of concubinage in Republican China. Eventually, several women's organizations successfully pushed Nationalist lawmakers to categorize concubinage as adultery in the regime's 1935 criminal code, which allowed a wife to divorce her husband for adultery if he took a concubine.[35] Still, a wife often stood to lose more than she could gain in a divorce, while her husband would then be free to marry his concubine. Lisa Tran notes that the civil code had many loopholes and was not evenly implemented across regions. Republican society continued to view the concubine as a minor wife and women continued to become concubines, though we lack statistics on their exact number.[36]

Communists took over China in 1949 and the central government issued a new Marriage Law in 1950, which defined concubinage not as adultery but unambiguously as bigamy. For a marriage to be considered legal, regional courts required couples to register with the government and receive an official marriage license. At the same time, the government conducted investigations to determine which living arrangements constituted de facto marriages, making concubinage easily identifiable as bigamy. This prompted many concubines to sever their relationships with their masters in the 1950s, paving the way for the abolition of concubinage as a social practice by the 1960s. Lisa Tran cautions us about the limits of what we can know from official documents, which were often tainted by political ideology and propaganda. Nonetheless, it is clear that the importance of concubinage in public discussion had largely faded by the 1960s.[37]

However, beyond the Communist-controlled mainland China, the legal abolition of concubinage in the jurisdictions where Chinese immigrants settled took much longer and involved more complicated processes. For example, in Hong Kong, concubinage was only outlawed in 1971, despite continuing efforts and frequent calls for its abolition. Under British colonial rule, the institution was protected under the category of "Chinese customary law" (together with other customary Chinese rules on marriage, succession, and divorce, all of which were largely based on the Great Qing Legal Code) until the demise of this legal category altogether in 1971. Similarly, Singapore only abolished concubinage in 1961, several years before its independence from the British. As for Taiwan, during its Japanese colonial era (1895–1945) concubinage was condemned but not legally prohibited. Therefore, its abolition only came after the end of the Japanese occupation and the adoption of the civil code from the Republic of China in 1945.[38] The late abolition of concubinage in these places was likely due to the colonial regimes' initial reluctance to actively interfere with Chinese customary practices. Therefore, they took a "hands-off" attitude to Chinese family matters – giving Chinese men the power they wanted inside their homes to soften the removal of their power outside the home. On the other hand, Chinese people living in places where they held the demographic advantage kept concubinage going, perhaps as an assertion of their right to Chinese culture in the face of colonial overlords, unlike those overseas Chinese living in Western countries (such as the US and Australia) whose status was marginal and under attack, hence they felt keenly the need to eradicate concubines from public spaces as soon as possible.

An important but limited body of work has focused on the concubine in Republican China. Most of this work examines the attempts by reformist movements and governments to stamp out concubinage, while acknowledging its persistence until the Communist takeover in 1949.[39] Scholarship on family reform discusses the New Culturalists' drive to replace the traditional joint family with the conjugal nuclear family – an ideal predicated upon companionate, monogamous marriage – as well as examining efforts by women's rights groups to liberate concubines from domestic oppression.[40] Other scholars have studied concubinage as a social custom and noted the rising domestic status of the concubine from the Qing to the Republican period.[41] These findings have significantly enriched our understanding of the concubine issue; however, they are mostly centered on the theme of abolition. As a result, the public activities of concubines have received little attention, especially during the Republican period, when domestic seclusion was no longer a marker of virtue and status and many women began to enter new public spaces. Consequently, we often overlook the broader significance of concubines' public presence and the important connections between the two realms that they occupied and frequently traversed.

Using well-documented case studies rather than compiling a comprehensive survey, this book investigates how elite men's concubines emerged in new public contexts and modern institutions in the Republican era. It draws our attention to the changing social and educational backgrounds of concubines and shows how some elite concubines became not less but *more* important as – and after – concubinage was outlawed, moving further into the public sphere and honing their social skills to become increasingly instrumental to elite society. These women exploited the emergence of a new role for Chinese women – what I call the modern "social wife" – at a historical juncture when main wives were either unwilling or uncomfortable playing that part themselves. In addition, the book highlights the tensions generated by the presence of concubines in new public spaces such as progressive women's organizations and modern public schools. Due to the increasing social stigmatization of the category of the concubine during the Republican period, concubines who were active in public experienced varying degrees of intolerance from women's groups that were preoccupied with the virtue of their members and thus determined to exclude concubines from membership. The politics of excluding concubines reveals divisions within progressive women's circles and liberation movements – divisions based on class hierarchies and sexual morality that threatened the much-needed unity among Chinese women necessary to fight the entrenched gender inequalities they all faced.

THE RISE OF MODERN SOCIAL WOMEN

One of the major historical developments that contributed to shaping the stories told in this book is the rise of modern social women in Republican China. By this, I refer to the increasing freedom that Chinese women exercised in attending public functions and social occasions, where they mingled and interacted with male strangers. In late imperial China, the dominant influence of Confucian gender norms, which emphasized domestic seclusion and gender separation, required women from "good families" to be sequestered at home, never to mingle or socialize with men beyond the confines of their immediate family. In reality, women sometimes traveled long distances or attended religious festivals, but they often did so in the name of fulfilling familial obligations, carefully avoiding inappropriate contact with male strangers to retain their virtuous reputations.[42]

By contrast, courtesans were frequently seen in public: Often taught poetry and music, they conversed with elite men, regularly entertained officials, and performed for private parties. During the late Qing, courtesans occupied an ever-expanding public space as they became the subjects of an emerging print and pictorial press, embodying the growing reading public's idea of sophisticated urbanity. They were trendsetters and trend-followers at the same time, dressing in the latest fashions and attending banquets at Western-style restaurants. Some even learned a smattering of foreign languages or received a little modern education.[43] These women played an important role in the lives of elite urban men, particularly the scholar class, serving as their social and sexual companions, a significant position that was documented in poems, guidebooks, and novelettes written by these men about courtesans and their culture.

The Republican period witnessed a general decline in courtesan culture. In his study of the rise of singing and dancing hostesses (courtesans' new competitors and substitutes) in Republican Shanghai, Andrew Field succinctly summarizes the factors that led to the decline in the popularity of courtesans. It is worth quoting him in full:

> The decline in popularity of courtesans rested on a number of interrelated historical changes that took place in urban China in the early twentieth century. These included the official abolition of the examination system in 1905, the slow but inexorable dismantling of its institutions, and the subsequent decline of the scholar class; the heavy commercialization of prostitution stimulated by a rising male-to-female ratio as the city industrialized; progressive government regulations and social attitudes countering the practice of prostitution and concubinage in the 1920s; the rise of a new commercial and political elite that followed Western trends; and the increased social freedom and mobility of urban women.[44]

Among these factors, the last three pertain directly to the rise of modern social women. Indeed, since the late Qing, prostitution and leisure activities had grown increasingly commercialized, while the courtesan was concomitantly sexualized rather than being valued chiefly for her performance or conversational skills.[45] Hence, the distinctions between a courtesan and a sex worker gradually blurred. Although prostitution was not legally banned in Republican China (mostly due to the significant tax revenues that brothels generated for the government),[46] it came under severe attack by progressive social groups, was regulated by governments, and was widely regarded as a "backward" custom, a site of moral danger, physical disease, and a marker of national decay.[47] Consequently, it became increasingly socially unacceptable for respectable men, especially government officials, to be seen frequenting brothels and associating with courtesans – though such a phenomenon never completely disappeared.

Contributing to the decline of courtesan culture, urban women were gaining social freedoms and mobility in the public sphere, further diminishing the need to hire courtesans for social occasions. As women's domestic seclusion came to be regarded as an outdated practice hindering China's modernization, social and cultural constraints began to relax and women from various backgrounds gradually stepped into the public realm. As Paul Bailey has pointed out, the decades immediately before and after the 1911 Revolution were marked by the "growing public visibility of women" as students, teachers, workers, consumers, revolutionaries, and activists, marking "one of the most striking social and cultural changes of the period."[48] Particularly in the wake of the New Culture Movement, which denounced gender segregation and women's seclusion for slowing social progress, urban China witnessed a dramatic rise in women's active engagements with the public sphere. However, controversies and viciousness abound during this period surrounding the public activities of "good women." Social conservatives criticized the fact that girl students and prostitutes were often indistinguishable on the streets when schools first opened to young women from good families.[49] Early radical Chinese suffragettes were frequently portrayed as violent, obscene, and unconstrained shrews in print media and failed to gain public sympathy.[50] Therefore, women who were brave enough to venture out to the public had to carefully ensure their virtue remained intact. Otherwise, they might be denied access to the various new public places they fought hard to participate in, be these public schools, sites of employment, or political arenas. This concern generated a strong sense of sensitivity among some progressive women about being seen mixing in public with the highly stigmatized concubine, as Chapter 4 shows.

Significant scholarship has focused on the so-called "new women," examining the activities, achievements, and controversies of their public presence.[51] However, the public activities of women from other backgrounds have received far less attention. I have examined elsewhere how married, nonprofessional women without modern education moved beyond their sequestered domestic lives by engaging in charitable, philanthropic, and religious activities, repositioning themselves as effective public actors in urban Chinese society during this period.[52] However, little scholarly attention has been paid to the concubines who also became more visible during this period. Did their public activities carry a similar symbolic weight to those of the new women? Were they equally welcomed in this new public realm? What were the contentions and controversies surrounding their public engagement in Republican China? This book answers these questions by examining not only the novel role of the modern social wife played by elite men's concubines, but also the tensions and divisions within progressive women's organizations and women's public schools in response to the concubines' presence. I focus on these two types of public engagements because they were the most noteworthy and can draw our attention to some important, understudied historical changes during this period.

During the Republican period, as gender separation ceased to be the social norm, Chinese women began mingling and socializing with male strangers they encountered in public spaces. How did Chinese women and men learn to socialize with one another outside the confines of their families? What were the special challenges and risks for women? What were the necessary skills involved and how was sociability gendered? Answering these questions is crucial to understanding the phenomenon of the rise of social women in modern China.

First and foremost, coeducation in public schools provided girls and young women with opportunities to gain substantial experience interacting with boys and men, without the supervision of their parents. In 1912, coeducation was introduced in primary schools for the first time in Chinese history, and by 1920 women were permitted to enroll in universities. During the May Fourth New Culture Movement, an effort centered on college campuses in major cities such as Beijing to encourage "free social intercourse between men and women" (*shejiao gongkai*) became both a hotly debated topic and a much-touted new slogan.[53] Despite social conservatives' disapproval, *shejiao gongkai* quickly became an electrifying social trend, especially among students. As they participated in patriotic and other mixed student organizations, they were able to practice interacting with both women and men, while enhancing their speech-making skills – an increasingly important component of public occasions in the Republican era.[54]

As more women attended social and public occasions with men, print media outlets began publishing short essays that introduced modern social etiquette (*shejiao lijie*) to urban readers, catering to the needs that proliferated from the 1920s onward. Largely borrowed from the West, these advice columns gave concrete tips for interacting with the other sex during public occasions.[55] Though some columns aimed to teach young men how to behave like gentlemen, more emphasis and urgency were given to how women should properly conduct themselves. In 1934, *Nüsheng* (*Women's Voice*), a journal based in Shanghai, published a special series of eight articles on social intercourse (*shejiao*) between men and women, discussing its importance for gender equality and women's liberation.[56] In 1937, *Jiating zhoukan* (*Family Weekly*), a reformist journal based in Tianjin, referred to social etiquette as "the essential general knowledge of modern family," and offered a detailed list of eleven social tips for women, such as: "When a man is speaking to you, you should be natural and poised. Do not behave bashfully, and do not bend your body."[57] Popular leisure magazines, such as *Linglong* – a leading weekly women's magazine based in Shanghai, devoted considerable space to the discussion of socializing with men in the 1930s, promoting open social interactions by presenting Chinese practices as "moderate" when compared to excessive American behavior.[58] Knowing how to skillfully interact with men in social and public settings had become an important marker of the modern woman in Republican China.

The rise of modern social women was closely tied to the rise of a new commercial and political elite in China that consciously followed Western trends. Marie-Claire Bergère has shown that the years between 1911 and 1937 were "the golden age of the Chinese bourgeoisie." Capitalizing on the uniquely advantageous economic circumstances created by the First World War, Chinese entrepreneurs invested energy and resources in building Western-style industry, commerce, and banking, gradually forming a specific and coherent social class in cosmopolitan cities like Shanghai, with its own ideology and style of political activism.[59] This new bourgeoisie business class eagerly consumed Western cultural customs and products.

A good example of how the new commercial and political elite followed Western trends in socialization was the rapid spread of social dancing in China. In the 1910s, social dancing was limited largely to upper-class officialdom for the purpose of entertaining Western guests or practiced by returned overseas students.[60] Even in the early 1920s, such dancing was still deemed an "exotic" practice. However, by the 1930s, urban elites had enthusiastically adopted it as a favorite pastime and Western-style social dancing soon swept through urban China. Dance halls emerged like "bamboo shoots after spring rain" in major cities from Shanghai, Beijing, and Tianjin to Guangzhou.[61] Dance schools and academies were hastily set up and classes were offered in colleges, universities, and beyond.[62] The special appeal that dancing held for college students is evident in two of the major conservative backlashes it elicited. In May 1930, Dean of the Women's School at Peking University, Liu Bannong (1891–1934), issued an official ban on female students frequenting "suspicious" dance halls, believing that close and constant body contact could harm morale and distract students from serious academic pursuits.[63] Shanghai also saw a ban on college students frequenting public dance halls, the start of a series of efforts by conservative officials during the New Life Movement of 1934–1937 to crack down on the "decadent" influence of dancing.[64] Both bans reveal not only official anxieties but also the evident popularity of dancing among college students seeking new forms of social interaction.

The emergence of the term "social butterfly" (*jiaoji hua*; literally, "flowers of social intercourse") captures the growing public attention given to women who were particularly well known for their social skills and their active involvement in the so-called "sphere of socialization" (*jiaoji chang*). These women were usually well educated, beautiful, graceful – especially on the dance floor – and skillful in social interactions, often the shining stars of high-society gatherings. The two most well-known *jiaoji hua* in the 1930s were Tang Ying (1910–1986), from southern China (Shanghai), and Lu Xiaoman (1903–1965), from the north (Beijing); both were subjects of frequent newspaper reports, not all of them positive.[65] At its height, in the 1930s and 1940s, the term *jiaoji hua* acquired a negative connotation; the women it described came to be seen, in print media, as decadent consumers – morally suspect and vain women who used their social and dancing skills to flirt and seduce men for their own gain. This image revealed not only the anxieties of social conservatives but also seems to have been a byproduct of leftist writers employing the trope of *jiaoji hua* to criticize the decadent lives of the bourgeoisie in metropoles like Shanghai and Tianjin. Leftist novels and plays often featured stories of innocent female students forced by circumstance to degenerate into deplorable *jiaoji hua*.[66] Such an image had much in common with the courtesans of late Qing and early Republican era.

Elite men, too, including military officials, sought new ways to socialize. On December 1, 1927, Chiang Kai-shek (1887–1975), the promising new national leader in the wake of the Northern Expedition, set a precedent by holding his highly publicized wedding ceremony with Song Meiling (1898–2003) in the *ballroom* of the Majestic Hotel in Shanghai, with thirteen hundred guests in attendance.[67] An article in *Shenbao* described the cultural moment this way: "As the European wind blew to the East and socialization became free and open, social dancing has nearly become an essential social skill."[68] The article continues with the example of Guo Songling (1883–1925), a major general of the Manchurian Fengtian clique. Seeing other military officials dancing in Tianjin made him eager to learn; he hired a female teacher and started practicing daily.[69] Meanwhile, some observers realized that the craze for social dancing could be used to promote public welfare and the charity ball became not only an important venue for socialization and networking but also an accepted and trendy fundraising format, organized frequently by elite women to collect donations for relief efforts such as aid for disasters and war.[70]

The rise of modern social women provided a conducive social and cultural environment for the novel role of the modern social wife. By "social wife," I refer to a role played by two types of Chinese women in social functions: a wife who appeared on social occasions beyond the confines of family or a concubine who appeared in social functions in the nominal role of wife. The cases I selected for this book primarily concern the concubines of government officials and military men, as there are far more sources available on their experiences and public reactions to them. As social wives, these concubines stepped into the spotlight, gained new privileges, and sometimes generated controversies. They also sought to improve their domestic status through their modernity and public recognition, though, as we will see, the role of the social wife had its limits.

Although the book focuses on concubines married to elite men on whom we have more available sources, it does not mean to suggest that women from non-elite backgrounds did not play the role of the social wife in Republican China. Elite women's public activities often drew wide public attention and controversy, as they were frequently reported in the press. Therefore, elite men's concubines' playing the role of the social wife had broader social consequences and importance because they often set the trend for concubines and wives of non-elite men to follow. As time passed, a growing number of concubines and wives of non-elite men assumed the role of the social wife, too, albeit less frequently and on less privileged and publicly visible urban platforms. The aforementioned proliferation of the publication of essays in print media introducing modern social etiquette to urban women on how to socialize with men suggests that since the 1920s, an ever-increasing number of them (married and unmarried women) had begun to attend various social occasions where male strangers were present, a phenomenon we rarely see in the imperial period. However, we need many more sources to understand this phenomenon on a larger scale. In addition to the major cases, I have provided evidence of other concubines and wives playing this role throughout the book, even though information about these women tends to be very fragmentary and sometimes does not even reveal their names.

In addition to officialdom, sources also suggest that some Chinese businessmen seem to have gradually realized the appeal of a social wife for public occasions, as Westerners with whom they regularly interacted frequently brought their own wives to such occasions. Before the Qing Empire was defeated by the British in the First Opium War (1839–1842), the Qing government stipulated that Western traders leave their Western female companions and children in the enclave of Macao, while the Western husbands conducted business in Canton. This regulation was due less to the inherent cultural differences in gender norms but more to discourage foreign merchants from settling in China, according to historian Rachel Tamar Van.[71] However, this policy frequently caused marital tension and anxiety for the couples who lived apart.[72] After the Opium War and the subsequent signing of the Treaty of Nanking in 1842, Western women were finally admitted into select Chinese cities, introducing new gender dynamics to Sino-Western interactions. Van points out that Western wives played an instrumental role in their husbands' businesses as they socialized and entertained in the foreign communities of the Pearl River Delta. By 1846, "the kind of socializing within the predominantly Anglo-American foreign community increasingly included Chinese merchants as well."[73] Accounts of European wives who accompanied their husbands in late Qing and Republican China reveal that they felt privileged to meet the assumed "wives" of their husbands' Chinese business or official acquaintances on social occasions, only later realizing that they may have been incorrect about these Chinese women's identity (Chapter 2).[74] However, I have not seen a sufficient number of sources that fully reveal how the new role of the Chinese social wife played out in the business world. Overall, I hope the book can serve as a preliminary study to draw historians' attention to and stimulate further research on a significant, understudied, broad new social trend: the rise of the social wife in modern China.

This study demonstrates that the new role of the social wife had a particular beginning in late Qing diplomacy. In the late Qing, as Chinese diplomats realized the importance of following Western social norms, they began bringing their wives or concubines to public functions, in order to socialize properly in Europe or the United States (Chapter 1). However successfully their wives or concubines performed this role, they still generated controversy at home, since Chinese social norms dictated that women remain domestically secluded and segregated by gender. Nonetheless, some open-minded Chinese officials later adopted this custom in order to receive and entertain important Western guests in China's treaty ports, improvising just how a Chinese official's wife should appear in public functions without blatantly breaching Chinese rules of gender separation.

In the early years of the Republic, only top government officials and diplomats felt obliged to take their wives or concubines to public functions and social gatherings, principally those involving foreigners. By the 1920s, this practice was increasingly widespread, and over the next decade it became acceptable – even customary – for a man to attend social occasions with his "wife," especially in educated and reform-minded urban circles. These occasions could include *chahui* (receptions, balls, and parties, also called "*chahua hui*" in the Republican period), a format borrowed from the West and examined in Chapter 1. However, they could also include celebrations of festivals, birthdays, weddings, and other parties where friends, superiors, coworkers, and relatives were invited. Probably many more concubines from middle and lower-class backgrounds accompanied their husbands to these types of social gatherings than appeared at high-level public functions, to which only elite men's concubines had access.

A survey of contemporary newspaper reports shows that political and military officials frequently attended (and sometimes hosted) social events such as banquets, receptions, and balls accompanied by their "*furen*" (madam; literally, "husband's person").[75] The term "*ru furen*" (like a wife, used exclusively to politely refer to concubines) was rarely used in public after the 1930s, replaced by the more respectful "*furen*," which was not specific enough to reveal whether a woman was a wife or a concubine. Probably only those in the inner circles of an elite man knew who his wife and his concubine(s) were, as social stigma increasingly adhered to the traditional institution of concubinage. From the mid-1920s onward, an increasing number of Chinese officials, especially the younger men, were able to marry modern-educated women and have them as their only spouse – women who could attend public functions without difficulty. The best-known wives in the public eye during the Republican period were those of Gu Weijun (also known as Wellington Koo, whose wife was Oei Hui-lan, 1889–1992), Zhang Xueliang (Yu Fengzhi, 1897–1990), and Chiang Kai-shek (Song Meiling). News about and fashionable images of their public activities could be seen in a range of contemporary press accounts.[76]

From the perspective of an official, the mere presence of an educated and elegantly dressed spouse who accompanied him on public occasions lent his image a modern edge, not to mention the social networking she could accomplish to advance his career. Susan Glosser has noted that beginning in the 1920s, the New Culture Movement changed the expectations of an ideal wife. Younger generations of elite men, particularly the relatively affluent, well-educated urbanites in the Jiangnan area, increasingly "wanted their wives to take active social roles" while still fulfilling traditional responsibilities such as childcare.[77] But what of the elite men who had married young and later desired a partner who could be active in public? Their wishes could only be realized by introducing a concubine endowed with such qualities into their households.

A concubine who played the role of a modern social wife was a rare phenomenon in Chinese history, both before and after the Republican period. During the late Ming dynasty, talented courtesans who associated themselves with scholar-officials attracted broad public attention due to the cult of *qing* (passion, love) and became symbols of political loyalism. Still, once they married into elite households and became concubines, they faded into the domestic sphere and were rarely seen stepping out of their inner quarters to play a public role.[78] Some concubines during the imperial period provided company at private parties and played some sort of entertaining role for guests (since wives were not supposed to socialize with their husbands' friends).[79] But the role these concubines performed was decidedly different from that of a modern social wife, who received the public respectability and privilege accorded only to a man's legal wife, whose role at these functions was *not* an entertainer.

This book chronicles and examines how concubines exploited the emergence of a new role for Chinese women: the modern social wife who was expected to function with ease on diplomatic, social, and official occasions. Chinese diplomats since the late Qing, borrowing Western social norms, needed their wives to appear at public functions. This posed a challenge to many main wives for whom strict adherence to the Confucian principles of gender separation and domestic seclusion was well established. Consequently, an unprecedented opportunity arose for younger concubines to assume the role of social wives on social and diplomatic occasions, both at home and abroad. In other words, China's particular historical circumstances gave birth to a unique phenomenon: A significant number of the earliest and most daring social wives in modern Chinese history were, in fact, concubines. By the Republican period, despite the fact that domestic seclusion was no longer seen as a necessity for virtuous women, some main wives still felt uncomfortable or unwilling to play the role of the social wife in public; concubines thus continued to attend various public functions with their husbands. In the early years of the Republic, many of these women were former courtesans or entertainers. However, from the late 1920s and 1930s onward, new generations of women with uncompromised social backgrounds had grown up and achieved a modern education; some of them became elite men's preferred choices to serve in this role. Only with the Communist takeover and effective banning of concubinage did these concubines disappear completely from public and social occasions.

In her study of the role of the "diplomatic wife" in the US Foreign Service from 1905 to 1941, Molly Wood points out that the role has often been overlooked by feminist scholarship that regards it as essentially retrograde – "feminine" and dependent – rather than seeing these women as having pioneered their own careers while challenging established gender hierarchies and stereotypes.[80] I believe this view is helpful in explaining why the role of the modern social wife has been overlooked in the historiography of China as well. This book argues that gender historians need to broaden their perspectives, going beyond well-studied professional women or revolutionaries when discussing new models of Chinese womanhood. In particular, some models of Chinese womanhood, such as the modern social wife or the "diplomatic wife" (a role I have examined elsewhere),[81] were based more on gender difference than gender equality. The fact that this role did not require women to challenge men's social authority and political power made it easier for women to find a suitable platform from which to be active in public, sometimes even to start a career, to discover their own imperfect routes to fulfillment, and to realize personal ambitions. Undoubtedly, this role had its limits. As we will see in Chapter 2, Li Benwei (a courtesan turned concubine) successfully served as Li Yuanhong's social wife during his rise from lower-level commander to high-ranking official in the first two decades of the twentieth century, thereby gaining public prominence and Li's trust. Still, when Li died, Benwei's weak legal status as his (sonless) concubine could not protect her from social prejudice, reminding us that the auxiliary and dependent nature of the role of social wife did not provide concubines with a fully independent identity, no matter how long and how well they played their role.

INTRODUCTION

As a new model of Chinese womanhood, the role of the social wife emerged due to a new need for gender difference rather than gender equality in modern China's social occasions and public functions. Gender differences had long been a foundational principle in Confucian ideology during the imperial period, primarily used to justify the idea that women should devote themselves to the domestic sphere and remain secluded. However, late Qing and early Republican China witnessed a new public function for women emerging as a result of China's increasing interaction with European and American customs: A social wife was needed to serve as a public companion to an elite man, using the soft refining influence of the female sex to assist him in advancing political or business interests through socialization. The earlier roles that courtesans performed, as a social glue for men within the entertainment quarters, were no longer sufficient in the age of modern international trade and diplomacy where Western norms prevailed. A series of new "wife-specific responsibilities," such as serving as party hostess, emerged, requiring a new type of public-facing woman. Since many Chinese principal wives were either unwilling or unable to assume this new role, concubines with public skills stepped into the position. Men allowed their concubines to take advantage of gender differences to play the role of the social wife because it benefited them without challenging them for their authority and power. Appearing together in public with an elegantly dressed and educated spouse could increasingly lend a man's image a modern and civilized edge, as I have mentioned before. In addition, having social wives engage in public charities and social relief could also help soften and improve the public perception of military men (Chapter 3).

Concubines accepted such a role based on gender difference, despite its auxiliary and dependent nature, not only because they saw the opportunities it could provide them, but also because they knew they were not in a position to demand equality with their husbands at the time. For various reasons, many concubines were unable to become main wives, let alone equal to their husbands. They had no better choice but to accept their subjugated position to their masters. We only occasionally hear the voice of Yao Wenyu (the concubine in the opening of the book), who asked the question on gender equality: "How could 'distinguished men' who had concubines, thereby violating the principle of monogamy, continue to hold public office while the women who became concubines were immediately fired?"[82] However, her question was never answered and she was dismissively fired. The majority of concubines in this book understood that it was difficult for them to individually defy a patriarchal society and hence, at most, they attempted to maneuver to challenge the well-established superiority of the main wives rather than their own husbands, upon whom they had to rely for economic and social support. The book illustrates how these concubines seized the opportunity to assume the role of the social wife, thereby carving out a space for themselves to demonstrate their indispensable value and, in the process, enhance their domestic status. However, fundamentally, gender differences could not enable these women to transcend gendered power dynamics. The rise of the modern social wives still took place within the confines of the patriarchy rather than by asserting a role for themselves outside of it.

Examining how concubines played the role of the modern social wife in Republican China can remind us that rather than judge women's histories based on modern (often masculine) standards of gender equality, women's specific lived experiences should be interrogated in the context of their own time and understood in their own terms, if possible. This means acknowledging that sometimes roles based on the principle of gender difference were shrewdly utilized by women, especially those in subordinate positions, to carve out a new space or platform of their own, finding agency and (limited) empowerment. Only then can we truly understand how a variety of women found their place in the newly opened public realm and repositioned themselves in modern Chinese society.

CONCUBINAGE IN REPUBLICAN CHINA: CONTEXT AND CONSEQUENCES

Concubinage did not cease to exist in the Republican period, no matter how much social progressives wished and legal reformists worked to see that happen. Instead, the institution innovated. Three broad and intertwined developments in the Republican period serve as the larger context for the case studies in this book: (1) the increasing social stigmatization of the concubine and the rise of her domestic status; (2) the emergence of modern-educated concubines and their active but controversial public presence; and (3) the democratization of concubinage and the emergence of the Anti-Concubinage Movement. This section offers an overview of each development, with further discussions provided in individual chapters. Although some scholars have noted these changes, none have connected these issues and given them concentrated treatment, investigating the broader impact of concubines' public presence on the society, culture, and gender politics of Republican China. This study aims to weave these trends together to present a new perspective on a significant phenomenon and its implications for modern Chinese history.

INCREASING SOCIAL STIGMATIZATION AND THE RISE OF THE CONCUBINE'S DOMESTIC STATUS. The first noteworthy trend tracked in this account is the increasing social stigmatization of the concubine as a category, despite her upgraded domestic status during the Republican period. Historian Cheng Yu notes that the customary terms used to address concubines changed over time, which suggests that the domestic status of the concubine was drawing equal to a main wife's by the early Republican period. In *Dream of the Red Chamber* – one of four great classical novels composed in mid eighteenth-century China – concubines were called "*yi niang*" (aunt mother, since *yi* originally means mother's sisters), already a flattering term. However, Cheng points out, they were never addressed as "*taitai*" (Mrs.) or "*furen*," two terms reserved exclusively for main wives. In the late Qing satiric novel *Exposure of the Official World*, concubines are generally referred to as "*yi taitai*" (aunt Mrs.). By the early Republican era, the term "*yi niang*" was used exclusively for servants, while "*yi taitai*" had become widespread as a general term for concubines and had developed an undertone of social contempt. Behind the concubines' backs, servants were known to use the term derogatorily. Yet, in front of these women, *taitai* was widely used for both concubines and main wives, with the addition of a number to indicate the order by which each woman had joined the household. In news media and on formal occasions, out of politeness, the alternative "*ru furen*" (meaning "like a wife") was often used to refer to individual concubines.[83] These terms suggest that by the early Republican period, the concubine was viewed less as a servant and more as a spouse. This corroborates historian Katherine Bernhardt's findings and echoes the period's general and related trends: loosening status boundaries and increased commercialization and social mobility.

In terms of her *public* reputation, by the Republican era, the concubine as a social category had become a relic of the old society, a marker of male decadence, and a contaminating influence on anything she touched. Even concubines avoided calling themselves "*qie*" (concubine), choosing instead to identify themselves by other terms, such as "*yi taitai*," "*ru furen*," or "*xiaoqi*" (small wife).[84] To be sure, many concubines were former courtesans, prostitutes, maidservants, or entertainers from the so-called debased (*jianmin*) social class and were thus accustomed to scornful treatment.[85] Their traditionally low status formed the foundation of Republican-era discrimination.

However, in the early twentieth century, social progressives applied a new rationale to explain their contempt: Concubines lacked "*ren'ge*," they argued, adding a new layer of social stigma to this category of women. According to historian Tani Barlow, *ren'ge* was a word borrowed from the Japanese near the end of the nineteenth century. *Hanyu wailaizi cidian* (a dictionary of Chinese borrowed words) defines *ren'ge* as "the sum and substance of a person's individual disposition [*xingge*], temperament [*qizhi*], capabilities [*nengli*], and special qualities [*tezheng*]."[86] Barlow believes the translation that best explains the intellectual sense of the term is "personal standing," and provides evidence that "*ren'ge* played an important role in establishing the analytic standing of women as a category" in a range of progressive intellectual debates during the early twentieth century.[87] Historian Bryna Goodman confirms that *ren'ge* was coined during the New Culture Movement to capture the key modern virtue that new women were expected to possess. This highly elusive term evoked independent thinking, self-reliance, and individual moral rectitude. The ability (or inability) to achieve *ren'ge* was hotly debated, and derision of dependent women (such as concubines) for lacking *ren'ge* was common in the progressive press of the 1920s.[88] In Chapters 3 and 4, we will see specific examples of the social progressives who regarded concubines as morally dubious and socially parasitic: the near opposite of the New Woman.

INTRODUCTION

Many progressive women's organizations barred concubines from becoming members on the grounds that they did not possess *ren'ge*.

The increasing stigmatization of the concubine in Republican China also resulted from a series of unprecedented, vehement attacks launched by progressive intellectuals on the Chinese traditional custom of concubinage since the late Qing. In 1911, an editorial in *Dongfang zazhi* (*The Eastern Miscellany*), one of the most important Chinese journals, called concubinage "a major stain" on Eastern civilization after comparing the "lineage-centered Eastern societies" with "individualistic and independent Western societies."[89] In a 1924 issue of *Rensheng zazhi* (*Life Magazine*), another critic referred to concubinage as a "prominent mark" of "barbarian nations" in the twentieth century.[90] In a specially compiled 1922 issue of the journal *Fei qie hao* (*Abolish Concubinage*) – which seems to have been the first journal dedicated entirely to the issue of concubinage – the author of an article entitled "The Concubine is an Obstacle Obstructing Human Evolution" called concubines "social parasites" and described their existence as poisonous to the nation's evolution.[91] These discourses often indiscriminately conflated criticism of concubines as individuals and a social category with criticism of concubinage as an institution, allowing both to become symbols of degeneracy and revealing progressive intellectuals' deep sense of shame about the Chinese custom.

This book examines the public presence of concubines in Republican China, situating it within the context of the increasing stigmatization of concubinage and revealing the contested gender politics surrounding these women. It shows how and why concubines' public presence on the international stage came to be denounced as a "national disgrace" (Chapter 2). It analyzes the fears of "contamination" and the politics of women's virtue that drove progressive women to exclude or ban concubines from public schools and women's organizations (Chapter 4). And yet, despite the social stigma they faced, it was still possible for individual concubines of elite men – under the right combination of circumstances (such as having a clean social background, a modern education, and a powerful husband) – to avoid major controversies and enjoy a degree of respectability, particularly as social wives. In other words, concubines were not all equal, and not all were discriminated against equally. This calls our attention to the discrepancy between a concubine's collective and individual identities as well as the space she could carve out for herself in the contentious gap between theory and practice in modern China (Chapter 3).

THE EMERGENCE AND RAMIFICATIONS OF MODERN-EDUCATED CONCUBINES. Inquiring about what drew women to become concubines in Republican China prompts us to consider a second noteworthy development: the changing social backgrounds of concubines. Cheng Yu argues that, during this period, more concubines came from poor families than the traditionally degraded occupations – such as courtesans and entertainers – from which they had previously been drawn.[92] Since poverty was not inevitably linked to immorality, these concubines were regarded as less "stained" than those who had once been courtesans or prostitutes. Meanwhile, women's public schools were becoming more widespread and affordable (see Chapter 3); there were concubines in the younger generations who had received a modern education (which often included knowledge from and about the West), whereas the older main wives tended to be Confucian-educated or completely illiterate. In some cases, this dynamic reversed the long-held distinction between a main wife and a concubine, by which the main wife was more likely to be associated with literacy and education.[93] Some concubines who attended modern coeducational schools learned cross-gender mingling skills and modern social etiquette, enabling them to assume privileged public roles, such as serving as the modern social wives of elite men at official and social functions. Furthermore, educated concubines tended to have a heightened awareness of social issues and some of them chose to be active in the public world. Instead of relying completely on their husbands' support, some concubines sought independent employment; others devoted their wealth and leisure time to social causes by participating in women's civic organizations (Chapter 4). However, their membership requests split several progressive women's groups, which could not reach a consensus on whether to ban these women based solely on the stigmatized category to which they belonged.

Some contemporary commentators believed that the emergence of modern educated concubines signaled the rise of a new type of institution, as new domestic arrangements were required. We can see this view in a 1932 editorial written by Yiwei, the female editor of a well-known Shanghai-based women's journal *Nüsheng* (*Women's Voice*). In "Super Concubinage," Yiwei notes that women who became concubines had traditionally been prostitutes, servants, and daughters of humble families. This kind of "primitive" concubinage prevailed for four thousand years, until the 1928 Northern Expedition, a military campaign waged by the Nationalist Party against regional warlords to reunify China. Alongside various reforms, the institution of concubinage began changing as well. The reformed version of concubines – "modern misses," "campus beauty queens," and "bachelorettes with foreign degrees" – now seen among the upper classes could not simply be purchased with money, as they had in the past. This "new" concubine had conditions: First, she demanded the title of *taitai* (Mrs., a form of address previously used exclusively to refer to main wives); second, she wished to live separately from the main wife, which required a master wealthy enough to afford two or three separate mansions while providing each concubine with a separate living stipend. Other than "VIPs of the government," this was a scenario few men could manage.[94]

The phenomenon that Yiwei noted, with a degree of exaggeration and sarcasm, suggests several important changes that accompanied the modern educated women who became concubines. First, her domestic status changed, at least in elite households; she was no longer the humble servant who provided sexual services to continue the patrilineal line of her master. This corroborates Cheng Yu's argument that the domestic status of concubines rose in the Republican period. Educated in the modern style, she challenged the traditional domestic hierarchy, demanding recognition of her status as equal to that of a main wife, starting from modes of address. Sometimes, such women were not even willing to accept the degrading label of concubine. The case studies seen in Chapter 3 confirm this observation: By playing the novel role of modern social wife, some of these women – such as Guo Dejie (1906–1966), the concubine of Li Zongren (1890–1969), a major military official – demanded more than mere improvement in their domestic circumstances. Through their modernity, their untainted origins, and their public recognition, some of these concubines sought to be recognized as wives. This illustrates how modernity altered the dynamics of competition between wife and concubine.

Second, Yiwei observed, she did not always live with the main wife. This, too, is consistent with the trend noted by Cheng Yu: separate living arrangements for wives and concubines, mostly in urban areas. In big cities like Shanghai, as more and more housing became apartmentized, fewer people could afford a large house for the women to share. Instead, men rented several apartments and let one or two concubines live in one apartment while the main wife resided in another. Sometimes, wives and concubines were even settled in different cities; most often, the concubine lived with the husband in his work city while the main wife lived back in his hometown, looking after his parents if needed.[95] For concubines who did not live with the main wife, this arrangement meant they were no longer under her direct control and watchful eye and did not have to rely on her for food and clothing. For families in which wives and concubines lived together, a practice more prevalent in rural areas, the main wife typically still enjoyed more authority and a higher domestic status. In other families, a favorite concubine could become the domestic manager and control the family finances, weakening the actual power of the main wife despite the fact that they all lived under the same roof.[96] As Rubie Watson has pointed out in her study of concubines in early twentieth-century Hong Kong, "through force of personality or favoritism, a concubine might become a powerful household figure effectively usurping the position of the wife herself."[97]

Among the variety of modern educated women who became concubines in Republican China, "female students" (*nü xuesheng*, that is, women who enrolled in modern schools) received a disproportionate amount of public attention and criticism. Historians have not examined this phenomenon closely or analyzed its broader social impact. As I will show in Chapter 3, female students becoming concubines was widely viewed as a shameful matter, symbolizing to some the downfall of modern Chinese womanhood and a failure of national education reforms, despite the fact that some students willingly became concubines after having fallen in love with married men, thereby acting according to the new ideal of "free love." A student who became a concubine was believed to have brought "shame" not only on herself but on all Chinese women and the other communities to which she belonged, endangering her membership in those communities – such as public schools – as conflict and political tensions arose among students, faculty, and administration. Moreover, social progressives often blamed the students themselves for lacking moral principles by becoming concubines and rarely addressed the larger social and cultural issues that compelled some students to make this move. Public schools, particularly those exclusively for girls, became frequent sites of intolerance and discrimination against known concubines. Student leaders organized protests and strikes across campus, demanding that the concubine in question be immediately removed so as to cleanse the contamination inflicted on every "innocent" student (Chapter 4).

THE DEMOCRATIZATION OF CONCUBINAGE AND THE ANTI-CONCUBINAGE MOVEMENT. The third trend concerns the types of men who had concubines and how these men were portrayed in contemporary Chinese print media. Once viewed as a status symbol for Chinese men – a vehicle for displaying wealth, prestige, and sexual prowess – men with multiple concubines had long been subjects of admiration and envy. Despite the fact that only about 10 percent of the male Chinese population from the late Ming to the late Qing period could afford to practice polygamy, this cultural and sexual ideal, according to Keith McMahon, had far broader importance: Possessing concubines defined successful Chinese manhood.[98] Little wonder then that during the Republican period, military men, officials, and merchants continued to have concubines. In his study of urban women's marriage issues in Republican China, historian Yu Hualin notes the economic precarity that forced women into concubinage with men of modest means. Compared to earlier periods, ordinary men could more easily afford concubines because severe economic pressure forced more women to resort to prostitution (and concubinage) for survival.[99] In contrast to the imperial era, the economic climate during the Republican period meant that a man did not need a substantial amount of money to acquire a concubine.

Contemporaries' accounts confirm Yu's point. Zhu Caizhen, editor of the 1922 collection of concubine-abolition writings, lamented what he called "the popularization" (*tongsu hua*) of concubinage a decade into the Republican era:

> People are infected by an epidemic: concubine-taking madness. Taking concubines has been popularized. During the Qing dynasty, those with "three wives and four concubines" were mostly big merchants or high officials. Taking concubines was limited to an [elite]. Not so in the Republic. There are innovations in form. The germ of the concubine has been disseminated throughout popular society... Look! Small merchants [and industrialists] take concubines; principals and teachers ... take concubines; [university] students take concubines; doctors, lawyers, and painters take concubines; miserable poor scholars who [win a lottery] immediately take concubines. Most distressingly, legislators who preach Marxism also take concubines... Hasn't this become a world of concubines? Alas! I have not heard that people in our country have popularized the right to vote. But the evil of taking concubines has been spreading rapidly and ... distributed equally.[100]

In addition to Zhu, Western observers such as Sidney Gamble (1890–1968) observed that concubine ownership "has apparently become more prevalent." In his social survey of Beijing, published in 1921, Gamble elaborated: "It is even estimated that at least 80 percent of the officials have secondary wives and the taking of concubines has become a fad in Peking [Beijing] ... the custom of taking secondary wives is also spreading among the lower classes. A foreigner's cook was even found to be supporting three wives at the same time."[101] Although we do not have comparable surveys on Beijing in the 1920s to confirm the accuracy of Gamble's numbers, various other sources suggest that an estimate of 80 percent of the officials in China's capital city having concubines is reasonable. After all, this social group had long enjoyed special wealth, status, and privileges. As for the foreigner's cook, his earnings were likely much higher than those of ordinary Chinese cooks due to his special skills (preparing Western cuisine, possibly understanding a little English); it is hardly surprising that he would be able to afford more concubines than low-income cooks.

Although the phenomenon of "concubine possession" (*xuqie*) became more widespread during the Republican era, men who had concubines were no longer overwhelmingly viewed with admiration as they had been in the imperial period. As the progressive elite increasingly linked concubine possession with gambling and opium – the lingering social ills of traditional China – men who practiced such "evil" customs were regarded as morally problematic. Cai Yuanpei, a well-respected educator and progressive intellectual, established The Society to Advance Virtue (Jin de hui) in 1918 while serving as President of Peking University. The Society's founding was widely praised in the contemporary press and its membership included more than seventy faculty, ninety staff, and three hundred students. The Society's three basic requirements stipulated that members abstain from taking concubines, gambling, and prostitution.[102]

However, only in the early 1920s did critiques of concubinage culminate in a radical new wave known as the Anti-Concubinage Movement (Fei qie yundong), which resurfaced in debates over the Nationalist Party's adultery law in the 1930s. As Bryna Goodman has shown, the movement's major participants were "women's rights and suffrage groups and legal and family reform activists," who published articles on concubine abolition, held meetings to discuss campaign strategies, and demanded investigations of legislators' personal lives in order to dismiss those with concubines.[103] It is noteworthy that China's concubinage abolition movement peaked much later than the Japanese counterpart. Since the beginning of the Meiji period (1868–1912), the issue of concubinage had been a major topic of discussion in Japan, initially among the elite and later spreading to the general population. The significance of the issue was believed to be such that it risked endangering Japan's goal of becoming a "civilized" and independent nation. However, overseas Chinese students in Japan (most of whom were men), whether loyalists or revolutionaries, chose not to introduce the anti-concubinage movement to China, suggesting that they did not deem it a priority at the time.[104] By 1882, concubines had been removed from Japanese household registries, and by 1898, Japan had legally embraced monogamy.[105] However, in China, it was not until around 1929–1930 that the Nationalist government finally enforced a new civil code to insist on the principle of monogamy and disqualify concubines as wives. Even after the code was implemented (unevenly and with various loopholes), the issue of concubinage remained a public preoccupation and concubines continued to exist throughout the Republican period.

Under the influence of the Anti-Concubinage Movement, positive portrayals of concubinage in print media after the early 1920s became increasingly rare. Far more common were depictions of men with concubines as a class with special power and privilege: wealthy, avaricious, and evil. Such portraits did not mirror social realities, but they did influence the tone of public opinion. Reports charged that "eight or nine out of ten [of these men] were bourgeois, in particular those in the political, military, and business world."[106] They were probably "bandits, evil merchants, thieves, corrupt officials, warlords, and businessmen" – broadly speaking, "those special elements and evil forces."[107] In this way, the prevailing tone of the Anti-Concubinage Movement became a battle against anti-revolutionary social forces: corrupt, polygamous characters who caused social chaos and national degeneration while harming women and families. Sensational depictions related to concubine possession circulated in print media, playing an instrumental role in constructing and reinforcing the public image of decadent men wielding disproportionate power and obstructing the nation's march to modernity.[108]

To be sure, not everyone viewed the possession of concubines as immoral. Even among the intellectual classes, there were those who continued to support concubinage and were not afraid of expressing their views publicly. The eccentric Qing loyalist Gu Hongming (1857–1928) was probably the most well-known advocate for concubinage. He famously used the analogy of one teapot matched with multiple teacups (rather than the other way around) to justify why there could be only one husband but many concubines. However, Gu's defense of Chinese customs (not only concubinage but also footbinding and keeping the queue) was largely intended to defend Chinese "honor," as other scholars have pointed out. It was his way of venting his anger at Westerners' use of concubinage to ridicule and attack Chinese civilization.[109] Gu did not draw his conclusions after a careful examination of concubinage as an institution, nor did he pay any attention to the domestic hierarchy and class issues between a principal wife and her husband's concubines or the jealousy, conflict, and suffering they often caused. His defense of concubinage was hardly persuasive.[110]

Even among social progressives, there were those who opposed the Anti-Concubinage Movement. The most vocal and visible examples engaged in a series of intellectual debates about a "new sexual morality" (*xin xing daode*) in the Republican periodical press. In 1924, Zhang Xichen (1889–1969), a well-known publisher and editor, included an article titled "The Shallowness of Abolishing Concubinage" in a supplement to *Chenbao* (*Morning News*), a leading newspaper during the New Culture Movement. Zhang quotes several renowned Western intellectuals, including Arthur Schopenhauer and Leo Tolstoy, to prove that men had long practiced polygamy worldwide. Citing the fact that in monogamous Christian countries, a man was not held legally responsible for promiscuous relationships with women outside of marriage, Zhang suggests that Chinese concubinage offered women sturdier legal protections and social status. Historically speaking, Zhang notes, women tend to outnumber men, and men favor sexual variety; forcibly abolishing concubinage before a revolution of "new sexual morality" would simply create more social problems.[111] The "new sexual morality" Zhang anticipated would be founded on the principle of gender equality: Men and women should be free to choose their love objects regardless of whether they were married, and neither society nor the law should punish consensual, nonmonogamous relationships that did no harm to others.[112]

A year after Zhang first presented it, his concept of a "new sexual morality" came under criticism from Chen Bainian (1886–1983), a psychology professor at Peking University. Zhang and a fellow intellectual who shared his view, Zhou Jianren (1888–1984), engaged Chen in debate through a series of articles published in influential journals such as *Funü zazhi* (*The Ladies' Journal*) and *Xiandai pinglun* (*Modern Review*). Chen argued that Zhang and Zhou were simply creating a new excuse, or "talisman" (*hufu*) for the principle of "one husband, multiple wives." Love itself is possessive, Chen argued, quick to cause jealousy and fights. The sexual morality defended by Zhang and Zhou could end in tragedy, even murder and suicide. Strict adherence to monogamy and the principle of the conjugal nuclear family were superior to China's outdated "one husband, multiple wives institution" (*yifu duo qi zhi*), which Chen hoped to see abolished.[113] In their responses, Zhang and Zhou cited notable Western scholars to support their argument for a new sexual morality and suggested that if Chen disagreed, he should protest directly to these Western figures. Other public intellectuals supported Zhang and Zhou in the press.[114] Eventually, Chen retreated from the debate. Feeling victorious, Zhang and Zhou collected their writings and published the debate as a book in 1926.[115]

Zhang and Zhou's position was more idealistic than realistic. They urged people to follow the principle of free love and free choice, taking little account of whether a woman was a wife or a concubine, or whether a man was already married – treating these essential facts as mere formalities. Zhang seems to have forgotten that the starting point for men and women in a patriarchal society was already unequal. Concubinage, an institution created out of inequality and subordination, could never fit neatly into a "free love" paradigm. Moreover, Zhang and Zhou barely examined the practical implications for domestic and familial life, such as women's domestic status hierarchy, child-rearing, and other family responsibilities that women shouldered on a daily basis. Chen made valid points about the potential psychological fallout of the new sexual morality: namely, mistrust stemming from jealousy, which has been a dangerous and violence-prone emotion pervading many polygynous households throughout Chinese history. Overall, the public impact of the debate likely remained largely within intellectual circles, as the scholarly articles would have been difficult for a general readership to comprehend. However, sources suggest that outside of intellectual circles there were others who felt that the ideal of free love could justify concubinage. Some female students chose to become concubines in the pursuit of "free love," believing they were acting according to a romantic model promoted by the New Culturalists to replace traditional modes of arranged marriages, despite thereby becoming concubines, ironic relics of the past (Chapter 3).

In fact, during the early Republican period, far more people were ambivalent about concubinage than were staunchly supportive or vehemently opposed to it. But few people publicized their views in the press. Zhu Caizhen was one of the few male intellectuals devoted to eliminating the custom. When he posted an ad in a major provincial newspaper, *Zhejiang minbao* (*Zhejiang People's Daily*), to solicit articles on abolishing concubinage, few readers responded. Aside from invited contributions,

Zhu received only three items from the public and lamented that he could not blame ordinary people for their indifference when even his close friends, whom he saw on a daily basis and were part of "the intellectual class" – immersed in new thoughts and active on social issues – would not pick up their pens for this issue.[116] Yu Hualin has pointed out that although the 1920s gave rise to the Anti-Concubinage Movement, mainstream public opinion during this period was by no means unequivocally anti-concubinage. Compared to their strong support for ideas of free love, women's independence, and free divorce, much of the public remained ambivalent about concubinage.[117] After all, there were a variety of reasons that men kept their concubines during this period, such as being unable or unwilling to abandon them and/or to freely divorce their wives.

Indeed, the most forceful support for abolition often came from women suffragists and women's rights activists.[118] Despite their relatively small number, these educated, mostly female activists were the most persistent and vocal advocates for the abolition of concubinage. The age-old emotion of wifely jealousy likely played no small part of a role in their devotion to the cause. After all, it was mostly men of their husbands' social classes who could afford to bring concubines to their homes. The wives might have feared personal redundancy if their own husbands felt they could blithely take concubines without consequences. Their opinions enjoyed wide circulation in the press, and they often held leadership roles in women's civic organizations and public schools for girls. As Chapter 4 shows, they often proposed excluding or banning concubines from membership to protect the virtuous reputations of themselves and their groups, citing lofty and elusive terms from the New Culture Movement, such as *ren'ge*. Ignoring the manifold differences between individual concubines, they treated the entire category of *qie* as women of low moral worth and a contaminating influence. When challenged by other members of the groups, who argued that concubines were victims of oppression who could themselves be virtuous, the leaders refused to compromise, resulting in internal divisions that threatened the unity needed to advance their collective feminist causes.

Consequently, during this period, concubines who were eager to devote themselves to public causes or pursue meaningful professions frequently encountered hostile, discriminatory group environments. Occasionally, we see evidence of individual concubines expressing their indignation at the intolerance and discrimination they faced, but with little help and few allies, they often had to accept their expulsion or forced resignation (Chapter 4).

SOURCES, METHODOLOGY, AND STRUCTURE

Few concubines wrote about themselves, and in many cases, we do not even know their full names. Since most concubines came from humble or deprived origins, many were illiterate. Outside of the urban social and political elite, it is very difficult to find sources to examine the public lives of concubines in lower-class households and the countryside. These women also had far less leisure time to engage with public affairs beyond their endless rounds of chores. This reminds us that the category of concubine was itself a highly variegated one, and that a divide separated the experiences of concubines who married well-to-do urban elite men from the much larger number who married into poor rural households. However, even those concubines who lived in urban areas and were fortunate enough to receive a modern education rarely wrote extensively about their own lives. Nor did officials, military, or businessmen leave extensive records about their concubines, as they tended to view family matters as inappropriate for public discussion and trivial compared to national political affairs. The lengthy memoir of Li Zongren, a prominent military official during the Republican period, mentions his concubine Guo Dejie only eight times, mostly in passing (he does not mention his main wife at all, likely aiming to project a positive, monogamist image).[119] Guo was an active and highly visible woman who accompanied him on many social and public occasions. Despite her modern education, Guo did not write about her own life and activities either: The voices and subjectivities of concubines remain difficult to find.

The encouraging news is that there are enough miscellaneous, sometimes fragmentary, sources on the concubines' public presence to carefully piece together their experiences. These include contemporary memoirs, newspaper reports, foreign travelers' and visitors' accounts, officials' journals, recorded oral histories, and (auto)biographies. I have chosen to study the public engagements of elite men's concubines by selecting and analyzing the better-documented and most illuminating cases. Generally speaking, concubines who married elite men stood a much higher chance of being mentioned, if not by themselves, then by those who interacted with them or by being reported on by the press. Through these channels, we can uncover their public activities and sometimes public reactions to their activities as well. Though Li Zongren left few sources about his concubine – and Guo did not record her own life – it happened that Li's barely literate main wife, Li Xiuwen (1891–1992), left a valuable oral history of their family life, including important information about why Guo and Li married. In addition, as a high-ranking official's social wife, Guo's public engagements, especially those related to women's issues, were frequently covered in contemporary news accounts. This book thus assembles perspectives gleaned from a rich body of underutilized materials to examine the unprecedented public appearances of concubines, both as modern social wives and as members of public organizations.

News reports and articles related to concubines were frequently seen in the popular press of the Republican period, which not only demonstrates the frequent public attention given to concubines but also provides important source materials for this study. Scholars have noted the "striking" rise of the periodical press after 1895 and its exclusive role in circulating information and ideas to people across Republican China.[120] According to Perry Link, from the beginning of the twentieth century to the early 1930s, Shanghai's print media industry experienced a sixfold expansion while the urban literacy rate at least doubled.[121] Urban readers could access news in a variety of ways – from commercial dailies and weekly periodicals to specialized journals and small-scale publications. Meanwhile, the reach of this press far exceeded what its circulation numbers suggest, since people shared newspapers, read bulletin boards hung at important urban junctions, and spread information by word of mouth. The rapid growth of the urban press and other forms of print media increased the public visibility of a diverse range of women, from concubines and courtesans to female students, all of whom were frequently featured. After the "woman question" became an issue of national urgency in the late Qing, the drive to transform "parasitic" female consumers into productive modern citizens – both to strengthen the nation and to promote gender equality and women's liberation – prompted the founding of a large number of women's journals and magazines. By the late 1930s, about 250 women's journals had begun publication.[122] Women played new and important roles not just as readers but also as writers and editors for these magazines in a new "mixed-gender public space" for idea and intellectual exchange.[123] Among various issues on women, concubinage quickly became a frequent topic of discussion in the women's press as well. All of these journals and magazines played a central role in circulating ideas about concubines and shaping popular understandings of new forms of womanhood in the new era.

A point to clarify: By referring to concubines in "public," this book does not intend to wade into the debate about whether China had a "public sphere" independent of the state.[124] Instead, I use the word to refer to a physical world beyond the home, the opposite of the domestic sphere. As this book will demonstrate, concubines actively engaged in the urban public realm in Republican China. I focus particularly on their presence in two types of public platforms: first, novel forms of social gathering borrowed from the West (often referred to as *chahui*), such as parties, balls, receptions, and public occasions in which the presence of an official or other social notables' wife was assumed, and second, women's new civic organizations and public schools. The presence of concubines in these arenas has been largely overlooked by historians and an examination of their activities on these platforms is long overdue.

Gender historians have long noted that Chinese conceptions of the public and the domestic were never rigidly separated, largely due to the profound influence of Confucian ideology, which viewed order in the family as the foundation for ordering the whole of society.[125] Although the focus of this book is concubines' activities in the public realm, it also pays close attention to the connections between an individual concubine's domestic and public lives: the consequences for – and conversations between – the two realms. By fulfilling the new and important role of the social wife, some concubines improved their domestic status despite having produced no children. On the other hand, their high public profiles were not without personal cost, as Chapter 2 illustrates through the case of Li Benwei. After years of serving as a social wife,

INTRODUCTION

she could not easily remarry after her husband's death due to public expectations that she demonstrate continuing loyalty to her deceased husband, an expectation that was traditionally associated with a wife rather than a concubine.

The book is organized into four thematic and roughly chronological chapters, preceded by this Introduction and followed by an Epilogue. Chapter 1 begins with the first well-known case of a late Qing imperial official, Guo Songtao (1818–1891), who brought his concubine abroad and attended public functions with her during their stay in London from 1877 to 1879. Ambassador Guo was criticized by conservative factions at the Qing court and later recalled as punishment, partially for breaching Chinese gender propriety. Chapter 1 also examines the gradual realization among Qing elites that gender separation posed a liability in international diplomacy as well as their improvisational adoption of Western gender etiquette. Although these rapid adaptations reflected practical diplomatic concerns rather than wholly new conceptions of gender relations, they facilitated the emergence of the role of the social wife, opening an officially sanctioned platform from which Chinese women could be seen and sometimes even heard in public.

Chapter 2 continues to explore the ways that, both at home and abroad, shifting Chinese mores demanded that politicians appear in public with their wives, examining several cases of high-profile public concubines to illustrate the tensions involved. As this change took hold in the new Republic, courtesans and entertainers-turned-concubines emerged as some of the few contemporary women with the social skills and experiences to interact with male strangers; they served as modern social wives when main wives found the transition from domestic seclusion to the public stage too challenging. In the early twentieth century, the novel public status of concubines ran contrary to the increasingly virulent critiques of concubinage as backward, oppressive, and anti-revolutionary. The traditionally degraded class status of these former courtesans and entertainers worsened their stigmatization. Social protests arose against their appearance in public, particularly on the international stage, branding it a "national disgrace."

Chapter 3 investigates the new phenomenon of "female students" becoming concubines and the reasons behind it, leading to social progressives' outcry against "social degeneration." Unlike the concubines who were former courtesans or entertainers, these women graduated from modern public schools, rarely came from stigmatized social classes, and otherwise closely resembled the modern "new women." Due to their modern education and social skills, they became the preferred choice of politicians and military men, serving as their indispensable social wives and as domestic helpers who lived separately from the main wives. By playing this novel gender role, some of these concubines were emboldened to seek – in their modernity and through public recognition – to elevate their domestic status to that of a main wife despite their supposedly subordinate position within the traditional familial hierarchy.

Chapter 4 focuses on the various attempts to exclude concubines from public schools and progressive women's organizations. It examines incidents in public schools, where strikes were organized to protest against those students and administrators who were concubines. These incidents reveal deep anxieties about the concubine's tainting influence and the politics of women's virtue within campus communities. The chapter also examines the debates and conflicts surrounding concubine membership in progressive women's organizations, revealing overlooked divisions rooted in class hierarchy and sexual mores within Chinese women's liberation movements.

Underlying the stories of individual women, families, and group politics of which this book tells are the little-studied but important implications of the concubines' public engagements for the diplomatic, social, and cultural history of late Qing and Republican China. In addition, these case studies shed new light on the state of flux and clashing social dynamics experienced by a Republic caught between legacies of the past and the ideals of modernity. They also reveal how individual women and men translated powerful, perhaps inescapable, historical trends in light of their own lived realities.

CHAPTER 1

The Emergence of the Social Wife in Late Qing Diplomacy

WHEN LORD GEORGE MACARTNEY (1737–1806), the first British envoy to China, led a large delegation to Beijing in 1793, his refusal to "kowtow" to the Qianlong Emperor erupted into controversy, highlighting the importance of ritual in both Qing and British diplomacy.[1] Less well known were Macartney's reflections on the absence of women from Chinese social occasions and the effects that exclusion had on the country's social life:

> Where women are excluded from appearing, all delicacy of taste and sentiment, the softness of address, the graces of elegant converse, the play of passions, the refinements of love and friendship must of course be banished. In their place gross familiarity, coarse pleasantry, and broad allusions are indulged in, but without that honesty and expansion of heart which we have sometimes observed to arise on such occasions among ourselves. Morality is a mere pretence in their practice, though a common topic of their discourse.[2]

It was in this moral vacuum, according to Macartney, that Chinese men had developed two "cardinal vices": their passion for gambling and their appetite for opium.[3]

Macartney saw women's presence in public as an important part of the nation's social and cultural life and disapproved of Chinese women's relative invisibility. Macartney's gender ideals – particularly his belief in the refining influence of the female sex – were common to late eighteenth-century cultural commentary. In fact, Chinese men had long expressed a similar need for feminine presence. The fact that Chinese courtesans were traditionally active in social and public occasions – where they entertained scholar-officials with conversation, art, music, and other talents – is the best evidence of this, although it may not have been what Macartney had in mind.[4] Confucian gender norms required that a "good woman" – one from a respectable family – not show herself publicly nor have any physical contact with men outside her immediate family, since her chaste reputation was of paramount importance. What Macartney did not realize was the crucial class component of women's public presence in Qing China. As we will see, this class factor played a role in deterring some Qing officials' wives – who were often from upper-class, respectable families – from appearing in public and accompanying their husbands abroad.

By the mid nineteenth century, after suffering defeat in the Opium Wars, China was forced to open for trade and deal with various foreign and domestic crises through diplomatic means. A new institution, the Zongli Yamen, was created in 1861 to temporarily meet the demands of Western powers for diplomatic relations on an equal basis. The agencies it replaced, the Ministry of Rites and the Lifan yuan (Board for the Administration of Outlying Regions), had dealt mostly with affairs concerning tributary states and Inner Asia with a condescending and paternalistic attitude.[5] In this way, China's weakness in the face of the Western military might have led to the Qing government's first reluctant step in conducting diplomacy according to a new "international protocol," which meant mostly adhering to Western criteria. As interaction with the West intensified, issues of ritual and etiquette frequently caused concern in Qing official circles and were also contested by Western diplomats. Although the Qing court was forced to acknowledge its government's dramatically changed relationship with Western powers – and hence the need for reform and flexibility on matters of ritual – little consensus could be found on important details such as procedure, location, format, and the formal rituals involved in allowing Westerners to meet with Qing royalty and officials of different ranks.[6]

Studies of the diplomatic and international history of the late Qing pay little attention to the gendered aspect of China's foreign relations, except for cases in which an individual woman of extraordinary ability and special authority, such as the Empress Dowager Cixi (1835–1908), ascended to become a major actor and decision maker.[7] However, in

1 THE EMERGENCE OF THE SOCIAL WIFE

reality, diplomats of the late Qing were often among the first groups of people who had the earliest direct encounter with Western gender-related social norms and etiquette. To fulfill their official duties while stationed in Western countries, they had to frequently attend social and public functions where Western officials' wives were also present, and they could not simply ignore these women when being greeted. Furthermore, they were also expected to bring their wives to attend those social occasions together or to host receptions with their wives. Thinking from this perspective, it is not surprising that the role of the social wife, as this chapter will show, first came into being in the realm of Chinese diplomacy as a result of practical political necessity in the late Qing. In addition, it is also worth asking: What if the wives of the Qing diplomats were unwilling or felt uncomfortable attending these social and public occasions where gender mingling was common?

To better understand these little-explored issues, this chapter traces the emergence of the role of social wives in late Qing diplomacy and shows how concubines became the earliest Chinese women to play this role. It examines how Chinese diplomats and officials then gradually realized that gender-related Western social norms were essential etiquette that they had to learn to effectively socialize in order to carry out their diplomatic tasks. In particular, by focusing on their experience with *chahui*, an important form of Western social gathering that was mostly hosted by officials' wives, it shows how Chinese diplomats observed and learned about the important role of the social wife in the official world of the West. Specifically, the chapter first presents the case of late Qing Ambassador Guo Songtao bringing his concubine to London to serve as his social wife. This case was chosen because it was the first and best documented of its kind. This case also specifically demonstrates how the presence of a Chinese social wife in public functions invited political criticism and ignited controversy in the Qing court at a time when court conservatives and reformers were still battling about the degree to which China should be Westernized and the continued legitimacy of the Confucian principle of gender separation. Then, the chapter moves on to examine how other diplomats, such as Guo's successor, Zeng Jize, and his family adjusted to the expectation of a social wife's presence in diplomatic and official functions. The last section investigates how *chahui* and its gender-related etiquette were borrowed by China to entertain Western dignitaries and how it was adapted to suit late Qing China's particular cultural contexts, allowing Chinese officials' wives to attend without breaking the long-time Confucian norm of gender separation.

WOMEN IN *CHAHUI*

Despite the trend toward professionalization and bureaucratization in the mid nineteenth century, diplomacy continued to be conducted largely through sociability and conversation.[8] Historians have examined how the salon remained a key site for the gathering and spreading of news in European society.[9] Qing envoys in Europe quickly realized the importance of attending various social functions such as banquets, receptions, and balls. Among these social functions, *chahui* – whose closest English translation was probably "party" – stood out as a unique form of social gathering in which women played important and highly visible roles that caught the particular attention of Chinese officials. Not only were women expected to attend *chahui* together with their husbands, but also it was customary for officials' wives to serve as the hostesses of *chahui*, sending out invitations in their names. As we will see, this format of social gathering was later borrowed and adapted by Chinese officials to receive and entertain foreign dignitaries in late Qing China.

The term *chahui* was not foreign or borrowed, but a word of strictly Chinese origin, whose literal meaning – a gathering to taste tea – can be seen in the writings of the literati as early as the Tang and Song dynasties.[10] By the late Qing, however, the term had acquired new meanings in the journals of Chinese diplomats, as if pouring new wine into old bottles. Liu Xihong (?–1891), an assistant envoy to Britain in the 1870s, described in his journal a Western *chahui* he had witnessed: "[hosts] brew coffee and tea, add sugar and milk, and put some cookies on the side. Then [hosts] decorate the living room and wait until guests arrive to drink. When many guests are present, people mostly stand and chat."[11] In the West, Liu added, the *chahui* were all planned and hosted by wives.[12] Later, Zeng Jize (1839–1890), a Qing ambassador to Europe during the 1880s, shared similar observations of the key differences between European *chahui* and the traditional Chinese version.

As someone who often went "to a *chahui* hosted by a certain Mrs.," Zeng clearly understood that most of the *chahui* he attended were held in the names of the wives of officials, which differed from Chinese *chahui*, which respectable women were not supposed to attend as they were not meant to mingle with men publicly. Moreover, like Liu, Zeng mentioned that a central feature of *chahui* in the West was what he called "stand and chat," which was contrary to the traditional Chinese format of *chahui*, in which everybody sat down. The "stand and chat" format was especially true when the room was crowded, he noted.[13]

Cai Jun (1850–1908), another Qing envoy, offered the most thorough explanation of *chahui*. Cai's extensive diplomatic experience traveling abroad made him very familiar with Western etiquette.[14] In 1885, he published a short handbook in Shanghai titled *Things to Know as an Envoy* (*Chushi xuzhi*).[15] Cai introduced *chahui* by noting that Western countries placed great emphasis on it. State balls (*chaonei chahui*) were typically held twice or three times a year in the state palace, with major nobles, officials, wealthy merchants, and envoys from different countries all invited to attend. A general understanding prevailed that women would also attend, in accordance with Western social norms. Typical state balls could be attended by as many as two or three thousand people and were thus considered grand events. The king and the queen usually began the ball by leading a dance, followed by ambassadors, officials, and their wives, with more dances.[16]

As for nonofficial *chahui*, Cai explained, there were usually two types: large and small. The purpose was not to seek pleasure but to "cultivate friendship." A large *chahui* could have as many as hundreds or even thousands of people. Music and dance were typically included, and they were held at night with no set end time.[17] As for small *chahui*, the number of guests ranged from dozens to over a hundred and were held as frequently as once a week. The gatherings originated from a type of entertainment popular among Western gentry and official families. They were later adopted by envoys from various countries to facilitate social interaction and keep in touch. Though not as lively as the larger version, a small *chahui* sometimes involved dancing as well. The hostess would introduce all female guests, to whom one should bow first and then offer a handshake. Women sometimes played piano and sang; male guests could compose and recite poems to express themselves. In small *chahui*, guests usually arrived around two in the afternoon and left around six that evening, though some *chahui* were held from five to seven. Guests mostly sat and chatted, with a few refreshments.[18] To make sure his readers did not forget the importance of feminine presence in Western *chahui*, Cai further noted that a host with no female family members should ask a Western woman with whom he is familiar to act as hostess. The invitation to a *chahui* should include both the husband and wife, and a couple must attend a *chahui* together.[19]

In addition to handshaking, Cai further elaborates on the details of gender-related etiquette on how to attend Western dinner parties:

> At Western dinner parties men and women usually attend together [contrary to Chinese custom], but you may not sit next to your own wife. There maybe someone you know well who will sit with her to convey his respects, or wives may politely talk to each other as an expression of attentiveness. If you find yourself seated next to a female guest, when the meal is over you should say to her, "I am honored by *ma-dan*'s kindness; may I be permitted to take your arm?" Ma-dan is an honorific term for Western ladies; it means "lady." If she gives you permission, use your right hand to hold her left arm and accompany her to the living room. If she wants to stroll, walk slowly with her. If she wants to sit down, you should take her to a chair; after she is seated, she will thank you and you should then bow politely in return and step away. If you want to leave, you must wait until all the female guests have left before you can thank your host and say good-bye ...[20]

Considering the fact that, at that time, most Chinese officials rarely had any experience of interacting with unrelated women in public functions, Cai's detailed guidance here could be very shocking (but helpful) to them, given their Confucian education. Therefore, beyond the handshake, gender-related etiquette was the most challenging aspect of Western social intercourse for Chinese officials to learn and adjust to.

Unlike other forms of social gatherings, *chahui* were customarily hosted in the names of officials' wives rather than the officials themselves or the couples together, highlighting the uniquely important role of the social wife. By the late nineteenth century, *chahui* seemed to have become a part of diplomatic protocol in Europe: Upon an ambassador's arrival in the country where he was posted, it was expected that a *chahui* would be hosted in the name of his wife to entertain the country's

1 THE EMERGENCE OF THE SOCIAL WIFE

major officials as well as diplomats and their wives from other countries, demonstrating friendship and facilitating diplomacy.[21]

At *chahui* and other types of social gatherings, Qing officials observed that women were omnipresent in Western diplomatic socialization, playing an important and highly visible role in public functions. Merely to accomplish their official duties required attending these social occasions. Qing envoys, therefore, had to deal with gender-related issues, not only learning how they themselves should interact with Western women in public but also, more challengingly, deciding whether to follow Western etiquette and allow their own wives and daughters to attend public events that could include shaking hands with men, conversing with them over the dinner table, even dancing with them. As this chapter will show, one solution to these challenges was for a Chinese official to bring his concubine, often a former courtesan long active in elite social gatherings in China, to attend and host *chahui* as his social wife. In other words, late nineteenth-century China's particular historical circumstances led to the development of a unique phenomenon: Several of the earliest social wives were, in fact, concubines.

As more Western diplomats and officials began visiting or residing in Chinese treaty ports such as Shanghai, the question of how to properly receive and entertain them became a vexing issue for late Qing officials. As we will see later in this chapter, by the end of the nineteenth century, some officials started summarizing their earlier experience in Western *chahui* and applying this new formula to welcome Western dignitaries and their wives to China, gradually replacing outmoded and cumbersome Chinese rituals and etiquette. On a personal level, this adjustment helped to foster positive perceptions of Qing officialdom and forge friendly relations with Western powers. However, rather than simply copying Western etiquette, adaptations had to be made carefully to avoid blatantly breaching Confucian norms of gender separation, which court conservatives could use as a political issue.

CONCUBINES AS SOCIAL WIVES

In September 1875, Guo Songtao, a scholar-official from Hunan Province, was appointed by the Qing government to serve as the first

Chinese ambassador to Britain. Part of the reason for this appointment was the Margary Affair from earlier that year. Augustus Margary (1846–1875) was a junior British official who had been sent to southwest China to explore overland trade routes between British India and China's provinces. Margary was murdered in the frontier province of Yunnan, prompting lengthy negotiations between the Qing and British governments. Eventually, it was arranged that a Chinese emissary would be sent to Britain to apologize and to establish a Chinese Legation in London, thereby marking a significant stage in China's foreign relations. Guo's experience is worth examining because it was the first well-known case of an imperial official bringing his concubine abroad and attending *chahui* with her during their two-year stay in London, causing domestic political controversy for violating the Confucian codes of gender separation and domestic seclusion. Scholars have pointed to Guo's case as the first in modern Chinese history in which a Chinese official conducted "wife diplomacy" (*furen waijiao*).[22] However, I am concerned here less with women's impact on Chinese diplomacy and more with the emergence of a new type of social and public role for Chinese women in the late nineteenth century: the social wife, a role first played by a Chinese official's concubine.

On December 1, 1876, Guo and his embassy sailed from Shanghai on their unprecedented mission. His entourage included assistant envoy Liu Xihong, English interpreter Zhang Deyi, secretary Halliday Macartney (Chinese name Ma Geli, 1833–1906), a British citizen who worked for the Qing government, Guo's concubine (surname Liang), and another ten members of the retinue. On January 21, 1877, after fifty days at sea, Guo and his entourage arrived at Southampton. They quickly became a curiosity in the eyes of the British public: Londoners stared and followed them as they left the embassy. Most newspapers spared some space to introduce Guo, "the lion of the season," and his activities in England.[23]

Sources do not say why Guo's concubine accompanied him on the voyage rather than his principal wife. Neither do we know much about Liang. One source suggests that she was a maidservant of former Guangxi Governor Su Fengwen (?–1889) and was taken as a concubine by Guo in 1871; I have seen no other sources to verify this suggestion.[24] According to J. D. Frodsham, Guo "had originally planned to take both his secondary wives to England with him, but must have been persuaded by Halliday Macartney that such an indiscretion would prejudice his being received in polite society."[25] In addition, Frodsham explains, "the Western diplomatic community in Peking [Beijing] was aware that Madame Kuo [Guo] was not Kuo's principal wife, as we may see from a report submitted by one of the Secretaries of the French legation in Peking."[26] Liang's concubine status can be confirmed by the fact that the English interpreter of the Chinese embassy, Zhang Deyi, referred to her as *ru furen* (like a wife) in his journal, a polite term reserved exclusively for concubines.[27]

As Madame Guo, Liang attracted particular attention from the London media, not for any actions she undertook, but as the living representation of an "oriental lady" (see Figure 1.1). According to the *Illustrated London News*,

> Kuo-Ta-jên [Guo daren, Mandarin Guo] is accompanied by Lady Kuo, who may be said to be the first lady of position who has ever ventured beyond the shores of the Central Kingdom. During her voyage to England, in conformity with Chinese ideas of propriety, she remained during the whole time in the strictest seclusion, never once having even taken a seat on deck.[28]

Punch called Madame Guo "the Tottering Lily of Fascination" and depicted her "in the guise of simpering Japanese geisha in an outrageously décolleté kimono," expressing the hope that her bound feet would not start a national fashion in Britain.[29] The *Standard* mentioned Guo's possession of "two wives" (only one of whom was entitled to be called Lady Guo), Liang's small feet, and the slave girls who attended her.[30] British media was quick to identify every "oriental" feature of Madame Guo – seclusion, footbinding, concubinage, slavery – and make them into the ingredients of sensational news.

News that Liang was not Guo's principal wife but a concubine spread, possibly at the behest of Liu Xihong, the assistant envoy. Liu had not been on good terms with Guo, starting from Liu's dissatisfaction with the rank that Guo offered him in the embassy. Additionally, the two held very different attitudes toward the West: Guo was generally open-minded; Liu was a member of the court's conservative faction. While they were

1.1 "Madame Kwoh (Wife of the First Chinese Minister in London)" – Guo Songtao's concubine, from Demetrius Charles Boulger, *The Life of Sir Halliday Macartney K.C.M.G* (London: John Lane, The Bodley Head, 1908), 290.

still in London, in March 1878, Liu impeached Guo before the Qing government for "ten misdeeds" committed in Britain. These included the charge that Guo "socialized everywhere obsequiously and adopted the etiquette of handshaking";[31] that "he was keen to learn English, but, as he was too old to learn it, he told his concubine to learn it; and that he brought with him one of his wives to England and observed western diplomatic protocols by bringing her to some of the official functions."[32]

Indeed, the Guo couple socialized frequently in London. Liang, who was only in her twenties,[33] studied English, attended some

1 THE EMERGENCE OF THE SOCIAL WIFE

official functions, and visited the wives of British officials, all with Guo's approval. She even visited a public zoo and accepted an invitation to the "Embroidery House" from the wives of some British officials.[34] Compared to Liang, Guo and his staff were fully occupied by the hectic commitments demanded of ambassadors. They attended numerous parties, formal receptions, balls, and banquets held by the wives of officials. Shortly before the ambassador's return to China in January 1879, Queen Victoria herself granted the Guo couple a special audience, thereby affording Liang the seal of respectability in the eyes of the British media and high society.[35]

During these interactions, officials from the Chinese embassy noticed the British forms of social gathering and the prominent role played by the wives of British officials in social functions and diplomatic circles. In his journal, Liu Xihong described how different gender relations were in England: When couples went out to parties, "the husband serves his wife much as the filial son in China serves his parents."[36] Zhang Deyi shared similar observations: "In family regulations, the wife proposes, and the husband follows."[37] As J. D. Frodsham has pointed out, it seems that Liu confused deference with subservience in terms of an English husband's attitude toward his wife.[38] Neither Liu nor Zhang seems to have fully grasped the public–private dichotomy and its significance for British gender relations. In Victorian England, elite women were often viewed as "the angels in the house," and it was not surprising to see women making decisions as the managers of the household and the domestic realm. This in no way meant that women enjoyed equal status to men: Wives were still expected to devote themselves to their husbands and families. In the public realm, women were not allowed to hold official positions and could only attend salons and parties as the family members of male officials.[39]

After being repeatedly invited as a guest, Guo decided to follow the British custom and host a *chahui* in the name of Madame Guo to return the hospitality shown to him and his staff. In April 1878, he told Zhang Deyi to prepare a guest list and print invitations. Zhang expressed his reservations: "According to Western customs, *chahui* indeed should be held in the names of wives. However, this time, when hosting a *chahui*, the Chinese ambassador can be more flexible and does not have to follow British local customs strictly." Zhang explained further, "In Western countries, if you host a party in the name of your concubine, naturally, it violates no rules. However, if this news spreads into China, I am afraid that people will criticize you."[40]

Guo initially decided to heed Zhang's advice, but then changed his mind. On June 19, 1878, a grand reception was held in the name of "Madame Guo" at the Chinese embassy in London. The event was widely reported in Britain and China. What freed Guo from his fear of domestic criticism? The short answer is that Guo had by then determined to resign from his post and, therefore, no longer cared whether his activities conformed to Chinese gender norms. Guo's relationship with Liu had deteriorated such that they attacked each other in several memorials to the Zongli Yamen.[41] Their personal conflicts were also entangled with the struggle between reformers and conservatives in the Qing court. After reading Liu's account of Guo's "ten misdeeds" committed in Britain, Zhang Peilun (1848–1903), an attendant reader at the Hanlin Academy who had made a name for himself as an uncompromising critic of fellow officials, submitted a court memorial in December 1877 titled "Embassy Officials Should Not Be Allowed to Take Family Members Abroad." Zhang argued that Western custom did not separate men and women. Guo Songtao took his family abroad to fill his post, Zhang continued; While there, Guo insisted on imitating barbaric customs, made gender-mixed trips, and blatantly sought publicity to please foreigners. Consequently, when news of his activities spread, Guo was widely criticized. Hence, Zhang petitioned the government to prohibit Chinese officials from traveling with their families so as to "preserve our propriety and respect the honor of our country."[42]

Zhang's memorial suggests that even before Guo had the idea of hosting a party in the name of his concubine, he was already being criticized domestically for violating the Chinese custom of separating men from women and keeping women secluded. What further disappointed Guo was that the domestic court showed him little sympathy; many officials felt that he expressed overly strong opinions on a range of issues. Seeing this, Guo requested permission to resign and return to China, which made him care even less about whether his activities during the remaining months of his term contradicted Chinese ideas of propriety.[43] He decided to proceed with the party as originally planned.

1 THE EMERGENCE OF THE SOCIAL WIFE

The *chahui* held at the Chinese embassy in London in the name of Guo's concubine was a major success. More than 600 guests attended and *The Times* reported details of the party the next day:

> Last night the Chinese Minister and Madame Kuo [Guo] had a reception at the Chinese Legation, 45, Portland-place, the first time the representative of the Celestial Empire has given such an entertainment in Europe. The Minister had caused his residence to be arranged in accordance with English taste and usage. The entrance-hall and staircase were covered with crimson carpeting, and in every disposable place beautiful flowers were grouped in tasteful forms. The two principal saloons and anterooms were brilliantly lighted, the balcony fronting the mansion being enclosed and arranged with flowers and lighted with Chinese lanterns. The Chinese Minister and Madame Kuo received their guests in the usual European manner in the drawing-room, the hostess being dressed in the toilette of a lady of rank in her country. *The reception was especially interesting from the fact of its having been the first occasion on which a Chinese lady had appeared in general society, where gentlemen as well as ladies were present.* The dining-room and connecting apartment on the ground floor were thrown open for refreshments. The company invited numbered about 800, and about three-fourths of that number were present, including all the principal members of the Corps Diplomatique. Raimo's band was retained, and during the assembly played a selection of music.[44]

The report highlights how unusual it was for "a Chinese lady" to appear in public, receiving men as well as women.

In contrast to the Chinese court's critical reactions, some domestic press – including the highly influential *Shenbao*, one of the earliest modern Chinese newspapers – reported positively on the event. Three articles published in *Shenbao* in the second half of 1878 not only expressed their approval of Guo's activities in Britain but also seemed to defend Guo against domestic criticisms. This was probably due in part to the fact that the newspaper was founded in Shanghai (in 1872) and owned by an Englishman, Ernest Major (1841–1908). The first short report, published on August 6, 1878, and titled "Imperial Envoy Gives Reception," begins with a sketch of the June event detailing the dazzling arrangement of flowers, lights, and carpets. It continues: "The Ambassador and his concubine (*ru furen*), with the British advisor [to Guo] Mr. Ma[cartney], entered the reception hall to welcome the gentlemen and ladies." Here, the use of the exact Chinese term "*ru furen*" to address Liang – rather the more general term used by the British media, "Madame Guo" – shows that *Shenbao* did not try to cover up Liang's status as a concubine. After listing the illustrious guests gracing the reception, the report described the "banquet" ("*yan*," clearly the reporter had not learned to use the term "*chahui*"), which offered a variety of delicacies accompanied by music. The hosts and guests exchanged toasts, implying that Guo's concubine sat and interacted with the visitors. The report ends: "We note that this [type of reception] is a firmly established way of social intercourse for ambassadors stationed in other states; that in this case, Ambassador Guo has also done it along these lines. It is definitely the way of friendly and cordial relations."[45]

Three days later, *Shenbao* added an editorial, "On the Ritual Rule of Separating Men and Women," praising Guo for adopting Western customs of hosting banquets in London and receiving British guests together with his concubine. The editorial notes how much the reception was appreciated by his British guests and laments that Guo could only have done this in London; such hospitality that would be impossible in China owing to the ritual rule of separating men from women. The editorial harkens back to the history of the Spring and Autumn period (770–476 BC), arguing that Chinese women with talent and virtue were not then sequestered in the inner quarters; instead, they often received guests and officials. This original ritual, the rule of previous kings, was neglected in later eras as women's talents were belittled and they were separated from men.[46] By reinterpreting Chinese gender traditions, the editorial found a further rationale to support Guo's choice to co-host the reception with his concubine: Not only had Guo daringly adopted Western ways of social interaction when necessary, but he had also demonstrated a true grasp of the ritual essence of Chinese sage-kings.

Despite the positive evaluations of Guo's actions both abroad and domestically, on August 26, 1878, both Guo and Liu were recalled by the Qing government. Guo was ordered to return and replaced by Marquis Zeng Jize. Zeng was the eldest son of the well-known official Zeng Guofan (1811–1872), who played a leading role in suppressing the Taiping

1 THE EMERGENCE OF THE SOCIAL WIFE

Rebellion and restoring stability to the Qing Empire. In September or October 1878, rumors must have reached *Shenbao* that Guo had lost his position because he was attacked in court for failing to keep men and women apart and for adopting Western customs. On November 15, *Shenbao* reacted with another long editorial, "On the Proper Rules of Men and Women Interacting." It defended Guo by pointing out that the reception had been a diplomatic success. Since no one sits at a *chahui* (note the use of this term) in London, critics who accused Guo of allowing his concubine to sit with male guests at the banquet were simply ignorant.[47] The editorial's author was clearly familiar with the differences between a *chahui* and a traditional Chinese banquet.

The case of Guo Songtao and his concubine is the first and best-documented instance of a Chinese official's concubine playing the new role of social wife in gender-mixed social occasions. It demonstrates not only a Chinese diplomat's need to adjust and adapt to Western forms of social interaction but also the particular tensions and politics involved in a Chinese official's "wife" appearing on an international stage during the late Qing. Liang's visibility brought an unusual degree of respectability to a concubine but also subjected her to intense cultural controversy and immersed her in the political struggles surrounding Guo's actions abroad. Throughout the controversy, domestic criticisms were mostly centered on Guo having broken Chinese standards of propriety by failing to keep men and women apart, rather than on the fact that he brought his concubine instead of his principal wife abroad, thereby losing face for the Qing Empire internationally. By contrast (and as I will show in Chapter 2), some progressive Chinese elites in the 1920s (when concubinage was under vehement attack as a backward institution) reacted with a sense of shame and humiliation to the public presence of a Chinese concubine rather than a main wife on the international stage. As for the British media and high society in the 1870s, they paid only fleeting attention to the fact that Liang was not Guo's main wife and seemed more fascinated by exotic oriental gender customs (such as footbinding) than by Ambassador Guo's questionable morality.

We know of at least one other Qing official (Hong Jun, 1840–1893) who brought his concubine (Sai Jinhua, 1874–1936) rather than his main wife abroad for official duties. Sai met Hong, then a metropolitan degree holder, when she was a courtesan in Suzhou, southern China. She soon became his concubine and moved with him to Beijing in 1887. Sai accompanied Hong on diplomatic missions to Russia, Germany, Austria, and the Netherlands, spending three years in Europe and visiting St. Petersburg, The Hague, Vienna, Paris, London, and Berlin. She spent the longest time in Berlin (from 1887 to 1891), where she met Emperor Wilhelm II of Germany, Empress Augusta, and Chancellor Otto von Bismarck.[48] It seems that Hong learned from Guo's experience and took extra precautions to keep his concubine from mingling with other men. Hong's journal during this period mentions Sai's activities only a few times: on one occasion, entertaining female guests upstairs in a gender-segregated setting at the Chinese embassy during a New Year's party held by Hong; celebrating Hong's promotion with several diplomats' wives over drinks; and going for tea at the house of a German official's wife. It seems that Sai never attended a formal public reception as the social wife of a Chinese envoy, as Guo's concubine had, though we do not know if Hong deliberately omitted any mention in his journal (which would have been reviewed by the Qing government) of activities that might have been deemed "inappropriate."[49]

Although we do not have sources that explain directly why Hong took Sai abroad instead of his principal wife, we can speculate from the revealing descriptions in a best-selling late Qing novel, *Niehai hua* (*Flowers in a Sea of Retribution*), which fictionalizes the travels of Hong (as Jin Wenqing) and Sai (as Fu Caiyun). First published in 1905, about two decades after their journey, the novel is set in the 1880s and provides a fictional example of a principle then in operation: a wife calling on a concubine to accompany a husband on a trip abroad – a practice that was more common than a wife herself taking on the duty.[50] One scene is particularly illustrative. On the eve of Jin's journey abroad, Fu "steps out of the wedding sedan in the official garb ... of the principal wife."[51] Friends and relatives standing in the hall immediately notice the anomaly and start whispering, prompting Jin's principal wife to step forward and speak:

> "Dear friends and senior relatives, you may find today's ceremony and the costume of the bride surprising. Please allow me to explain. It stands

to reason that I should accompany Wenqing when he goes abroad. However, because of my physical indisposition, I will be unable to travel. The new bride of today will take over my responsibilities. Since the wife of an ambassador becomes the visible representation of the whole country, no attention to detail should be spared. Therefore, I am willing to lend her my power and my official costumes. When they return from abroad, of course, she will then return them to me." When her clear voice died down, everybody murmured praise.[52]

The public excuse used here by the principal wife was "physical indisposition." However, as Hu Ying has pointed out, an earlier scene in the novel describes the main wife "talking to her husband behind closed doors," stating her resolve not to go abroad due to principles based on "cultural differences": "I have heard that, following foreign customs, an ambassador's wife is also expected to receive guests, attend parties, and even shake hands and kiss foreigners. Having been brought up properly in a distinguished household, not in a thousand years would I ever get used to this sort of business."[53] The novel's main wife views traveling abroad and interacting with foreigners in public as an outright transgression of the Confucian norms of gender separation and domestic seclusion. The concubine is seen as the appropriate candidate for the role of an ambassador's social wife because she had already violated the boundary between the domestic and the public in her previous position as a courtesan.

ADJUSTING TO WESTERN GENDERED NORMS OF SOCIALIZING: ZENG JIZE'S FAMILY

Succeeding Guo, Zeng Jize was appointed Minister to Britain, France, and Russia in 1878. Zeng lived in Europe for seven years and, like Guo, followed the court's order to keep a journal detailing his activities abroad. Zeng's journal further illuminates how a Chinese official observed and participated in various Western social formats and how his family members gradually became more engaged with them as well.

The term *chahui* appears frequently in Zeng's journal, indicating how often Zeng socialized with European officials in this manner.[54]

ADJUSTING TO WESTERN GENDERED NORMS OF SOCIALIZING

During the first two years of Zeng's time in France, his journal entries record his attendance at a *chahui* every few days. Sometimes, he went to several in a single night. In January 1879, Zeng saw "the ritual of men and women dancing together" for the first time in his life.[55] At first, he shared Liu Xihong's misgivings, but one month later, Zeng attended another ball and began to understand the purpose behind it, especially one held for charity. He not only watched the dancers for a long time but also donated funds to the charity.[56] On April 19, 1880, after a ball at Buckingham Palace, his journal entry describes the features of the ball in detail and notes that the men and women who danced together "had dignified deportment and noble expression."[57] Such positive remarks show Zeng gradually adjusting his original views.

At the start of his European journey, Zeng seems clearly to have learned from Guo's "mistakes" and felt determined to forbid the women with him from mingling with men. We know that Zeng took his wife (surnamed Liu; Zeng did not have any concubines at the time), two daughters, and a sister with him to Europe.[58] According to his journal, before they boarded their ship to France, Zeng wrote a letter for his interpreter to forward to the French government, explaining that Confucian gender codes forbade Chinese women from mingling with men. Despite the friendly relationship between China and Western countries (and the personal friendships Zeng himself had cultivated), he could not allow the women traveling with him to follow Western etiquette: mingling with men and shaking their hands – or worse, dining together – would be regarded "a great shame in their lives." Female family members of Chinese envoys could, however, meet Western female guests.[59] In November 1878, Zeng's ship arrived in Hong Kong, where the Zeng women faced their first challenge in attending public functions when Hong Kong Governor Sir John Pope Hennessy (1834–1891) came to welcome them. Zeng immediately informed the governor that Chinese etiquette differed from Western norms; that the Zeng women could not meet male guests, and especially could not dine with them. The governor showed understanding and the next day ordered two separate banquets to welcome them, having arranged for the Zeng women to dine in a gender-segregated room with female servants to forward on mutual greetings.[60]

1 THE EMERGENCE OF THE SOCIAL WIFE

Soon after they arrived in Europe, the Zeng women were busy meeting Western women, mostly the officials' wives who called on them. Each year, Zeng spent about half his time in France and half in Britain as ambassador to both countries. When he was appointed ambassador to Russia as well, he sometimes stayed there for extended periods, and his family members always accompanied him. In the second year, during his stay in Britain, Zeng set aside a separate room in his house, designating it the "female reception room" to facilitate these social interactions, while indicating that he was still upholding the Confucian principle of gender separation. Sometimes, the Zeng women would meet ten to twenty Western women in a single day.[61] Zeng played the role of interpreter in these meetings when he could; after about two years, the Zeng women (especially his young daughters) had learned sufficient English to carry on conversations with guests on their own.[62]

Like Guo, Zeng soon realized that after attending so many *chahui*, he and the Chinese embassy should do something to reciprocate the hospitality. In January 1880, his journal entry shows that he and his subordinates discussed, at great length, over several successive days, how to organize a *chahui*. On February 4, a *chahui* was held at the Chinese embassy, with more than twelve hundred guests in attendance. It began with a banquet and finished with dancing. The entire procedure – including time, format, and content – followed Western custom.[63] Despite his earlier disapproval of men and women dancing together, Zeng followed local custom by incorporating dancing into his own *chahui*. His journal does not reveal whether the Zeng women joined in and danced as well, but it is difficult to imagine that the host and hostess of the *chahui* did not follow Western etiquette, appearing publicly to welcome the guests as Guo and Liang had at their own *chahui*. From then on, the Zeng women began attending more *chahui*. One journal entry reveals the pressure Zeng felt and his eventual compromise. On May 22, 1880, he took his wife and sister to Buckingham Palace for their first concert. His journal entry for that day explains why he decided to do so: Since the beginning of that year, his family had received invitations from Buckingham Palace twice for balls and twice for concerts. The first three times, he did not bring his family with him. But for the fourth visit, his secretary Halliday Macartney advised him to take his family, as it was important for the

Zengs to accept the British monarch's great generosity.[64] Zeng agreed; his struggles suggest that the longer he stayed in Europe, the more difficult it became to strictly forbid his family members from attending public occasions where men were also present. From 1880 to 1881, the Zeng family attended four to five *chahui*. On June 3, 1883, Zeng recorded taking his wife to Buckingham Palace for a ball.[65]

We do not know whether the Zeng women mingled or shook hands with men at these occasions, or if they dined and danced. Zeng's journal left out all relevant details. He must have known that his journal would be reviewed one day by conservatives at court and that he must be very careful not to mention any "inappropriate" activities related to the Zeng women. It is also possible that he felt these were trivial details not to be dwelt on in the journal of an ambassador. In addition, he often reexamined his journal to transcribe, delete, and revise its content. None of the Zeng women expressed themselves in writing, so we do not know how they felt about these experiences either.[66]

In addition to demonstrating the gradual process by which a Chinese official and his family adopted the gendered etiquette of the West, Zeng's case shows that a Qing official's wife did sometimes accompany her husband for official duties abroad and serve as his social wife. The decision seemed to depend on individual situations. Zeng did not have a concubine when he left for Europe and he was relatively flexible about Western customs. It did not take him long to realize that adhering strictly to rigid Confucian rules of gender separation and refusing to accommodate Western ways of socializing would be neither beneficial to Chinese diplomacy nor practical for their own lives. After all, his family lived in Europe for seven years, from 1879 to 1886. Nonetheless, Zeng was careful to avoid mentioning any detail of his wife's public presence in his journal, particularly if she mingled with men, to avoid any controversies in the domestic court. He was also fortunate not to have a hostile subordinate like Liu Xihong, who reported in detail on Guo and his concubine to the Qing court. Consequently, although Zeng's wife and daughters probably attended many *chahui* in Europe, people in China generally knew nothing about it. Their reputations as respectable women remained intact.

In addition to Zeng's wife, we know that later, another Qing diplomat's wife, Shan Shili (1856–1943), accompanied her husband, Qian

Xun (1853–1927), on several of his trips abroad. However, I have not seen any sources showing if she had ever played the role of a social wife in *chahui* and other public functions. It seems that Qian did not have any concubines at the time, either. Unlike Zeng's wife, Shan herself later wrote two works about her travels. The first is a travelogue *Guimao lüxing ji* (*My Travels in the Guimao Year*), which is a record of the author's eighty-day trip through China, Japan, Korea, and Manchuria en route to Moscow and St. Petersburg in 1903. The other is a ten-volume *Guiqian Ji* (*Writings on Returning to a Life of Seclusion*) from 1910, which explores Italy, ancient Greece, Roman art, and cultural exchanges between China and the West. Hu Ying has pointed out that Shan skillfully justified her activities abroad not as a transgression against propriety but as fulfilling family obligations and broadening knowledge. This suggests an important potential way for respectable women like Zeng's wife and daughters to justify their trips to Europe if necessary. Although Shan acquired a general knowledge of Western civilization through these trips, there is no mention in her work of whether she hosted parties and entertained foreign officials, as a diplomat's wife was expected to do in the West. Chances are that even if she did, she would wisely avoid writing about it.[67]

HOSTING *CHAHUI* IN LATE QING CHINA

Chinese ambassadors living in Europe frequently received invitations to socialize, but what of the Western diplomatic corps residing in China? Until the end of the Second Opium War (1856–1860), the Qing government basically maintained the policy of "*renchen wu waijiao*" (officials in private have no diplomatic power). This principle, issued at the beginning of the Qing dynasty, stipulated that as the ruler's subjects, officials without direct orders from the ruler should not engage in social and diplomatic interactions with foreigners, either through writing, meetings, or exchanging gifts. Officials who did so could be suspected of colluding with foreigners and blurring the traditionally established boundaries between the Chinese and "barbarians." However, after Qing's defeat in the First Opium War (1839–1842), government officials gradually realized that this policy of simply refusing to meet and communicate with foreigners could not continue. Their duties demanded frequent meetings with Westerners, as well as the exchange of gifts as tokens of goodwill.[68]

Treaties signed after their defeat in the Second Opium War finally obliged the Qing government to allow Western countries to maintain resident ministers in Beijing who could interact on an equal standing with Qing officials. (It was also at this time that the Qing court began sending envoys to Western countries.) On June 29, 1873, the Tongzhi Emperor received Western ministers at court, and from that point on, the old principle of *renchen wu waijiao* was nearly dead.[69] Still, many Qing officials hesitated to break this rule and venture into uncharted territory, well aware of previous cases in which officials who had no choice but to accept Westerners' gifts or attend their banquets – or even to allow their female family members to meet with Western officials – were punished by the central government or impeached by their fellow officials.[70]

It is in this context that we can fully appreciate the importance of a major breakthrough. In 1897, Chinese officials in Shanghai, then a major treaty port where many foreigners resided, hosted the first ball for Westerners in China. On November 4 of that year, Shanghai Daotai (Shanghai Intendant of Circuit, an official title), the aforementioned Cai Jun, used the occasion of Empress Dowager Cixi's birthday to host a grand Western-style ball at the Bureau for Foreign Affairs. The premises had been specially arranged for dancing: The ceiling was decorated with bunting and a hardwood floor had been laid for dancing.[71] The Daotai's office sent out six hundred invitations to the consular body and about five hundred Western guests attended, including "the British, French and German Admirals and the Captains and officers of all the foreign men-of-war in port, and to the leading and representative residents of Shanghai."[72] The event's Western style is clear from the fact that nearly all the guests attended with their female family members, that Chinese officials adopted Western-style handshakes as a way of greeting (instead of the traditional Chinese way of shaking their own hands); that the banquet served Western food; and that a band led by a Western conductor played Western music, performing all twenty dances on the program. The ball broke the rule of domestic seclusion by allowing Chinese officials' female family members to attend, but it improvised by setting aside a separate room for these women, who did not participate in dancing but watched through curtains, dressed in their most formal

1 THE EMERGENCE OF THE SOCIAL WIFE

and elegant attire. This compromise allowed respectable Chinese women to attend a public occasion without breaking the Confucian strictures on men and women mingling.

The ball seemed to have successfully impressed Westerners and achieved other friendly results. The *North China Herald*, one of the most influential English newspapers in Shanghai, not only sang Cai's praises personally but also highlighted the significance of the birthday celebration with great enthusiasm, lauding the event as "a new departure," the dawn of "a new era." Finally, an "enlightened Chinese official" "broke down the barrier" of "cumbersome" and "exclusive Chinese etiquette," entertaining and interacting with Westerners in their own style.[73] Clearly, the social etiquette adopted by Chinese officials in this ball was no small matter to the Westerners but indicated how open and inclusive Chinese officialdom was fast becoming.

Once Cai set a precedent – hosting official events in the Western practice to entertain Westerners – other Qing officials followed suit, particularly in Shanghai. In mid-April 1898, Prince Henry of Prussia (1862–1929) visited Shanghai. With the help of Cai Jun, Jiangsu Provincial Governor Kui Jun and Treasurer Nie Jigui hosted "a brilliant reception" for the prince. Due to limited space, only 150 invitations were issued; the great majority of those present were German residents. It was after midnight when the gathering dispersed, "the function having been highly gratifying to all concerned," according to the *North-China Herald*.[74]

In October 1907, William Howard Taft (1857–1930), then Secretary of War and soon to be a US president, visited Shanghai with his wife. For the first time, the leaders of the foreign concessions and those of the Chinese city collaborated to welcome and entertain them. When former US President Ulysses S. Grant (1822–1885) and his family visited Shanghai in May 1879, the concession leaders hosted a ball with only foreign guests in attendance. On a separate occasion, Chinese officials entertained the visiting Americans in traditional Chinese ways: a Chinese opera performance and a grand Chinese banquet (accompanied by some Western-style drinks, such as coffee). Although Chinese officials also arranged for some Chinese women to accompany their guests and watch the opera together, no cross-gender mingling occurred and no Chinese officials' wives appeared publicly.[75]

CONCLUSION

In contrast to Grant's visit, the welcoming banquet held for President Taft was attended by prominent Chinese officials, gentry, merchants, and leaders of the foreign concessions. With 230 guests in total, it was said to be the largest reception ever held in Shanghai. Chinese and foreign guests also sat and mingled together at the seven dining tables. It is noteworthy that twenty to thirty female Chinese students in attendance were from the Tianzu hui (Natural Feet Society), an anti-footbinding society founded in 1895 in Shanghai by Mrs. Alicia Little (1845–1926), a British national.[76] Two female students also presented Taft with a "handsome silver punch bowl" at the conclusion of his address. The students placed the bowl on a table and bowed low to the Tafts. The presentation took place amid tremendous applause.[77] The *New York Times* did not let the appearance of these Chinese girls in such a public event go unnoticed, singling the incident out for comment:

> This reception marked an epoch in the matter of the status of women in China, for today Chinese women of aristocratic families were present at the reception and even presided at tables, where they served refreshments. This was the first time such a thing had happened in China. This Chinese welcome to the American visitor was most significant ...[78]

Chinese women's public presence in this new style of social interaction was taken as an important symbol of progress – even honor – by the commentator. In 1907, the Qing government had just officially approved Chinese women's public school education. Female students were still very rare and their families tended to be socially progressive.[79] Furthermore, these students were members of an anti-footbinding society, which suggests that they (and maybe their families too) were brave enough to challenge traditional gender norms. Despite their being of a special cohort, the public appearance of these girls at the reception signaled that by 1907, at least near the end of the Qing dynasty, the rules forbidding respectable Chinese women from attending *chahui* and interacting with men in public had begun to relax.

CONCLUSION

It was largely the need to attend social diplomatic occasions – and confront or compromise with Western etiquette – that forced Chinese officials in the late Qing to break the Confucian stricture of gender separation and bring their concubines or wives to public functions. But these rapid changes in diplomatic practice should not be understood merely as a story of progress. The daring actions of these Chinese officials did not result in their rejection of Confucian gender norms and their acceptance of more egalitarian models. Even in the late nineteenth-century West, women were still viewed as belonging primarily to the domestic sphere despite not being required to seclude themselves from the public. Instead, the changes described in this chapter were adopted out of practical diplomatic necessity in the context of the Qing Empire's military defeats and the ensuing national crisis, as Chinese elites gradually realized that gender separation might be a liability in international politics. It was no light matter or easy process for the officials involved – or for their family members – as evidenced by their initial bouts of resistance and hesitation and by their eventual compromise and adaptation. It was a sensitive, politically charged issue, as evident from the punishment meted out to Ambassador Guo. Not until the iconoclastic New Culture Movement (the so-called Chinese Enlightenment), from the mid-1910s to the 1920s, do we begin to see progressive Chinese intellectuals systematically attacking Confucian gender doctrines and calling for gender equality and women's rights, leading to a wide-scale intellectual awakening.

It should also be pointed out that this process of adaptation did not consist simply of passively copying Western gender-related etiquette but included improvisations based on long-standing Chinese traditions and customs. The most notable example of this was the solution of temporarily bestowing a concubine with the authority and status of an official's main wife to represent China abroad. Since many concubines were former courtesans with experience of interacting publicly with men, they tended to behave more comfortably in various *chahui* than long-sequestered main wives. By tapping concubines as substitutes, their wives' reputations as "good women" under a Confucian definition remained intact. We also see other examples of improvisation, such as Cai Jun's strategy of setting aside a separate room for Chinese officials' wives to watch a *chahui* through curtains. Another solution, used in the early twentieth century, allowed modern-educated Chinese girls (rather

CONCLUSION

than older women with Confucian upbringings) to appear at *chahui*, providing just the refined influence that Lord Macartney desired while representing a new generation of Chinese women. Through these ingenious adaptations, *chahui* and women's public role in its development gradually became integral ingredients of modern China's diplomacy.

Paying attention to the role of gender in cultural diplomacy and state matters may not always yield a stark new interpretation of any one diplomatic event. Still, using gender as an analytical framework can provide substantial help in illuminating, for example, the little-known cross-cultural exchanges and adaptations that occurred during the process of diplomatic socialization, a topic that has been largely overlooked in late Qing diplomatic history.[80] Without due consideration of these historical issues, we are not able to fully understand what the complex process of modernizing China's international relations entailed. This chapter also shows that despite the lack of sources in these women's own voices, we can still find productive angles to witness their agency, such as through the lens of the gendered norm of socializing, utilizing existing sources to make new discoveries in the history of gender, such as the emergence of a novel role in late Qing diplomacy: the social wife.

CHAPTER 2

From Courtesan to Social Wife

THE 1911 REVOLUTION COMPELLED the Qing dynasty's last emperor to abdicate his throne, and on March 10, 1912, Yuan Shikai (1859–1916) was sworn in as President of the newly founded Chinese Republic. Among the daunting array of challenges immediately facing Yuan was the need to officially receive greetings from foreign diplomats and their wives in Beijing during a celebration of the Chinese New Year. Viewing himself as a modernizer, Yuan followed Western social customs and summoned his main wife, Lady Yu – who was old-fashioned and illiterate – from domestic seclusion to attend this public occasion as the First Lady of China. As they stood receiving guests, a foreign envoy approached, intending to shake her hands. Unable to understand the envoy's intentions, Lady Yu panicked and put her hands behind her back, which stunned and embarrassed the envoy.[1] From that moment on, Yuan meticulously prepared for important occasions, hoping to avoid similar mistakes. He ordered two of his modern-educated daughters to accompany his wife at public functions, answering questions and acting on her behalf.[2] Sometimes, he also allowed his first concubine (among nine), a former courtesan in Suzhou, to join him on diplomatic occasions. Allegedly, she "charmed many foreign officials."[3]

The challenges that Lady Yu faced were not hers alone. Although she was willing to appear in public to serve as Yuan's social wife, she was not comfortable or skillful enough to play this role. This was mostly because most elite men's main wives at the time, like Lady Yu, had just barely emerged from their accustomed domestic seclusion and had not gained enough experience and social skills to interact with men in public functions. During the late Qing, the reluctance of these wives to appear in public functions was largely attributed to Confucian conceptions of "propriety," which required that men and women not mingle and that respectable women remain in domestic seclusion. By the early Republican period, as Western influences intensified in China, women's domestic seclusion gradually lost its legitimacy as a marker of virtue and respectability and, therefore, more women began to move freely in the public sphere. Meanwhile, Chinese officials who frequently interacted with foreigners found themselves in greater need of women who could skillfully play the role of the social wife. However, now less concerned with Confucian propriety and more with the difficult adjustment transitioning from a domestic to a public role, many main wives with Confucian upbringings seem to have willingly ceded the outside arena to concubines. As Elizabeth Croll has noted:

> Some [main wives] had spent all but the last few years of their lives in the seclusion of their homes. Now, because of their husbands' occupations, they were expected to accompany them and meet and talk with foreigners, make speeches and play independent public roles of their own. They had found this abrupt transition from a domestic to a public role very hard and were sometimes not even sure that they approved of the new trends which their own activities represented.[4]

In rare cases, a principal wife with a Confucian upbringing was able to learn and adapt to the new social and public roles expected of her during the Republican period. Zhu Qihui (1876–1931), the only spouse of Xiong Xiling (1870–1937), an official who held several high positions in the Beiyang government (including Premier of China from 1913 to 1914), is a good example. As I have shown elsewhere, a classically educated woman from a Qing scholar-official family, Zhu turned out to be exceptionally capable and flexible in both the domestic and public realms. She supervised her menu and kitchen and was a generous hostess who entertained a diverse group of guests, including officials, intellectuals, revolutionaries, reformers, bankers, entrepreneurs, missionaries, and educators. She wore long leather shoes to conceal her bound feet and, over the years, learned to conduct herself according to Western etiquette, becoming a much sought-after guest of honor, "a charming Chinese lady," at embassy and legation parties in Beijing.[5]

She was also a renowned philanthropist of the time and a key national organizer and fundraiser for the Mass Education Movement in the 1920s. Admittedly, though, her successful repositioning and accomplishment in the public realm were both remarkable and exceptional in early twentieth-century China.

For an official without a main wife capable of attending public events and socializing with him, a concubine with good social skills could serve as his social wife. And though such skills might not have been the sole criterion in his choice of concubine, they could prove an important benefit in the long run. As the new Republican bureaucracy became increasingly modernized, concubines accompanied their official husbands with more frequency to offices, public functions, and on formal trips both domestic and abroad. Moreover, the Beiyang government (1912–1928) in Beijing was dominated by different warlords at various times, resulting in frequent leadership changes that gave a larger number of officials' wives and concubines opportunities to appear, albeit briefly, at official functions. The intense competition for power among various political factions, either in the cabinets or within different ministries and parliament, prompted politicians big and small – as well as their various staff members – to use any means available to maneuver for power and influence. Conflicts that could not be solved openly sometimes saw officials asking their concubines to mediate behind the scenes, writes historian Wang Shaoxi. The women initiated friendly contacts and secretly asked for favors or illicit opportunities to make money, their "feminine" social skills and tactics often proving more successful than direct methods. Some officials who had no concubines, even hired courtesans to socialize with them temporarily.[6] Occasionally, a conservative official might disapprove of his wife/concubine's public appearance. During Cao Kun's (1862–1938) brief term as President of China (1923–1924), he was said to disapprove of "Madame Liu's [his third concubine] desire to cut a figure in foreign society." Any proposed meetings between her and foreigners were thereby continually postponed until Cao, like his predecessors, "was ejected from his exalted office."[7]

In the early years of the Republic, the most readily available category of social/public women remained the courtesan (later, as I will show in the next chapter, elite men began to prefer their public wives to be female students). Although the early Republican period witnessed a general decline of the courtesan culture, many elite men's concubines were still former courtesans. The social and public skills these women had cultivated over the years made them more suitable candidates for public functions than sequestered main wives. It is not surprising to see those courtesans-turned-concubines became valued partners, relied on by husbands in need of social wives.

This chapter focuses on how courtesans/entertainers turned concubines played the role of the social wife in the early Republican period. Using a wide range of primary sources, from foreign travelers' accounts to the memoirs of contemporary observers and newspaper reports, it analyzes the public activities and social controversies surrounding the public appearances of particular concubines. The first section focuses on a case study of Li Benwei, a courtesan who became the concubine of Li Yuanhong (1864–1928), a politician who served twice as President of China (1916–1917 and 1922–1923). Benwei acted as Li's social wife for over twenty years, while his main wife focused principally on domestic affairs. An examination of Benwei's long-time public service reveals the range of social activities that the social wife of a top-ranking Chinese official engaged in during the early Republican period. In addition, her long-time success in the role also helped her gradually win the trust and appreciation of Li, thereby securing and strengthening her domestic status, despite being a courtesan-turned-concubine with no male heir. Seen from this perspective, therefore, her case also illustrates the important connections between a concubine's public role and her domestic status, adding a previously overlooked dimension to the innovations to concubinage in Republican China.

At the same time, the concubines' novel public status and privilege in the early twentieth century ran counter to the growing virulent critiques of concubinage as backward, exploitative, and anti-modern. Particularly when a concubine's social origin was as a courtesan/entertainer – a traditionally degraded category – her public presence could cause unprecedented tensions and sensitivities, especially on the international stage. The section "A National Disgrace" offers a case study on Zhou Shunqin, the concubine of Zhou Ziqi (1869–1923), a high-ranking Beiyang official, to illustrate this issue. When Zhou took his concubine to attend the

Washington Naval Conference in 1921, overseas Chinese students in the US protested against her presence, arguing that her public appearance might be used to bolster international perceptions of China as backward. During this conference, Zhou Shunqin also collided with a Chinese official's main wife, who was herself playing the role of a modern social wife. Their class difference and the conflicts generated by it illustrated another type of tension around concubines and main wives acting as social wives on the same international stage.

The section "Life after the Death of a Husband" examines the lives of public concubines after their husbands had passed away. In particular, I follow Li Benwei's life after the death of Li Yuanhong to investigate the two controversies that put her back in the limelight: her property dispute with Li's children and her failed attempt to remarry. Behind the widespread public condemnation of Li Benwei's remarriage lay her long-time role as Li's social wife: She was no longer treated as an ordinary courtesan-turned-concubine who usually could freely remarry without experiencing much moral judgment. Instead, she was expected to demonstrate traditional wifely virtues of loyalty and chastity. In other words, her new role as the social wife brought societal expectations of her continuous demonstration of wifely virtues, but could not provide her, a sonless concubine, upon the death of her husband, much-needed real-life protection against her weak legal status and social prejudices. After all, it is a role that cannot give a woman an independent identity, no matter how many years she has played it.

THE "NUMBER ONE CONCUBINE OF REPUBLICAN CHINA"

By all accounts, President Li Yuanhong's main wife, Wu Jingjun (1870–1930), was a typical secluded woman with no fondness for public activities. When Grace Seton (1872–1959), an American traveler, writer, and suffragist, met her in Beijing in 1922, she described the "First Lady of the Land" as "middle-aged, conventional, of the old order, who receives hardly anybody."[8] A "Mistress of Ceremonies" served as "the link between Madame Li and the foreign diplomatic world of Peking" and assisted her in arranging limited public activities. Bound-footed, Wu was a devout Buddhist who usually lived at the couple's home in Tianjin; Seton was able to see her only because she happened to be in Beijing to care for her grandson, who had a fever. Seton observed during their meeting that Madame Li was "much more reserved and showed less comfort in welcoming a foreign woman." Regarding her as a "representative of the old order," Seton heard from a woman in the Diplomatic Corps that "five years ago when her husband first became President, and Madame Li was dragged from the seclusion so beloved of Chinese women, she was terrified at the ordeal of having to meet half a dozen foreign women and to have to shake hands with them."[9] Though Li's main wife tried to fulfill her duty as the First Lady of China in the modern Western way, it seems clear that she did not enjoy it, preferring to stay at their home in Tianjin rather than live with her husband in Beijing.

In 1905, more than a decade before he would become president, Li Yuanhong met Li Benwei. He was then a lower-level commander under the eminent statesman Zhang Zhidong (1837–1909). Seeking to entertain a high-ranking official who had come to inspect the New Army that Li was helping train, he visited a brothel in Hankou, Hubei Province. By midnight, Li was said to be very drunk, and he slept in the room of a courtesan named Wei Hongbao. After that night's encounter, Li purchased Wei as his concubine and gave her a new name: Li Benwei.[10] By then, he was approximately forty-two years old and she was under twenty. Young, adaptable, pretty, and literate, Benwei proved adept at socializing and entertaining. Before long, she had become Li's indispensable assistant, accompanying him to public occasions while his main wife devoted her full attention to raising their four children. Newspaper reports suggest that during most of Li's political career, it was Li Benwei who accompanied him as "Madame Li" for public occasions and travel. She was later referred to as the "number one concubine of Republican China" (*minguo diyi rufuren*).[11]

The 1911 Wuchang Uprising, which led to the Xinhai Revolution that overthrew the Qing dynasty, dramatically altered Li Yuanhong's fate; it also elevated the public profile of his concubine. From then on, Benwei enjoyed a rare degree of visibility and privilege, attending and participating in a range of public activities. On October 11, 1911, when the uprising happened, Li was forced at gunpoint to be the new provisional military governor of Hubei Province, despite having killed several of the rebels attempting to overthrow the Qing dynasty. Li and his troops suffered severe casualties from attacks by the Qing government's army and navy. Benwei visited the injured soldiers on Li's behalf, boosting morale at local hospitals, offering comfort to the wounded, and explaining: "The Commander-in-Chief meant to come by himself, but the military situations are urgent, and he cannot leave the front. Therefore, he sent me to give his sincere regards." In this way, she became known as "Madame Li."[12]

Several other women who were publicly active in Hubei during this period were also concubines rather than the principal wives of male revolutionaries who were appointed to government positions after the victory of the Wuchang Uprising. These included Liu Yi (1891–1951), the concubine of Liu Gong (1881–1920), leader of the Gongjin Hui (a revolutionary organization) and central inspector of the Hubei government; and Xu Zonghan (1877–1944), the concubine of Huang Xing (1874–1916), the first army commander-in-chief.[13] Liu Yi set up a reception desk daily to assist the women who enthusiastically responded to the Wuchang Uprising and came to offer their help in overthrowing the Qing dynasty. Her successful collaborative work among the "women's circle" (*nüjie*) in the reception office convinced Li Yuanhong to entrust Liu Yi with organizing the women volunteers looking to join the army into a separate women's corps, and the Women's Northern Expeditionary Corps (Nüzi beifa dui) was born. Its establishment was widely reported in Hubei and elsewhere, prompting a wave of women to join the army to assist with the 1911 Revolution.[14]

The momentum of women's activism persisted into the early years of the new Republic. Meanwhile, Benwei continued to appear in public as Madame Li. Soon after successful negotiations between the revolutionary force in the south and the Qing government in the north saw the last emperor abdicate his throne (on February 12, 1912), the newly established Nanjing Provisional Government of the Republic dissolved the women's army and ordered the provinces to recruit no more troops. In short order, the leader of the Women's Northern Expeditionary Corps and other women leaders organized the Women's Suffrage Alliance (Nüzi canzheng tongmenghui) and elected Li's main wife as its nominal president, since Li had by then become Vice President of China. The

Women's Suffrage Alliance established the Women's School of Law and Politics (Nüzi fazheng xuetang) in Hubei, to which Li allocated over a thousand *liang* of silver currency. Both his wife and his concubine also made generous donations. In November 1912, the school officially opened its doors. Li attended the opening ceremony with Benwei (rather than his main wife) and delivered a speech emphasizing the importance of understanding the law and fulfilling civic obligations.[15] The founding of the Women's School of Law and Politics led to the establishment of a range of girls' schools across Hubei.

Benwei was a privileged concubine whose active public life was due mostly to her husband's position. Yao Wenyu, the accountant at the Women's School of Law and Politics featured in the opening of this book, faced different circumstances and was fired after becoming a concubine. Benwei was able to keep her position at the same school as its superintendent, and she went on to establish the No. 2 Women's Normal School in Hubei in 1913, together with the two daughters of Sun Yat-Sen (1866–1925), who had been forced to resign the presidency of China in 1912 (he gave the position to Yuan Shikai, whose wife then memorably offended a foreign envoy by refusing to shake his hand). Although Li was able to retain his vice presidency, he represented a potential threat to Yuan, who insisted in December 1913 that he move to Beijing. There, Li became a confined, passive bystander under Yuan's grip. Benwei accompanied him. According to a report in *Shenbao*, on the day they left Hubei, female students from across the province came to see Benwei off at the train station, regarding her as a "*taidou*" (leading figure) of women's educational circles. The students stood in a row in their uniforms along the Yangzi River, shook hands with her, and showed their reverence; Benwei exchanged gifts with them as tokens of respect before departing.[16] Benwei went on to become a socialite in Beijing and Tianjin, whose upper-class circles were aware that she had recently been studying English and French and would soon be able to hold direct conversations with foreigners.[17]

After Yuan Shikai died in 1916, Li became President of China twice (first from 1916 to 1917 and again from 1922 to 1923), further elevating Benwei's public platform. Benwei was often charged with entertaining female guests at parties and balls; she had become familiar with Western customs and could readily make her guests feel at home. Among the first five presidents of the Beiyang period, Li had the best relationship with the foreign diplomatic world in Beijing and it is highly likely that his concubine played a part in his success.[18] Li introduced her as his wife at informal meetings on an official trip to Japan, which surprised their hosts, who knew the truth. Although some Japanese officials also had concubines, they generally kept them out of the limelight and never presented them as wives.[19]

In June 1923, Benwei was entrusted with a crucial task at the center of a political incident. Cao Kun, the warlord and military leader of the Zhili clique, forced Li to resign his presidency and give it to Cao. As Li vacated the capital and fled to his home in Tianjin, his special train was intercepted by one of Cao's subordinates. Under pressure, Li confessed that he had taken the three presidential seals and secretly entrusted them to Benwei. When the head of the Beijing Police found Benwei hiding at a French hospital in the Legation Quarter of Beijing, she was not intimidated. Benwei refused to hand over the seals until Li called her from a train station in Tianjin and asked her to cooperate. Li was forced to sign an official resignation letter that had been drafted for him.[20] His official career was complete; Li devoted his energy to investing in industries and became very wealthy. In November 1923, he briefly took Benwei to Japan again for medical treatment.[21]

In 1928, Li died in Tianjin at the age of sixty-three. He left a large share of his property to Benwei, which indicates the great value he placed on her contributions and assistance during the twenty-odd years she spent with him. By successfully playing the role of Li's public wife, Benwei carved out a space of her own and strengthened her domestic position within the Li family despite having no children of her own. However, as I will discuss in the section "Life after the Death of a Husband," Benwei's public skills were no longer needed once Li died; as a sonless concubine, her domestic status within the Li family immediately became precarious.

A "NATIONAL DISGRACE"

Despite the public appearances of concubines like Li Benwei on official occasions, it should be noted that there seemed to be special situations in which an official might feel that his main wife had to be chosen over a concubine as his public consort. This sensitive matter arose if a concubine's presence in front of foreigners on very formal occasions on an international stage seemed in danger of arousing Chinese nationalist sentiments, given that a concubine could symbolize not only China's modernity but also its "backwardness." In her later years, Li's eldest daughter claimed that on very important occasions, such as formal receptions for foreign guests, it was invariably her mother, the main wife, who traveled to Beijing from Tianjin to play the public role of "Madame Li."[22] This possibility suggests that, as President of China, Li was highly attuned to how foreign dignitaries might perceive Benwei's status. But not all officials were as careful as Li. This section examines the case of Zhou Ziqi, whose concubine attended an international conference representing China, prompting public protests among overseas Chinese students. It also shows that most foreigners were not aware of a Chinese woman's actual domestic position. Instead, it was primarily a Chinese audience who felt uncomfortable – wary of potential foreign reactions to the concubine's true status.

Zhou Ziqi was another notable Beiyang official whose concubine frequently accompanied him on various functions, domestic and abroad, including formal occasions. Zhou was a Columbia University graduate who went on to hold key positions within the Beiyang government, including those of Minister of Finance, Acting Premier, and Acting Minister of Education.[23] His concubine, Zhou Shunqin, was a famous drum performer. He had purchased her from Tianjin and brought her along to Japan as his consort on official business, just as Li Yuanhong had traveled with Benwei.[24] Another Beiyang official – Liang Shiyi (1869–1933), who served as Premier of China from 1921 to 1922 – followed suit.[25]

In November 1921, Zhou took Shunqin to the Washington Naval Conference in the US, which caused a minor public outcry. Local overseas Chinese expressed great shame at the presence of an entertainer-turned-concubine in the Chinese diplomatic delegation. They called her a "national disgrace" (*guoru*) and protested against her attendance.[26] A contemporary Chinese newspaper also reported that during the three-month duration of the conference, "Madame Wellington Koo" (Oei Hui-Lan, 1889–1992) – whose husband, V. K. Wellington Koo (1888–1985), was an important member of the Chinese delegation – looked down on

Zhou's concubine. As a consequence of this discrimination, and to avoid Madame Koo, Zhou and Shunqin moved out of the accommodation leased by the Chinese delegation for the conference despite Shunqin's pregnancy. She gave birth to Zhou's first son in the US, which greatly pleased him; Zhou was then over fifty.[27]

To understand why the fleeting presence of a Chinese concubine in a foreign country could arouse such strong social protests among overseas Chinese, we must first understand the significance of the Washington Conference itself and the public sentiment that surrounded it. The conference took place at a particularly patriotic and anxious moment for many Chinese, domestically and abroad. In addition to establishing a naval balance of power, the conference aimed to resolve international entanglements in the Far East. The Chinese delegation's primary task was to reclaim China's sovereignty in Shandong Province. During the Paris Peace Conference and subsequent Treaty of Versailles in 1919, Shandong was transferred from the hands of the defeated German army to Japan, which aroused angry public protests against both foreign imperialist powers and the weak performance of the Chinese government. These protests directly induced the May Fourth Movement. The Washington Conference, occurring only a few years later, was invested with high expectations by the Chinese as an opportunity to reach a just settlement through diplomacy. Chinese communities in the US shared this desire. According to Madame Koo, when negotiations between Japanese and Chinese delegates became deadlocked during the conference, a group of angry Chinese students broke into the drawing room of their residence, loudly berating Wellington Koo, then Minister of Foreign Affairs, for the Chinese delegation's supposedly weak-kneed policy toward Japan. It was only after he had calmly explained the challenges and made clear that a firm stand was being taken by the Chinese delegation that the students were reassured and left peacefully.[28]

Within this political context, Shunqin's stigmatized status and background made her presence at an important international conference seem inappropriate, even humiliating, given that a strong and positive image of China was believed to be desperately needed for diplomatic success. According to Madame Koo's memoir, the wives of diplomats were expected to attend endless rounds of parties and social engagements during the conference, including a dinner hosted by President Warren Harding (1865–1923) and his wife at the White House. Shunqin may well have attended these events as the "wife" of a Chinese diplomat. Madame Koo would surely have been aware of her presence at these social occasions and was unlikely to contain her disgust, putting further pressure on Shunqin to move out of the official residence.

Madame Koo's memoir also reveals that Shunqin was not the only concubine to show up at a Chinese embassy or legation:

> According to those in the inner circles of Chinese diplomacy, anyone visiting a Chinese embassy or legation for the first time would meet a diplomat's wife who was roughly the same age as her husband. The next time around, the wife would be 20 or 30 years younger. I was living in an age when Chinese women were struggling to be freed from a long-term yoke of oppression such as Western women have never had to endure… Now, in diplomatic circles, I was watching the concubines, who had seen how foreign women were treated, rebelling against their substatus [sic]. Because divorce still was not recognized in China unless it was blessed by the ranking elders of both families, the liberation of the concubines involved sleight-of-hand tactics. The genuine wife was sent away, usually back to her family, while the concubine, formerly the number two wife, stayed on and took the wife's place and authority. It was as simple as that and, so far as the legitimate wives were concerned, as humiliating.[29]

Madame Koo's account suggests, first, that it was not uncommon for Chinese diplomats to bring their concubines to live with them at a Chinese embassy or legation abroad and, second, that the concubines with public experience were gradually learning Western gender norms and practices. Rather than simply enduring their low domestic status, as previous generations had, some demanded better, more equal treatment. Often, the practical and tactical solution was to set up separate households at different locations rather than for men to divorce their wives. Consequently, the concubine was able to "take the wife's place and authority," particularly when the wife was absent.

In addition to the national interest, it was also possible that the protesting overseas students were simultaneously concerned about their own reputations being tarnished in the US, despite denouncing Shunqin as a "national disgrace" without mentioning their personal concerns. As I have shown in the Introduction, Chinese Australians at the beginning of the twentieth century were very sensitive about how the Chinese custom of concubinage could negatively affect white Australia's public perceptions of them. Therefore, it was likely that the overseas students in the US had similar personal concerns in mind, although they did not share them publicly.

Madame Koo's resistance to the presence of concubines in official parties was probably not due merely to her concern for China's reputation, either. She had her own unpleasant family experience with concubines. As a main wife, Madame Koo's mother suffered a lifelong unhappy marriage filled with jealousy, rivalry, and intrigue due in no small part to the many concubines kept by her husband, an extremely wealthy Chinese merchant in the Dutch East Indies (nowadays Indonesia).[30] More importantly, Madame Koo's concern for her own status and reputation trumped any putative female solidarity. A cosmopolitan speaker of six languages, Madame Koo was one of the few modern-educated wives of Chinese officials who actively accompanied her husband to public and diplomatic functions and served as a hostess during the Beiyang period.[31] Over the years, she must have realized that the efforts of modern Chinese women to break the traditional gender norms that required "good" women to stay in the domestic realm were jeopardized by the simultaneous presence of concubines, who were often former courtesans, particularly in front of Western audiences in new social spaces. Courtesans already had a public life in China; now "good women" wanted some of that space too. When they met in Beijing in 1922, Grace Seton recorded Madame Koo explaining that she had been "nearly everywhere" and was at present "only assisting Minister Koo in social diplomatic duties, hoping to introduce the Chinese feminine sphere to the Western world."[32] Madame Koo seems to have been keenly attuned to representing modern Chinese womanhood positively on the international stage. "The Chinese feminine sphere" that Madame Koo tried consciously to promote and represent had no space for concubines, who could only amplify the already huge social risks of daring to appear as a "proper" wife in public. Seen from this view, Madame Koo's resistance was not mere snobbery or old-fashioned loathing of low-status concubines; it was also about protecting her own reputation while forging new public roles for respectable women.

On the other hand, it seems that the overseas protests had little impact on Shunqin's social life in China. After returning from the Washington Conference, Shunqin continued her role as a social wife and hostess. In December 1922, she invited Seton to tea in her Beijing home. Thanks to Seton's published account of her trip to China, we gain a closer glimpse of a woman for whom there are few Chinese sources. After entering "a very large drawing room charmingly furnished in the French manner," Seton describes her hostess:

> Young, in the twenties, very pretty with a satisfying taste in dress, exquisite jewels and a winning smile, I found Mrs. Chow Tzu-chi [Zhou Ziqi] altogether charming. Educated in a fashionable girls' school in Tientsin [Tianjin], her native city, Li Yu [probably another name for her] developed a real interest in music, studying Chinese music at home and European music later, in Washington, where in 1921 she accompanied her husband on a diplomatic mission. In fact, music and charity are the two things which occupy most of her time. She is director of a school for poor children and a member of the Woman's Charitable Society. Mrs. Chow [Zhou] is an example of one phase of the varied social life in Peking [Beijing]. She likes movies and theatres, riding, skating and walking, although her big limousine seemed to be in no way neglected.[33]

The "diplomatic mission" to which Seton referred was, of course, the Washington Naval Conference. Her account also reveals that, despite Shunqin's background as an entertainer, she had received some level of modern education and was thus literate. Like Li Benwei, she was also active in charity work. These aspects of Shunqin's experience do not conform to the prevalent image of the "backward" concubine subscribed to by overseas students. But her tainted class origins and concubine status were probably shameful enough for the students to protest.

On the other hand, Seton seemed not only to know nothing about the overseas protest against Shunqin, but also to assume that her hostess – this "social" woman, whose English name was "Shirley T. C. Chow" (see cover image) – was Zhou's wife. In fact, after his first wife (surnamed Wang) died in 1916, Zhou married a woman named Tang Kangyu (1901–1966) in 1918.[34] But this second wife was rarely mentioned, whereas Shunqin became the woman most associated with Zhou. At Shunqin's Beijing party, Seton also met "an interesting group of women," including a "Mrs Tsai Lun [Zai Lun], a wife of the fifth brother [should be son] of the Imperial Prince Ch'ing [Qing], who was Councillor-in-Chief under the Empress Dowager Tzu His [Ci Xi]."[35] Actually, Seton was mistaken again. "Diana T'sai Lun" (Lun Qianru) was a concubine of Zai Lun, with an entertainment background (as a Peking opera singer) resembling Shunqin's.[36] Seton did not speak Chinese; it was up to the Chinese women present at the party to decide if they wanted to reveal information about the identity of a wife or concubine. Clearly, they chose to keep Seton in the dark, possibly out of fear of how a foreigner might react to the truth.

Croll has highlighted this common misunderstanding among Westerners in her study of European women writers in late Qing and Republican China:

> Even when it looked as if some rapport might have been established, there were instances of culturally-derived misunderstandings which could beguile the unsuspecting foreigner. For example, European wives often thought quite incorrectly that they had been privileged to meet the wives of their husbands' business or official acquaintances even though it was not usual for the women to accompany them to tea-house or restaurant meetings.[37]

Croll gives the example of an American writer who thought she was meeting the wife of her husband's business acquaintance, only to find afterward that "a flower girl had been hired especially for the occasion."[38] This suggests that, besides using concubines to play the role of a social wife, temporarily hiring other public women was another practical alternative adopted by Chinese men to meet the demand for social interactions with foreigners. Moreover, as Croll suggests, businessmen, as well as officials who frequently dealt with foreigners, often required a social wife for social functions; however, no sources have been discovered that shed more light on how this practice operated in the business world. Since many Westerners remained completely unaware that the Chinese women they met during social occasions were, in fact, concubines rather than wives, Shunqin's appearance at the Washington Conference probably did little damage to China's reputation. Mostly, it was the overseas Chinese students who felt shame and anxiety about the prospect of Shunqin's status being discovered by Westerners. This reminds us of the sensitivity and sense of urgency expressed by Wong Shee Ping around 1909–1910 in his novel *The Poison of Polygamy*, urging Chinese Australians to abandon concubinage to improve their public perception in the eyes of white Australia.

Nevertheless, Seton gradually grew suspicious about the exact status of the women she met in many large Chinese households: "Frequently some one was introduced as 'a cousin' whom I suspected of being a secondary wife, the fact being concealed from me out of deference to my Western prejudices."[39] Seton, who was a suffragist herself, eventually became aware of the concubine issue – which was heatedly discussed in 1920s China – and was informed on some occasions that the women she met were concubines. She was "puzzled," for she found that "Some of the sweetest, most attractive women I met were secondary wives."[40] So, she suspected that "these women must not be classed as concubines, as the Western mind understands the term."[41]

LIFE AFTER THE DEATH OF A HUSBAND

Because concubines were typically much younger than their husbands, they had to face the challenge of maintaining their livelihood, status, and legal rights after their husbands' deaths. In most cases I have encountered, the concubine quickly disappeared from public sight unless something unusual happened. A majority fell into obscurity and experienced some kind of hardship or tragedy. Hong Jun (mentioned in Chapter 1) died shortly after returning to China in 1893, leaving his concubine, Sai Jinhua, to become a courtesan once again as Hong's family refused to provide her with any maintenance.[42] Shunqin also disappeared from public sight soon after Zhou Ziqi died. When Grace Seton met her in 1922, her husband was at the height of his career, even briefly serving as Acting President of China after Xu Shichang (1855–1939) resigned. Only a year later, in October 1923, Zhou unexpectedly died of illness in Beijing. From then on, any historical traces of Shunqin disappear. The rise and fall from prominence experienced by these concubines reflects their auxiliary status. No matter how well known they became, their rise took place within the confines of the patriarchy rather than by them asserting a role for themselves outside of it.

After the death of her husband, a concubine often suffered because the main wife and her children refused to continue her support and drove her from the household, though this was illegal. Concubines who did not give birth to sons and consequently could not receive a share of property through their children were particularly vulnerable. The promulgation of the Nationalist government's civil code of 1929–1930 only made matters worse: Following Western models, the law promoted monogamy and did not recognize the legal existence of concubines. Having no legal status, a concubine had no inheritance rights within her husband's family and could only hope for maintenance, which depended on her being allowed to remain within the household.

During the early Republican period, a concubine's legal entitlement to maintenance was based on household membership documented in a contract, since her ties to the household head were no longer defined as marriage relations as they had been during the Qing period. When her master died, this obligation was transferred to the new head of the household. Later, the promulgation of the new civil code further limited a concubine's household-member status as a contingency resting on co-residence with the household head. In other words, a concubine now had to remain in the same (rather than a separate) household to continue receiving maintenance; once she left, she lost her status as a household member and, consequently, her entitlement to maintenance.[43]

Under the new civil code, a concubine who had a son gained legal rights over her own offspring, who were no longer considered the children of the main wife. This gave her room to maneuver through her children. With the new law giving equal status to every son in the family and the Chinese inheritance custom of equally dividing property among all sons (rather than the eldest inheriting all), a concubine now had access to economic resources and could enjoy the respect and care of her sons even after her husband's death. Chaste widow-concubines, though probably a small percentage of the total population, had been awarded rights and status approaching a principal wife's since the late Qing. But a concubine with no offspring whose husband died early lost any way to incorporate herself into the kinship structure; her luck probably depended on the mercy of the main wife and her husband's family members unless she had the resolve, resources, and patience for a lawsuit. Many ended up remarrying, either by choice or out of desperation.[44]

Compared to other public concubines, Li Benwei's life after Li Yuanhong's death was somewhat exceptional: not because she suffered no hardships as a widowed concubine in an intensely patriarchal society, but because she refused to endure the injustice and inequality silently, fighting instead for what she believed she deserved. Benwei returned to the limelight in the 1930s owing to two major controversies, which demonstrate, on the one hand, how a concubine's public profile over the years could make her more assertive on issues of gender equality and women's rights and, on the other hand, how that profile could constrain her life choices in the years after an illustrious husband's death.

First, Benwei sued Li's children for her share of the property Li had left her, and she won, largely due to the existence of Li's will.[45] In May 1928, as Li lay dying, he stayed at Benwei's place for about seven days before being moved to his main wife's residence (where he eventually died). However, while staying with Benwei, Li created a will, leaving her most of his properties in Tianjin, even though they had no children together. His principal wife was deeply displeased by this news, and within two years, she died as well. Around this time, Benwei changed her name to Wei Wenxiu and found a new lover, Wang Kuixuan, who worked at a local silk store and was about ten years her junior. Benwei did not try to hide the relationship. When Li's daughters and sons learned of the relationship, they criticized Benwei's behavior, accusing her of tarnishing the reputation of the late president and the Li family. They refused to give her the properties that Li had bequeathed her and provided a monthly stipend of only 300 *yuan*.[46] Angry, Benwei took the certificates of Li's will and left Tianjin with Wang to resettle in Qingdao, Shandong Province. She sued Li's children, claiming that they had deserted her and refused to hand over the properties that were rightfully hers. Major newspapers, including *Shenbao*, all reported the lawsuit. Benwei won her case due mostly to the existence of Li's will. The court ordered not only that the properties be returned to her, but also that the Li family pay her 25,000 *yuan* as a pension. In September 1934, Benwei (now using the name Wei Wenxiu) announced in the newspapers that she had officially severed her ties with the Li family.[47]

Several months later, while living in Qingdao, she once again attracted public attention, this time for a more controversial matter: her remarriage. After renting out some properties in Tianjin, Wei Wenxiu used the rent she collected to help Wang invest in the local silk business in Qingdao, which turned into a great success. So, around January 1935, they decided to get married in a grand ceremony. Wei Wenxiu was now forty-three and Wang was over thirty. But as the news spread, various social circles, including Li's old friends, began to criticize and ridicule her. In response to questioning from a close relative in Beijing, Wei allegedly wrote a letter explaining her reasons for remarrying. The letter was soon circulated in newspapers and journals, including the leading newspaper, *Shenbao*:

> Love is destined by heaven; therefore, its course cannot be stopped. In our current civilized world, where new morality is prevalent, widows are not forbidden by propriety to remarry. Those who still refuse to do so and thus are living difficult lives are stupid women. You criticized me for remarrying. This was because different people have different views. I appreciate your concern. Although Mr. Li treated me well, for the past over twenty years, I have served him with dedication. Although I cannot claim that I have repaid all my debts of gratitude, I did not fail my womanly duty. When Mr. Li was hardly cold in his grave, his descendants would not tolerate me. If I do not seek somebody to rely upon, how can I continue to survive? Those who are understanding probably would forgive me due to my difficult circumstances. As for those who would not, I only seek my peace of mind. Why should I care about their opinions?[48]

Wei gave three justifications for remarrying: First, she had fallen in love; second, the time's new standards allowed widows to remarry rather than remain chaste; and third, difficult life circumstances forced her to remarry. Was her argument widely accepted in 1930s China? We can get a sense of the era's moral yardstick in judging a concubine's actions after her husband's death from a contemporaneous case. In 1935, around the same time that Wei was being publicly criticized for her choice to remarry, a pregnant concubine with the surname Sha committed suicide by jumping from the roof of her building only hours after her husband's sudden death in Nanjing.[49] This incident was quickly reported by *Shenbao* because her husband, Lu Diping (1887–1935), a high-ranking Nationalist official, was the former provincial governor of Jiangxi and Zhejiang.[50] Although some scholars later claimed that the deaths of Lu and his concubine were the result of Lu's involvement in the investigation of the assassination of Shi Liangcai (1880–1934), a journalist and the owner of *Shenbao*,[51] newspaper reports of the time focused mostly on extolling Sha's suicide as a form of "chaste martyrdom" (*xunjie*).[52] If such a violent act was still popularly applauded in the 1930s, it is hardly surprising that public opinions of Wei's remarriage were generally disapproving.

A survey of the public discussion in print media surrounding Wei's remarriage reveals a major factor underpinning the hostility she received: her long-standing role as the public companion of one of the country's most respected men. Although it was not uncommon for a concubine (particularly one without a son) to remarry after the death of her husband, the heavy criticisms aimed at Wei indicate that she was not considered an ordinary concubine.

Three days after her explanations for remarrying were published in newspapers, another article in *Shenbao* raised the issue of the undue public attention given to Wei's remarriage. The author points out, first, that for ordinary families, a concubine's remarriage was not a big deal; even a main wife's remarriage was no longer rare. Because Wei was Li's concubine and she had now chosen to remarry, she was criticized for tarnishing the late president's reputation; Li's family members regarded her action as a great stain on their family's reputation. However, the *Shenbao* author argues that after Li resigned, he was supposed to be treated like everyone else. Why should people pay particular attention when his former concubine remarried? Additionally, the author continues, under the new civil code, concubinage was no longer defined as a legal marriage and Li had already died, leaving Wei "no inalienable relations" with the Li family. Remarrying or not was related only to Wei's own personhood (*ren'ge*) and had nothing to do with Li's "family reputation." The author concludes that Wei's remarriage would best be treated as "a very ordinary and common matter."[53]

Outside the pages of *Shenbao*, the reality was that Li and Wei were not treated as equals to everyone else. After Li died in 1928, major Nationalist officials, including Chiang Kai-shek, all went to commemorate him and unanimously decided that he deserved a state funeral. However, it was only in the early 1930s that the committee in charge of the matter finally selected his burial site near a mountain in Wuchang (Hubei Province, where the 1911 Revolution first started) and finished construction of his tomb. In April 1933, major newspapers like *Shenbao* reported in detail the transport of coffins for Li and his main wife (who died in 1930) from Tianjin to Hankou. One report mentioned that Wei and other Li family members accompanied the coffins south throughout the trip.[54] Photos of Wei, together with other Li family members wearing mourning white, were also circulated in major newspapers and journals,[55] which reminded the public of the close relationship she once had with the late president. The two coffins were temporarily placed in a Buddhist temple in Wuchang to await the completion of the mausoleum's construction. Finally, on November 24, 1935, Li's long-planned state funeral was held in Wuchang. The scale of the ceremony, including the cost and the number of participants (more than 50,000), was rarely seen in modern Chinese history.[56] Thus, in January 1935, just as Wei chose to remarry, public sentiment surrounding Li's commemoration was still strong. In addition, from 1932 to 1934, Wei waged a highly publicized inheritance lawsuit against the Li family, remaining highly visible in the media. Nobody forgot for a moment that she was the late president's public companion.

In this context, it is not difficult to understand why some groups and individuals who had been close to Li took special action to show their disapproval of Wei's remarriage. The Hubei Native Place Association in Qingdao (Lüqing hubei tongxianghui) petitioned the mayor of Qingdao, Shen Honglie (1882–1969), to banish Wei and Wang from the city.[57] The mayor did so, agreeing that Wei's remarriage "tarnished the reputation of the late president." Mayor Shen was not only from the Hubei Province (like Li); he also happened to serve under Li during his early military career in Hubei.[58] Their close connection is crucial to understanding why the mayor chose to use his administrative power to grant such a rare and illegal request. Wei was thus expelled from Qingdao, though not without voices raised in defense of her right to live in the city.[59] Her new husband, Wang, was arrested by local police, who confiscated and closed his shop and questioned whether he, a mere "merchant," intended to use the former concubine of the late president for certain unseemly purposes, especially considering their age difference. Under threat, Wang agreed to completely cut ties with Wei. After failing to resolve the issue with the Qingdao government, Wei intended to leave for Beijing. However, when she asked a relative to help rent a place to shelter her from attack temporarily, she was decisively turned down.[60] It was said that she went to Hangzhou in southern China, where she considered becoming a Buddhist nun.[61]

At the same time, the much-celebrated remarriage of a former Chinese premier poignantly exposed the double standard wielded against Wei. On February 9, 1935, following his wife's death, the sixty-five-year-old Xiong Xiling remarried a woman twenty-eight years his junior, Mao Yanwen (1898–1999). A grand ceremony was held at a cathedral in Shanghai and the union was celebrated by the media, friends, and relatives of both sides. Even Qingdao Mayor Shen Honglie invited the couple to his city to reside and establish new charities. Hearing the news of Xiong's remarriage, Wei published a sentimental poem in *Shenbao*'s "Women's Garden" section. In it, she used the same poetic tune that Xiong had once used to write a love poem to Mao. She expressed her sadness about how she struggled to have "a feminist new life" and how she hoped to remarry for love but could not due to the "cannibalistic" rules of "propriety" and the heated public discussion of her actions.[62]

The poem garnered Wei public sympathy and support, while sparking a wider debate about gender inequality in Chinese society. Some readers compared Xiong's remarriage to Wei's and noted the drastically different social and public reactions, as well as the unfair treatment to which Wei was subjected, especially considering the age difference between Xiong and Mao was larger than that between Wei and Wang.[63] In February 1935, several women's societies in Shanghai held a joint meeting to express their "righteous indignation" at the criticism Wei had endured. They decided to send Wei a letter of comfort and, if necessary, to visit Nanjing to petition the Nationalist government.[64] The Nanjing Women's Culture Promotion Society (Nanjing shi funü wenhua cujinhui) sent Wei a telegram, stressing that the law allowed widows to remarry and that the provisional constitution granted citizens the freedom to live wherever they chose. Editors of the journal *Funü gongming* (*Women's Resonance*) not only published the telegram but also encouraged Wei to fight back on behalf of all widows.[65] Still, these sympathetic comments and support seem not to have changed Wei's situation much. Wang had already left her, and after the remarriage controversy, she gradually fell out of public view. We know little about how she lived the rest of her life.[66]

Unlike many other concubines, Benwei spent over twenty years of her life as a public figure – "Madame Li" – and was often treated much the same as Li's wife. Her high public profile came with both benefits and costs. In the 1910s, her privileged status as the concubine of then-Vice President Li enabled her to assume a vaulted position in a modern women's school (which was denied to other concubines such as Yao Wenyu) and to engage in a range of public, progressive activities. However, this also meant that she could not remarry freely, her options curtailed by her well-established association with the former president of China. Dominant public opinion seems to have expected that she would dedicate the rest of her life to the commemoration of her dead husband, thereby embodying the long-valued virtues of loyalty and chastity more commonly associated with a widowed principal wife than a concubine.

However, she refused to follow this script. Wei had few options but to remarry in order to survive, in part because her ambiguous and precarious status as a concubine loomed large after Li's death. She was not on good terms with Li's children, who were reluctant to support her and mired in legal disputes about her status. Her public role was no longer needed, and with no children, she had no inalienable ties to the Li family. She was only in her mid-thirties; although she won the property lawsuit, what Li left for her was not enough to support her for the rest of her life. What happened to Wei after Li's death shows how easily a concubine could lose her privileges and face, alone, the cost and consequences of her previously high-profile public life. Although the social changes of the Republican period had given this former courtesan unprecedented new opportunities, it was still a time in which women's identities were, to a large degree, dependent on men.

CONCLUSION

During the early Republican period, concubines like Li Benwei and Zhou Shunqin were able to adapt and play the role of social wives because, among other factors, their former experience as courtesans and entertainers had equipped them with social and public skills that most of the hitherto cloistered main wives did not possess. This novel role gave them special privileges and social respect that ordinary concubines could rarely enjoy. However, the role and the benefits associated with it lasted only as long as their husbands remained alive. Its fundamentally auxiliary and dependent nature determined that this new role alone could not give concubines an independent identity nor any important protections after the deaths of their husbands.

Moreover, it seems that during this period, the concubine status of these women was not generally kept secret from the Chinese public, as evidenced by the fact that news media frequently used the term "*ru furen*" to address Li Benwei. It was probably not difficult to determine the social backgrounds of these concubines, as they had been public entertainers. The only sensitivity involved was about their appearances at official functions when foreign dignitaries were present, especially since the 1920s. Li Yuanhong wisely avoided any controversy by bringing his old-fashioned main wife from another city to meet foreign guests on those occasions. Zhou Ziqi, on the other hand, was less careful and brought his concubine to the Washington Naval Conference, which caused angry protests from overseas Chinese students who had strong anxiety about how the "backward" low-class concubine and former entertainer might tarnish China's international image (probably their own as well) in Westerners' eyes.

On the other hand, also on the international stage, Madame Koo's efforts to remove Shunqin from the Chinese delegation's official residence also suggest that some main wives during this period were simultaneously forging very similar new public roles. However, they clashed over their class differences. To keep her respectable reputation, the main wife could not tolerate the coexistence of her lower-class tainted sister and felt compelled to exclude the concubine from shared public spaces to protect herself. In Chapter 4, I will further demonstrate how this class-based discrimination gave rise to politics and divisions within progressive women's organizations and public schools.

After the early 1920s, as the Anti-Concubinage Movement gradually reached its height, press coverage of officials' social wives rarely disclosed their concubine status, as I will show in the next chapter. Instead, these women were indistinguishably addressed by the general term of *furen*, making it difficult for the public to know who were actually concubines. As new generations of modern-educated Chinese women grew up, some of them also ended up becoming concubines of elite men. The majority of these women did not have tainted social backgrounds as courtesans and their social and public skills were mostly developed through their experience in modern public schools. Closely resembling the much-celebrated "new women" and being very active in public, did they willingly accept their status as concubines? How did they become concubines? The next chapter will focus on this type of concubine and answer these important questions.

CHAPTER 3

From "Female Student" to Concubine

As for a female student who willingly became a concubine, it is totally due to the shallowness of her knowledge, being amazed by vanity, and thus voluntarily falling into degeneration; or it is due to her abnormal psychological development driven by erotic impulse, becoming a concubine by mistake; or she was deceived to be a concubine.

—A Chinese sociologist analyzing the new phenomenon of female students becoming concubines in 1931, from Guan Ruiwu, "Qie zhi yanjiu, 98."

I married Dejie so as to have a social companion to the frequent social public occasions I had to attend... She is a female student, thus educated and sensible. You can ask her to help you.

—Li Zongren, a military official from Guangxi Province, explains to his main wife why he took in a concubine in 1924, from Xiuwen Li and Tan Ming, *Wo yu Li Zongren*, 31.

THIS CHAPTER FOCUSES on a new social phenomenon that emerged in the Republican period: Some "female students" (*nü xuesheng*) became concubines, either forcibly or voluntarily. Although there were other types of modern educated women who became concubines, this category became the most eye-catching in public discussion and generated the most intense outcry among social progressives. It testifies to the persistence rather than the elimination of concubinage, revealing underexamined innovations of a traditional institution for a new era. Specifically, this chapter first examines the various reasons behind the phenomenon and the criticisms it generated, as seen through print media. It shows that although social criticism often blamed the students themselves for their own deficiencies (which can be seen from the first epigraph), in reality, there were a variety of reasons that led to the phenomenon, such as young women's lack of individual autonomy and freedom due to the continued tradition of arranged marriage and strong parental authority, the lack of employment opportunities for female graduates, and the desire to pursue the new ideal of "free love" with married men who could not seek divorces. Consequently, some female students found themselves caught between new ideals of love and marriage and the lingering influences of traditional constraints. Eventually, they had few other choices but to become concubines despite the strong social stigma associated with this category.

The second part of the chapter focuses on a case study of Guo Dejie (1906–1966), a female student who became a concubine, specifically, the concubine of Li Zongren (1890–1969), a major military official of the Republican period. In particular, it examines how she played the role of a modern social wife for Li for several decades. Though Guo was highly visible in the public eye as "Madame Li Zongren" (Li Zongren *furen*) from the 1920s to the 1940s, her concubine status was rarely mentioned in print media. Unlike courtesan-turned-concubines, Guo's untainted social origin made it difficult for the public to discover her concubine status. Her public image, as reflected in various newspaper reports, was that of a modern, educated woman with good social skills, which she utilized not only to engage with various women's, patriotic, and charitable causes but also to support her husband's official career. As we can see from the chapter's second epigraph, Li chose Guo largely so that he would have an educated social companion for various public functions and official events, a role that his barely literate main wife could not play. Whether or not this was his sole criterion in choosing a concubine, Li articulated an elite man's need for a social wife in the changing public sphere of Republican China, calling our attention to a new rationale for taking a concubine, one that differed from traditional reasons such as producing a male heir to carry on the family line. Unsurprisingly, by the Nationalist period, as the number of modern educated women increased, students-turned-concubines became the new preferred choice of many elite men for playing the role of the increasingly indispensable social wife and serving as domestic helpers who lived separately from the men's often old-fashioned secluded main wives. This case was chosen because it was one of the few well-documented ones due to the existence of a rare oral history account left by Li's main wife, which reveals the inner details of the domestic and public arrangements made by an official husband, his wife, and his concubine. As we will see, in this novel gender role, through their modernity, clean social origin, and public recognition, some concubines, such as Guo, demanded more than merely some improvement in their domestic circumstances – they were no longer willing to accept their concubine status and instead attempted to be recognized as wives.

FEMALE STUDENTS BECOMING CONCUBINES

Nü xuesheng – an entirely new social category that emerged in early twentieth-century China – generally referred to women who were enrolled in modern public schools from their primary years through to university.[1] In early twentieth-century China, this category of women enjoyed a privilege that most did not: They were allowed to leave their homes and go into the public realm for their education. The majority of Chinese women (and men) in this period were illiterate; some women acquired basic literacy only through home (but not public) schooling. So, although their time as students may seem like a transitory phase of life, it served as an important identity and marker that could define a woman long after she had left school, indicating a generally progressive outlook regardless of the number of years spent in formal education.

The category itself was a direct outcome of opening China's educational institutions to female students. During the imperial period, elite Chinese women could receive only limited private education at home from their parents or private tutors. Generally speaking, in their early years, they were taught Confucian classics and histories alongside their brothers. After age ten, girls studied separately, covering more "womanly skills" such as weaving and needlework to prepare them for future marriages. They were not allowed to take the civil service examination, even those who showed real talent in learning the classics.[2] According to historian Paul Bailey, China's first public school for girls was established in 1898 when the Chinese Girls' School (Zhongguo nü xuetang) was founded by a group of reformers (comprised of both men and women) at the height of the One Hundred Days' Reform.[3] Its curriculum included modern subjects such as law, psychology, and pedagogy, as well as traditional subjects like history, art, and "womanly skills."[4] In 1907, the Qing government officially approved public school education for Chinese women. Five years later, the new Republican government established an education system that provided secondary schools for girls and sanctioned coeducation in primary schools.[5] Around 1919, higher education for women was approved with the establishment of Beijing Women's Higher Normal School. Soon after, the prestigious Peking University allowed women to enroll. Throughout this period, however, the government viewed the purpose of women's education as an aid to fulfilling their future duties as virtuous wives, worthy mothers, and scientific managers of the household, not as a training ground for career women.[6]

The total number of female students in Chinese-operated schools (there were missionary schools as well) was small, especially in the early Republican period. According to Bailey, their number "increased from just over 141,000 in 1912–13 (constituting nearly 5 percent of the school population) to nearly 420,000 in 1922–23 (comprising just over 6.9 percent of the school population)."[7] A growing demand for female teachers meant that "normal" (teacher-training) schools now included a relatively large percentage of female students. In 1923, there were nearly "7,000 students at women's normal schools, constituting over 17 percent of the total attending normal school."[8] Cong Xiaoping has noted that for women from rural and remote inland regions, one of the few valid channels to economic self-reliance started with enrolling in a woman's normal school and then securing employment as a teacher.[9] And yet, some female graduates (even some students) found an alternative life trajectory: Rather than seek professional employment, they became the concubines of wealthy men.

Female students were highly visible in the early Republican period – a frequent topic of discussion, a new representational category, and a symbol of modern womanhood.[10] Equipped with practical knowledge and social skills, educated young women were expected to become productive citizens who could contribute to modernizing China. Over the years, however, their "outrageous" dress styles, "frivolous" and "coquettish" attitudes, and "disorderly" and "unrestrained" behavior became a source of consternation and condemnation in various press outlets, revealing the ambivalence and anxieties that many "modernizing conservatives" felt upon seeing the impact and consequences of early twentieth-century women's public education.[11] Notably, it was the public, rather than the educational, dimension of girls' schools, that raised the concerns of social conservatives.[12] Coeducational reforms that had always elicited fears about the potential dangers surrounding the school for girls now gripped officials and educators – particularly, the question of how to control girls' sexual behavior and preserve their chastity when the sexes were no longer segregated.[13] The constant denunciation of female students' behaviors in the press was a direct reflection of anxieties borne of the predicted breakdown of the existing moral and sexual order, as well as the looming danger of modernity.[14] We see similar anxious social reactions to the cultural figures of the Modern Girl and the New Woman in Republican China.[15] Other scholars have noted that the public image of female students evolved over time, shifting from that of a simple, innocent girl in the 1910s to a mature, fashionable, and materialistic woman in the 1930s, who increasingly resembled the popular stereotype of a concubine.[16]

The phenomenon of students becoming concubines was a highly visible one in the modern press and the writings of reformist intellectuals and social activists, often to their great dismay and sometimes even their contempt. One observer noted in 1922:

> Nowadays, as women's public schools are thriving, women with modern education are no longer rare. These women should prize their personhood (*ren'ge*). However, I used to see in my neighborhood women who had been to public schools and received civilized education carry themselves proudly, behave boldly, and talk about equality and freedom extravagantly; before long, they had bowed their heads and submissively become concubine servants (*jishi*).[17]

Here, the stark contrast between the students' demeanor before and after becoming concubines suggests that the observer viewed their transformation as representing the undesirable repercussions and failures of women's modern educational reforms. Even some conservative moralists lamented that such students "voluntarily degraded themselves" and that the phenomenon suggested a "moral depravity" in Chinese society.[18]

Even college graduates, the category of women who enjoyed the highest level of education available in China at the time, were not immune to the "lure" of concubinage, to the great dismay of progressive intellectuals. Lü Simian (1884–1957), a history professor, noticed while teaching at Shenyang Normal University in 1920 that some "graduates from women's normal colleges" chose to become concubines and that the locals did not seem surprised by their choice.[19] Lü made his observations and comments in a series during his sojourn in Shenyang, which was published by a journal based in his hometown of Jiangsu Province, southern China, namely, *Changzhou yuekan* (*Changzhou Monthly*).[20] What Lü noticed was hardly a local custom. Zhu Caizhen, the editor of the journal *Fei qie hao* (*Abolish Concubinage*), published in Hangzhou in 1922, also lamented in his preface that nowadays, even those "graduates from women's normal colleges" "married down" to become the concubines of military men.[21]

How can this phenomenon be explained? Cases of female students becoming (or refusing to become) concubines were highly visible in print media during this period. Most cases that ended up in newspaper reports involved lawsuits, deaths, or other forms of violence, thereby becoming sensational news that attracted public attention. These news reports provided valuable sources to analyze the reasons behind this phenomenon. A survey of these cases suggests that four scenarios accounted for the majority of instances in which a student became a concubine.

First, she was deceived and did not know the man in question already had a wife. In this scenario, the woman either filed a lawsuit against the man or had to bear the situation since she was already married to him. For example, in December 1931, *Shijie chenbao* (*World Morning News*), a newspaper based in Shanghai, reported the following: A male teacher surnamed Hu was drawn to the beauty of a female student surnamed Shou. However, she was already in love with a fellow student. Hu became very jealous and tried in various ways to win her over. He even sought the help of the school President, an artist who had returned after studying in France. Finally, with the president's persuasion, Shou agreed to marry Hu. They held their wedding ceremony at a hotel. Shou's family was wealthy, and therefore, it was also possible that

Hu was interested in her family's wealth. Before their marriage, Hu promised Shou that they would go to study together in Paris. However, once they were married, Hu shut Shou inside their home and would not even allow her to continue attending school. Unexpectedly, about six months later, Hu's first wife showed up at their doorstep. When Hu was young and poor, his first wife had helped him to finish his studies. So, their marriage did have an emotional foundation and now he dared not divorce her. In the end, the reporter notes, it was Shou who had to endure the situation.[22] Clearly, Hu was not living with his wife and Shou did not discover earlier that he was already married. It also seems that neither Hu nor the school president informed Shou that she would not be his main wife. They were probably afraid that Shou would not agree to be Hu's concubine, considering that she was from a well-to-do family. Finally, Hu's background reminds us that during this era, men who took concubines could also have had a modern education.

Second, a student was forced into becoming a concubine against her will by the arrangement of her parents or other relatives. These cases generated fewer public comments than those involving individuals who married for "free love" (discussed later), although they highlighted a different kind of social issue. According to *Dagong bao* (*L'Impartial*), a "very intelligent" nineteen-year-old student in Tianjin had "high aspirations" for marriage, which she frequently conveyed to her parents. But her father was stubborn and secretly betrothed her to be the concubine of a man surnamed Zhao. Knowing that her father would refuse to change his decision, she began a hunger strike. When that failed, on the day of her wedding in December 1923, she took a knife into her wedding sedan chair and used it to commit suicide. By the time the sedan chair arrived at Zhao's home, she was already dead. Shocked, Zhao got into an angry dispute with the bride's family. Relatives and friends reported the case to a local court; after an investigation, her death was confirmed as a suicide.[23] A similar story in *Shibao* (*Eastern Times*), another major newspaper, reported on a student in Zhenjiang, Jiangsu Province, who was set to become the third concubine of a wealthy merchant. On her wedding day, in February 1926, she went missing; her mother received a letter from the girl swearing that she would not acknowledge the "barbaric marriage."[24] In both accounts, we can see that despite being educated women, neither student had any control over her marriage. It was their parents who were arranging marriages for them (following the traditional custom) without their consent. However, their modern education inspired new aspirations for marriage and encouraged them to view concubinage as backward and unacceptable. The discrepancy between their ideals and reality resulted in tragedy.

Third, a student might choose to become a concubine largely out of practical concerns, such as material security, especially if she was from a family without means or resources. A typical story can be seen in the report that follows from *Minguo ribao* (*Republican Daily*), a major newspaper, in 1924: A married man named Qian in Jiaxing County, Zhejiang Province, was attracted to a female student from a local college and tried to "seduce" her. Because her family was poor and he had money, she agreed to be in a relationship with him. Initially, she asked him to divorce his wife, but he said his mother would not allow it. Later, she asked him to give her mother two diamond rings, two gold bracelets, and a betrothal gift of 1,000 *yuan*. He agreed. Then the two went ahead and decided on the date of their "cohabiting."[25] Considering that traditionally, concubines were often directly purchased by wealthy men, this type of news should not be surprising to many. However, in this era, this story ended up in the press probably because the concubine involved was a female student rather than a courtesan. Although not ideal, becoming a concubine was a deliberate decision made by the student as a practical way for her and her family to achieve material security.

Scholars have pointed out that despite having the good fortune to receive a modern education, many female graduates could not find jobs to support themselves during the Republican period.[26] This was not only due to the low number of available jobs in the Chinese economy at the time, but also because of the constraints imposed by popular perceptions of what jobs were appropriate for women. Only certain white-collar jobs were deemed suitable for educated women, such as teaching, nursing, and secretarial work, which further limited the employment opportunities of female graduates. Consequently, marriage became an alternative channel of social mobility for educated women who were unable to earn a living independently. However, for those female graduates who were from poor families, the chance of being selected to be the main wives of wealthy men was low as well, since many of these men already had arranged marriages based on matching family backgrounds. Consequently, if these female graduates still wanted to marry men from well-to-do families, becoming their concubines was often the only way. As we will later see from the case studies in the section "'Madame Li Zongren': A Concubine?" both Guo's family and Cai's family agreed to marry their daughters to military officials as their concubines, probably calculating that this could prevent their families from suffering poverty.

Fourth, a student might voluntarily become a concubine in the pursuit of "free love" – a romantic ideal promoted by the New Culturalists to replace traditional modes of arranged marriages. Among the four scenarios, the most eye-catching to the contemporary press were those motivated by "free love" since they represented a genuinely new social phenomenon. In March 1924, *Xinwen bao* (*News Press*), then one of the four major newspapers in Shanghai, reported on a student "voluntarily" becoming a concubine. Xiao (her surname), a student from a girls' school, became engaged to a rice merchant surnamed Xu, with whom she experienced "free love" (*ziyou lian'ai*). When Xiao's uncle learned of the match, he filed a lawsuit with the Jiangning regional court (in Nanjing, Jiangsu Province), requesting that the marriage agreement be nullified, as Xu already had a wife. Nonetheless, Xiao refused to abolish the engagement. Nor did she think Xu should divorce his wife. Instead, she was willing to become his concubine. The judge asked her why, as a "female student," she was willing to be a concubine. Xiao answered that legally, she was a free person; that in terms of human rights, men and women should be equal, and that free love was "the trend of the times." Even if she were to become a concubine, she would not be breaking any laws. Why must the judge interfere? Hearing this, the judge saw no option but to let her keep the engagement and become Xu's concubine. Her uncle reported the affair to her school president, who regarded it as a family matter in which he should not get involved. Eventually, Xiao's uncle had to admit defeat and leave the couple alone.[27]

In this case, the judge clearly thought it unusual for a student to choose, of her own free will, to become a concubine. Thus, he asked for her reasons. The student then used the new language of individual freedom, equal rights, and, in particular, the free choice of whom to love to justify her decisions. Since the May Fourth New Culture Movement, free-love marriages have been touted by progressive intellectuals as a new model that should replace outdated arranged marriages, symbolizing the triumph of individual will over parental authority in romantic relationships. The early 1920s saw the heyday of this ideal.[28] By following her own will to pursue love in a relationship, Xiao believed she was acting according to this new ideal despite thereby becoming a concubine, a relic of the past.

In the social and ideological flux of the Republican period, Xiao was only one of many women who willingly became concubines due to romantic attachments. Many similar reports can be found in the contemporary press, often with titles emphasizing the "voluntary" or "willing" nature of the cases.[29] Zhu Caizhen referred to these women as the "new-style concubine" (*xinshi de qie*): They chose to become concubines as a result of "falling in love" with men to whom they were unable to become wives. In Zhu's analysis:

> The relations between men and women are in a state of extreme instability. On the one hand, people vigorously advocate freedom in love... On the other, people with freedom in divorce cannot leave their spouses. People choosing free marriage cannot marry... Because the old custom of male superiority has not been abolished, there are regretful consequences, with many new-style concubines. Old-style concubines have not yet been abolished. How can we stand to add new-style concubines?[30]

What Zhu pointed out was a dilemma many men and women faced in the Republican period. They desired free love, but the men could not bear – or dared not attempt – to divorce their main wives, who had often been handpicked by their parents. Consequently, the progressive ideal was subjugated to a "backward" institution: concubinage. It should also be noted that some of these couples refused to acknowledge that they were practicing concubinage (a regressive custom), especially when they married for love (a progressive ideal) and lived separately from the main wives (thereby forming a nuclear family). Accordingly, these women often refused to be identified or addressed as concubines, despite their families, friends, and colleagues being aware of the circumstances of their situations.

Some contemporaries cast doubt on the expressed motives of love. In the well-known *Funü zazhi* (*Ladies Journal*), an observer wrote in 1927 that she had heard there was "no lack of" female students in Hangzhou (Zhejiang Province) willing to sacrifice the status of a main wife to become a concubine. But this, she believed, was not so much "sacrificing themselves for love" as it was "making a mistake for money."[31] In other words, this observer still believed that material concerns rather than emotional attachments were the real motivation. This view resembles the way that some female activists characterized the motive for becoming a concubine: "When a woman is willing to degrade her personhood and humiliate herself to become a concubine-toy, she is motivated by nothing but an obscene desire for wasteful extravagance."[32] According to Bryna Goodman, "such caricatures of concubines proliferated in the essays of activists who sought to liberate women."[33] Though such activists claimed moral superiority, the social reality was, in fact, far more complicated than they acknowledged.

As we have seen, there were at least four major types of realistic and complicated reasons that led female students to become concubines during this period. Some scenarios reveal the continued strong influence of parental authority and the lack of freedom and autonomy among young women. In this sense, the phenomenon of female students becoming concubines sheds new light on the state of flux and clashing social dynamics experienced by the people who lived in a Republic caught between legacies of the past and new ideals of modernity. Female students becoming concubines as an innovation to concubinage also reveals how individual women and men translated what they believed to be powerful, perhaps even inevitable, historical trends in the light of their own lived realities. However, these realistic factors were rarely discussed in social critiques of the phenomenon. The possibility of these women being victims of oppression due to the lingering social, cultural, and economic issues of the time was largely ignored. No realistic solutions were proposed to help these women escape such arrangements. In addition, the criticisms further sexualized the discussion of female students. Consequently, in the end, it was up to individual female students to face their various struggles and make necessary decisions based on their own life circumstances.

"MADAME LI ZONGREN": A CONCUBINE?

Unlike courtesans, the traditional category of social and public women, female students did not have a tainted reputation to overcome: They could play the role of a respectable public wife without causing social embarrassment for elite men. By the early Republican period, prostitution had come under heavy attack from China's progressive intellectuals and social reformers. For an elite man, especially a governmental official, to appear with a courtesan at formal public occasions, no matter how gracefully she behaved, was increasingly deemed inappropriate; however, in private, some elite men still frequented brothels. The former courtesan-turned-concubine Li Benwei played the role of a social wife in the 1910s and early 1920s, during the chaotic warlord era. But by around 1928, the Nationalists had defeated the "backward" warlords and established themselves as modern China's "progressive" political leaders. The social wives who accompanied their official husbands and enjoyed high public profiles were no longer former courtesans but modern educated women with unblemished backgrounds.

If the case of Zhou Ziqi's concubine Zhou Shunqin, discussed in the previous chapter, shows us the tensions and controversy surrounding concubines who served as social wives, the case of Li Zongren's concubine Guo Dejie tells a very different story. Li was a prominent Guangxi "warlord" and Nationalist military commander during the Northern Expedition (1926–1928), the Second Sino-Japanese War (1937–1945), and the Chinese Civil War (1945–1949). The high point of his career was serving as Vice President and later Acting President of the Republic of China from 1948 to 1949. From the time Li married Guo in 1923 until her death in 1966 (three years before Li's death), Guo was one of the most active social wives of Nationalist officials, known throughout China as "Madame Li Zongren." The public seemed completely unaware of Guo's concubine status. Almost no media reports addressed her as a "*ru furen* (just like a wife)" or used the word *qie* to indicate her concubine status, as they sometimes referred to Li Benwei and Zhou Shunqin.[34] Instead, newspaper reports over the years followed her various public engagements, ranging from accompanying her husband to official functions to establishing schools for girls to helping her husband run for Vice President of the Republic. Praising her capability and social skills, the press regarded Guo as a progressive New Woman rather than a backward, stigmatized concubine.

How to explain this phenomenon, especially compared to the controversial cases discussed previously? Among a variety of factors, it is noteworthy that before marriage, Guo was a "female student," a modern category of women in early twentieth-century China. Unlike Li Benwei and Zhou Shunqin, who could never fully conceal or shake off their former courtesan/entertainer backgrounds – no matter how high the status they eventually achieved through their marriages to powerful men – Guo did not emerge from a degraded social class.

Much of what we know about Guo does not come from her own words since she did not write about her life. Neither does it come from her husband; although Li Zongren left a lengthy memoir, he barely mentioned his family life. In this respect, Li's memoir resembles those of several other major Nationalist officials with whom he worked closely, such as Bai Chongxi (1893–1966) and Huang Shaohong (1895–1966). Ironically, it is through the recollections of Li Zongren's main wife – Li Xiuwen (1891–1992), who outlived both Li and Guo – that we know many rare details about Guo's life. Though Xiuwen herself knew only some basic characters learned from her husband in the early years of their marriage, in her later years, she narrated her experiences to her nephew's wife, Tan Ming, who recorded, edited, and arranged to have her life story published as a book, titled *Li Zongren and I*, in 1987. Xiuwen's oral account left us invaluable information about the world of a main wife, her illustrious husband, and his concubine, whom Xiuwen referred to as a "New Woman" (*xin nüxing*).[35]

Sources suggest that Xiuwen's marriage, though arranged, was a relatively happy one. Both parties came from rural farming families in Guangxi Province and they married around 1911. A diligent daughter-in-law, Xiuwen quickly gained the affection of Li's parents and siblings. After their marriage, Li traveled frequently to fulfill various military

3 FROM "FEMALE STUDENT" TO CONCUBINE

duties. Xiuwen accompanied him until she gave birth to their only son, Li Youlin, in 1918. As it became increasingly difficult to follow her husband, Xiuwen chose to stay with her parents-in-law in Shanghai. In 1924, her mother-in-law received news that Li had married Guo, so she encouraged Xiuwen, who was still kept in the dark, to visit Li with their son when his troops were stationed at Guiping in Guangxi during a temporary peace.

Xiuwen learned from her husband directly how he had met and married Guo. One day (he told her), Li and several of his officers visited a local girls' school when they were stationed in Guiping. There, two (relatively) older students caught Li's eye. Although he did not think much about it at the time, his battalion commander noticed and suggested that since his wife was at home taking care of their son, nobody was taking care of him; why not welcome in another "*furen*" (Madame) to do so? Li agreed, and through the commander's introduction, he met Guo, an ambitious and intelligent primary school student who had been studying there for two to three years. Though her father was merely a local cement artisan with a large family, and though she was already sixteen years old by the time it became fashionable for girls to go to school, Guo was determined to become an "outstanding New Woman." She enrolled immediately. Many of her peers preferred not to marry military men due to the frequent wars demanding their participation, but Guo did not hesitate. Li, a graduate of a provincial military school, was then a brigade commander with a promising career; Guo saw that potential and accepted his proposal.[36] Li joined the Nationalist Party in 1923. By August 1924, with his Guangxi Clique and their Pacification Army, he had driven the local ruler, Lu Rongting (1859–1928), and other rivals out of Guangxi and would soon become Guangxi's military governor.

Li told Xiuwen that he and Guo had a "civilized wedding" (*wenming jiehun*), a practice increasingly associated with female students and teachers since 1911, without performing ceremonial obeisances or paying their respects to the ancestral tablet.[37] But Guo's modest family did ask for a bridal sedan chair to escort her to her new home. Later, Li and Guo hosted a banquet for relatives and friends to celebrate their union, a practice that was increasingly common, even for marriages involving concubines, during the Republican period. This was because, by then, the ceremony itself no longer served as a clear mark of distinction between the main wife and concubine. What mattered then was the man's intent, not how the woman had been married. Therefore, in early twentieth-century China, it was not unusual for a concubine to go through the same elaborate wedding ceremony as a main wife.[38]

Seeing Xiuwen's silence as he told this story, Li explained that their child (then five years old) made it difficult for her to move with him constantly, as the military demanded. Furthermore, as a "high-ranking officer," he needed a domestic helper at his side who could serve as a "companion for frequent social occasions." "Isn't it good that these things that you could not do previously now could be handled by someone else?" he asked Xiuwen. Li emphasized that Guo was a "*nü xuesheng*" and was, therefore, "educated and sensible." If Xiuwen needed any help, she could tell Guo. Finally, he promised to continue providing for Xiuwen; she just needed to enjoy her life while raising their son well. Seeing that their union had already become a fact, Xiuwen accepted the arrangement albeit with complicated feelings. Then Li asked Guo to come out and greet Xiuwen in person.[39]

It should be noted that in addition to this account, there are several other extant versions of how Li met Guo. The difference relevant here is that one version describes Guo as a student from Guiping Women's Normal School (Guiping nüzi shifan xuexiao) rather than from a primary school and records her age as eighteen (instead of seventeen) when she met Li.[40] Later newspaper interviews quote Guo telling reporters that she was "a student of a women's normal school" (*shifan sheng*).[41] Xiuwen likely misremembered Guo's educational background, as she herself had never enrolled in a public school. Whatever the truth, these accounts confirm that Guo was an educated student from a poor family when she met Li. One source claims that she immediately quit school after her marriage.[42] As the daughter of an artisan, she probably recognized the need to find work after graduation because her avenues to living comfortably were limited. The opportunity to become a concubine of a high-ranking officer represented a major upgrade for a woman of her social and economic background.

Xiuwen also knew of other military men who made arrangements with their main wives by taking students as concubines. She described, for instance, the case of Huang Shaohong. Huang was a major general under Li Zongren while they were both in Guangxi Province. Together with Bai Chongxi, the three formed the core of the so-called New Guangxi Clique. After Guangxi was unified under their rule, major military officers gathered in its provincial capital, Nanning, and settled down for a while. Some officers brought their wives over to join them, but Huang's wife had duties at home – caring for her parents-in-law and young children – that kept her from following him to Nanning. Huang became depressed, began drinking, and even visited brothels. Li Zongren and other officers worried that his dispiritedness would harm the "revolutionary cause," particularly the collaboration between Guangxi and Guangdong provinces to embark on the Northern Expedition. They discussed the matter with Huang's lineage elders, agreed that he needed "the warmth of a family," and introduced him to a middle-school girl in Nanning. The student, surnamed Cai, was not only educated and beautiful but also socially skilled. Huang immediately quit drinking and, within a month, the two families had exchanged betrothal gifts, a practice suggesting that, for Huang, marrying his concubine was, in this case, treated like taking a wife. We do not know Cai's opinions on the matter, though her family likely viewed it as good fortune to see her marry such a high-ranking official. From then on, Cai accompanied Huang at almost all public functions; Xiuwen saw her in person at a banquet. Meanwhile, Huang continued to support his main wife, surnamed Wei, back in his hometown. According to Xiuwen, Wei accepted the arrangement and busied herself taking care of her in-laws and children.[43] This case reminds us that securing a modern social wife for public engagements was not the sole reason that officials took in concubines; however, in the new world of the 1920s, their choice of a woman to provide "the warmth of a family" to Huang was a young, educated student (no longer the courtesan/entertainer). It had to be a "good" woman who could play the role of social wife when needed, confirming historians' sense of the changing expectations of an ideal wife.

After Guo married Li, she became Li's social wife, accompanying him almost everywhere, while Xiuwen resided with Li's parents, taking care of them and Li's son.[44] Occasionally, Xiuwen brought their son to visit Li, allowing father and son to spend some time together. Guo and Li never had a son of their own, though Guo later adopted one.[45] Xiuwen sometimes stayed with Li and Guo; according to Xiuwen, she and Guo generally got along well (all evidence suggests that Xiuwen was a magnanimous person).[46] Li's professional rise, Xiuwen noted, meant that there were more frequent social events for military officials and their wives. She participated in some gatherings, especially the less formal occasions, but admitted that she was not adept at socializing or making speeches.[47] Still, whenever she came to visit her husband, even for a brief period, invitations arrived for Xiuwen and Guo to attend social gatherings at the same time, since they were both Li's *furen* and the local hosts did not want to offend either of them. However, Guo often seemed uncomfortable at these events, probably because it was clear to everyone present that she was merely Li's concubine. Later in their relationship, if Guo learned that Xiuwen planned to attend a public occasion, she avoided it, despite the respect shown to them both by those present, who usually referred to Xiuwen as "Madame No. 1" (*da furen*) and Guo as "Madame No. 2" (*er furen*), never addressing Guo as "*qie*" or "*yi taitai*," terms reserved exclusively for concubines.[48]

After several rounds of socialization in the officialdom of Nanning, Xiuwen noticed that as main wives became more familiar with each other, they tended to gather together to chat, drawn by similar life experiences and domestic status. She learned that many main wives, including herself, were nicknamed "*xiangxia po*" (the old woman from the countryside) or "*tu po*" (old-fashioned woman) by the concubines, to whom they seemed insufficiently fashionable, beautiful, and sociable; nor did they know how to dance in public. Xiuwen acknowledged that "men in officialdom needed *taitai* [Mrs.] with these skills to entertain and socialize."[49] Nonetheless, she expressed that she had no interest in "gaining status through social skills" (*shejiao diwei*) as many concubines attempted.[50] This comment suggests that Xiuwen was aware that, apart from Guo, there were other concubines (whose husbands probably were of lower ranks than Li) who purposefully seized the opportunities to play the role of social wives to gain public recognition and privilege and to elevate their traditionally inferior social and domestic status.

If Xiuwen sounded secure in her status, this arose not only from having given birth to Li's only son but also – as she herself pointed out – to the traditionally recognized domestic hierarchy. She married Li first, establishing her position within his extended family. Xiuwen was often addressed by Li's family members according to the birth order of her husband – in her case, "the ninth sister" (*jiu sao*). Li's extended family was a large one – whereas Guo, as a concubine, could only be referred to by her own surname, "Sister Guo" (*guo sao*). Xiuwen later heard that Guo was not happy with this custom, probably because it failed to recognize Guo's incorporation into Li's kinship networks; hence, the younger generation began referring to Guo as "the uncle's woman" (*jiuniang* or *boniang*), a term at least recognizing her relationship with Li.[51]

Xiuwen and Guo generally showed one another respect, but there were public occasions that highlighted their status difference and caused conflict. Two incidents illustrate this particularly well. First, when Li's mother died in 1942, a grand funeral was held in Guilin with hundreds of social notables in attendance. According to Xiuwen, when it was Guo and Xiuwen's turn to pay their respects to the deceased mother-in-law, Guo insisted on kneeling in front of Xiuwen rather than following the traditional order of kneeling behind her. Guo's hands brushed against Xiuwen's hair several times, angering Xiuwen. She blocked Guo's hands, gave her a stare, and told her to behave. Guo blushed at this public embarrassment. Rumors circulated that Xiuwen beat Guo, and although nothing ended up in the press, Xiuwen realized that her scolding had made Guo lose face in public.[52] As the main wife, Xiuwen had a personal relationship with her deceased mother-in-law that Guo did not, which could also have provoked Xiuwen's anger. The key to the incident lies in the domestic hierarchy on public display: When Xiuwen and Guo were both present for occasions like a big family funeral, which was governed by rules of seniority and propriety, Guo's concubine status was heightened, especially when Xiuwen publicly disciplined her. In addition, when Guo was not playing her role as the social wife (as at this family funeral), she could not use her social skills or modern background to gain the upper hand; nor could she, as the concubine, directly defy the disciplining of the senior main wife in front of many family members.

Their second public conflict occurred at the ninetieth birthday celebration for the mother of General Bai Chongxi, a major social event held in Guilin in the spring of 1944. Xiuwen and Guo each sent a birthday banner with a congratulatory message (*shouzhang*) to Bai's mother. On the day of the event, Guo discovered that the Bai family had neglected to put up her banner but had instead displayed Xiuwen's banner together with Li's. Guo angrily questioned Bai's wife, calling the choice a personal insult and demanding she take down Xiuwen's banner and replace it with Guo's. A number of the guests felt that Guo was being unfair and should not make a scene. They comforted Xiuwen, who responded (according to her memoir): "I am not that petty! I even allowed her [Guo] to take the title of 'Madame Li Zongren,' why do I care about the birthday banner matter?! If I also have to yield on giving birthday gifts, then just count it as if I did not bring any gifts." Bai's wife apologized to Guo and hung up her banner as well, quieting the incident. Eventually, "Madame No. 1" (*da furen*, i.e. Xiuwen) won praise for being the bigger person.[53]

In both incidents, the ambitious Guo challenged her traditionally subordinate position in a symbolic public gesture in front of the main wife Xiuwen. Instead of quietly accepting her concubine status and kneeling behind Xiuwen, Guo tried to occupy the space in front. Instead of having her banner displayed together with Xiuwen's, she demanded that her banner *replace* Xiuwen's. What emboldened her to do so? The short answer is that by the 1940s, almost twenty years after marrying Li, Guo had successfully established her public identity as "Madame Li Zongren" to the point that she dared to challenge Xiuwen's status as the main wife. By playing the novel role of a modern social wife, ambitious concubines without tainted backgrounds like Guo used public recognition to elevate their status to that of wives, despite their supposed subordinate position within the traditional domestic hierarchy. By the time of the two incidents, Guo would have been accustomed to appearing on public occasions as Li's *wife* rather than a concubine. A survey of press reports in the Republican period reveals how frequently Guo was referred to as "Madame Li Zongren," particularly in the 1930s and 1940s.[54] Some reports even unwittingly referred to her Li's wife (*qi*).[55] Li's main wife, Xiuwen, was not mentioned in print media until 1980 when Tan Ming published some of her interviews. Guo, who had always been very competitive since her student years, must have believed that with her clean background, modern education, and capable social skills, she could get away with acting aggressively and ignoring the presence of Xiuwen, an old-fashioned, barely literate country woman, at the aforementioned events. Clearly, she had miscalculated. On occasions like family funerals, the rules of tradition and hierarchy remained too strong to be easily overthrown. This reminds us how different contexts (modern or traditional) weakened or strengthened the hands of the wife versus the concubine relative to each other.

It is difficult to imagine that courtesan-turned-concubines like Li Benwei and Zhou Shunqin would dare to do the same as openly as Guo did. Although Benwei also used her good social skills to make Li Yuanhong rely on her and gain his favor, thus improving her domestic position, no sources suggest that she had ever attempted to publicly challenge Wu Jingjun's status as Li's main wife. Benwei probably knew that her tainted courtesan origin was too big a stain to enable her to ever replace Li's main wife in a respectable high society. At most, she could enjoy the privileges granted to her while playing the role of Li's social wife when he was alive. The public was aware from the beginning that she was only a concubine, as news reports then frequently used the polite term for concubine – *ru furen* – to refer to her. In contrast, Guo did not have any disreputable past holding her back and thus she probably believed that she was in a far more advantageous position to replace Xiuwen.

As Madame Li Zongren, the social wife, Guo was widely seen in Republican media as "very capable."[56] She played leadership roles in various causes and patriotic initiatives, promoting women's issues and social charity. During the Northern Expedition, she was appointed Chief of the Guanxi Female Students Northern Expedition Corps.[57] She took responsibility for women's work during the New Life Movement (1934–1936) in Guangxi Province.[58] During the Second Sino-Japanese War, she led the Guangxi Women's Resisting Enemy and Assistance Society (Guangxi funü kangdi houyuanhui), not only donating her own gold jewelry but also organizing many other donations.[59] In 1939, she established the Guilin Children's Home; a year later, she founded Dezhi Middle School in Guangxi. After the war with Japan ended, when Li was appointed Director of the Peiping Field Headquarters (Beiping xingyuan zhuren) from 1945 to 1947, the highest official representative of the Nationalist

Government in Peiping (today's Beijing), Guo was put in charge of women's work for the Nationalist Party. In 1948, Guo was elected a representative to the Nationalist Party's congress, paving the way for her husband's bid to become vice president.[60] In these leadership roles, Guo tirelessly advocated for women's place on all the front lines and argued that women's wartime contributions proved their social equality.[61] Her public profile became enhanced. Her contributions, however, like many other prominent Nationalist women, have not been recognized by the later Communist regime. Instead, she has been mostly remembered as "an elite warlord wife."[62]

Guo was most visible, among the various activities she assisted Li with over the years, during and after the period when she assisted Li's run for vice president. It was then widely acknowledged that her excellent socialization and mobilization skills contributed greatly to Li's election success on April 28, 1948, despite strong opposition from Chiang Kai-shek, the President of the Republic, who chose to support Li's opponent Sun Ke (1891–1973). According to contemporary newspaper reports, Guo conducted frequent campaign canvassing for Li in the newly formed National Assembly and was referred to as "an expert of social intercourse" (*jiaoji jia*) when she appeared with Li at press conferences and answered reporters' questions. When representatives of the National Assembly lined up to vote, Guo stood at the entrance to the site and shook hands with each representative.[63] Sun Ke (son of the founding father of the Republic, Sun Yat-Sun) also relied on his wife and even his mistress to help campaign and mobilize voters.[64] The two sides engaged in a dramatic series of behind-the-scenes maneuvers. A contemporary writing in *Xinwen zazhi* (*News Magazine*) noted the prominent role that women and women's organizations played in the vice-presidential campaigns, referring to "the wind of skirt blowing to every battlefield" and predicting that "if a man does not have a good *taitai* or girlfriend, his run for the Vice President position would be severely affected."[65]

After the election, according to newspaper reports, wherever she was in the capital, Nanjing, Guo attended banquets with Vice President Li. Socializing with "foreign upper-class ladies" taught her a lot about "international social intercourse" (*guoji shejiao*). Guo was said to emulate Song Meiling (1898–2003), the wife of Chiang Kai-shek, who received her early education in the US and was familiar with Western social etiquette.[66] This suggests that, unlike Li Yuanhong, who avoided taking Benwei, his courtesan-turned-concubine, to official public occasions to meet foreigners, Li Zongren did not have such concerns. This was probably because Guo was a former student rather than a former courtesan who could not easily hide her tainted past from the public. Hence, Li Zongren did not need to worry that Guo's background would cause any scandal or make him lose face. On January 21, 1949, Chiang resigned his presidency in the wake of several key military victories by the Communist Party in northern China. The next day, Li became Acting President and Guo the de facto First Lady, though real power still lay in the hands of the controlling Chiang. However, the Communists' swift victory in the Civil War and the subsequent founding of the People's Republic of China on October 1, 1949, in Beijing cut short Li's presidency and ambitions and, accordingly, Guo's position as the First Lady. After Chiang relocated his government to Taipei, Li and Guo went into exile in the US until their return to Communist China in 1965, which caused an international sensation. A year later, Guo died of breast cancer, and in 1969, Li died of duodenal cancer. After the Communist takeover, Xiuwen lived with her son in the US. In 1973, she returned to her hometown in Guangxi, where she died in 1992 at the age of 101.[67]

As Madame Li Zongren, Guo played an active and important role as Li's modern social wife without causing major public controversies despite her concubine status. This was probably due to a combination of factors. On the one hand, her established public image as an educated progressive woman was so strong that it obscured her status as a concubine. The public imagination could find no way to fit Guo into the popular stereotype of a concubine who was backward, parasitic, and unproductive. Without the tainted background of a former courtesan, she had no trace of a disreputable past. As a former student, she could confidently apply the modern education and social skills that Xiuwen lacked to carve out a space of her own. Domestically, she was a much-needed helper who could move with Li whenever military situations demanded, while Xiuwen had to settle down to take care of Li's son and parents. Guo was far more adept than Xiuwen at appearing in public, playing the role of Li's educated and attractive companion to enhance his image, socialize within elite circles, and advance his career. Few people, except those in their inner circles, seemed aware of Guo's concubine status. Those who knew chose to keep quiet about it. Throughout their married life, the couple mostly lived separately from Xiuwen, who gradually became the forgotten wife. Guo seemed unwilling to identify herself as a concubine, even though Li's family, Xiuwen, and other insiders knew. The general public might have heard of "Madame Li Zongren" only through media reports and assumed she was his wife. As for those who knew she was a concubine, nobody publicly exposed Guo or used that knowledge as a weapon to attack Li. Considering Li's powerful position, it may well have seemed unwise to disrespect Guo in public and risk offending Li. Furthermore, many other military officials also had concubines or mistresses. Therefore, playing the concubine/mistress card probably was not the best strategy to seriously damage and topple one particular official.

Guo was unusually fortunate during her lifetime: A girl from humble origins sought a modern education, became a concubine of a powerful man, and participated in the public realm without causing major controversies. Because she passed away three years before Li, she also escaped the challenges faced by many other concubines: starting a new life or facing inheritance disputes after the death of a prominent husband, as Li Benwei had to.

CONCLUSION

A significant new development in concubinage during the Republican period was the social origins of concubines: Many of these women were no longer confined to traditionally "degraded" categories such as courtesans or prostitutes but instead included young women who were the beneficiaries of modern, public school education. For social critics, although female students and concubines sometimes shared similar features in print media portrayals – such as materialism, frivolity, decadence, and being consumers rather than productive citizens[68] – these two categories of women were still perceived as being fundamentally antithetical. The female student was supposed to represent the future of modern Chinese womanhood; the concubine had become a stigmatized relic of backward

Chinese tradition. In reality, the two categories overlapped due to a variety of reasons that often had to do with the larger contemporary social and cultural constraints posed by legacies of traditions rather than merely women's own lack of moral principles, as social critics tended to emphasize. Meanwhile, although the social phenomenon of female students becoming concubines was widely collectively deplored and regarded as a type of social degeneration, individually, modern-educated concubines with uncompromised social backgrounds could serve as the social wives of elite men without generating major controversies. Some of them, as we have seen in the case of Guo, were emboldened to publicly challenge the traditional domestic hierarchy and attempted to be recognized as wives, a demand that those courtesans-turned-concubines rarely dared to make. In the next chapter, we will see another dimension of the ramifications of concubines' public engagement: how concubines' membership issues within progressive women's organizations and public schools ignited tensions, divisions, and class prejudice that fractured the movements for Chinese women's liberation.

CHAPTER 4

Excluding Concubines

The Politics of Virtue and Contamination

IN ADDITION TO PLAYING THE ROLE OF A SOCIAL WIFE, concubines also engaged in other public activities during the Republican period. This chapter examines their presence in two types of communal spaces: public schools and progressive women's organizations. These institutions were chosen because they witnessed the buildup and precarious resolution of tensions and conflicts surrounding attempts to exclude concubines from membership. Major incidents were publicized in contemporary newspaper reports, garnering broader social attention; however, a far greater number of minor cases likely went unreported and remained unknown. Therefore, news reports are an important source for us to uncover attempts to exclude concubines from public schools and women's progressive organizations and analyze how the issue was framed, debated, and resolved (or not). Examining these controversies reveals the contested gender politics and overlooked divisions based on class hierarchy and sexual morality within women's liberation movements in Republican China.

While teaching at Shenyang Normal University in 1920, history professor Lü Simian noticed that some "graduates from women's normal colleges" had chosen to become concubines. He indignantly proposed an intervention to put a halt to this phenomenon: "If I were to live in Shenyang for a long time, I would persuade each college to set up a committee to intervene with those students who were about to become concubines. If I were asked how to intervene, I would suggest: 'Report them to the local Inspection Office and let the Office file public lawsuits against these students.'"[1] In fact, lawsuits were not a feasible solution, since becoming a concubine in this period did not necessarily require a woman to break any laws. Most Republican lawmakers, reformers, and progressive intellectuals seemed to believe that concubinage continued mainly due to the initiative of men. Women were understood to play only passive roles and were rarely punished for doing so. Even the men who took concubines after the implementation of the Nationalist civil code (1929–1930) were treated, at most, as having committed "adultery" rather than bigamy.

This does not mean that women who became concubines suffered no public backlash. The Anti-Concubinage Movement reached its height in the 1920s and 1930s. When the American writer and suffragist Grace Seton traveled through China in 1922, she learned that an organized effort was underway to "give a social black eye to concubinage."[2] Bryna Goodman has examined the writings of anti-concubinage activists (most of them women) and notes that their divisive and discriminatory discourse created "fissures" in "the category of woman."[3] The critique of concubinage, a traditional institution, often spilled over to the women who became concubines, to the point that their very existence as individuals was spurned. Sources suggest that the trend of expelling and excluding concubines was especially prominent in progressive women's circles: More than any other social group, it was progressive women who would not tolerate concubines' public presence, especially when the concubines asked to share their stage.

This chapter examines the discrimination concubines encountered and their expulsion from public organizations in which they were (or hoped to become) members in Republican China. It zooms in on the often-obscured dimension of real-life politics when concubines stepped into the public arena and began engaging with progressive women's circles. Relying mainly on little-used newspaper sources, the chapter begins by examining the protests and strikes that arose against public school students and administrators who became concubines. These incidents reveal deep fears surrounding the tainting influence of the concubine and the politics of virtue woven within campus communities. The section "Concubines in Progressive Women's Organizations" focuses on concubine membership in progressive women's organizations. Their enthusiasm for feminist, patriotic, philanthropic, and other causes prompted some concubines to seek out progressive social organizations. However, many women's organizations in this era banned (or attempted to ban) concubines from becoming members, arguing that regardless of individual differences, all concubines had low moral worth. Still, other members maintained that concubines were victims of patriarchal oppression who deserved liberation and that some were, in fact, "virtuous" women.

CONCUBINES IN PUBLIC SCHOOLS

Since concubine was a highly stigmatized category of women in Republican China, both students and administrators in public schools who became concubines ran the risk of expulsion. Although there were also a few cases of female teachers becoming concubines,[4] I have not seen any news reports on attempts or calls to fire them, though both likely occurred. The aforementioned Yao Wenyu, a general secretary, was fired from Hubei Women's School of Law and Politics in 1913 for becoming a concubine. An educated woman who was active in the Women's Suffrage Alliance, Yao lost not only her job but also her progressive social credentials when she became the concubine of a wealthy man.

A similar incident occurred in Guangzhou in 1920; this time, the concubine involved held a position even higher than Yao's. According to a report in *Dagong bao* (*L'Impartial*), a major newspaper in Republican China, a woman named He Zhifen was appointed President of Guangzhou Women's Normal School in southern China in January 1920. On learning that He was the concubine of Yang Qusheng – a man from the Gaozhou area of Guangdong Province – students organized to protest He's appointment. They cited school policy that "servants and concubines were not allowed to be students" and expressed outrage that the school had allowed a concubine to become president. In the students' view, the decision betrayed a complete lack of consideration for a woman's *ren'ge*. They organized a meeting on January 4th to discuss the matter. The newspaper report ends by expressing the reporter's fear that another student strike was imminent.[5]

By March of that year, *Minguo Ribao* (*Republican Daily*), another major national newspaper, reported that the protests and strikes had finally stopped and students had resumed classes because He had resigned and a new woman, surname Zhu, had been appointed interim president. It was said that in her official resignation letter to the provincial authorities, He expressed indignation, criticizing the students' intolerance. Unlike Yao Wenyu, He did not dispute the decision that a concubine could not serve as school president. In fact, He did not even mention concubinage.[6] Chances are, she understood the social and cultural climate generated by the Anti-Concubinage Movement, especially in progressive educational circles. That climate was more hostile toward concubines in 1920 than that experienced by Yao in 1913.

Little is known about He Zhifen. But she was surely an educated woman who had been active in the public world despite being a concubine. She must also have secured a good reputation and won praise in local educational circles to be chosen for such an important position. The fact that students' objections to her appointment were based solely on her concubine status suggests that she must have been well qualified in other respects. At the same time, the school seems to have had an established policy specifically forbidding concubines from becoming students. This suggests that the school may have had previous incidents of concubines applying to become (or remaining) students but being rejected (or expelled), prompting the school to draft a policy regarding the matter to prevent it from happening again in the future.

In the students' view, a concubine could not be allowed to become a member of their community due to her lack of *ren'ge* (personhood), a term created during the New Culture Movement to capture the core virtues of a modern woman: self-reliance, moral rectitude, and independent thinking. Bryna Goodman has shown that the term was both elusive and exclusive. Women with *ren'ge* had to have a meaningful vocation; female factory workers did not count, as their work was not deemed sufficiently meaningful.[7] In other words, *ren'ge* represented a new standard of women's respectability, which abandoned the traditional Confucian emphasis on domestic seclusion and gender separation and replaced them with an updated emphasis on women having an independent, meaningful vocation in the public world. However, few women in early twentieth-century China, including those with modern educations and independent professions, could meet the criteria for *ren'ge*, as Goodman's case study of public discussions surrounding the suicide of

Xi Shangzhen – a young secretary working for the *Journal of Commerce* in Shanghai – has demonstrated.[8]

In the eyes of most women's rights activists and concubinage abolitionists, it was impossible for a concubine to ever achieve *ren'ge*. And the lack of *ren'ge* was frequently cited as a reason to exclude them from public schools and progressive women's organizations. This judgment was based on traditional assumptions about concubines' debased sexual morality and social status, but it was also drawn from the reality that most concubines were not economically independent. As a category of women symbolizing relics of the old society, the concubine, due to her social and economic dependency on her husband, was often viewed as the antithesis of the New Woman, whose essential qualities include her pursuits of personal independence and women's emancipation. But in many of the cases presented throughout this book, the concubines active in public arenas shared a number of similarities with the new women (especially in terms of their modern education), an irony that seems to have been lost not only on the progressive women themselves but also on the scholars assessing the often contradictory role the concubines played in this period of Chinese history. Some educated concubines who made efforts to find independent employment, such as working as administrators in public schools, were rejected due to their concubine status. They faced a conundrum: Even those seeking "meaningful vocations" and endeavoring to achieve *ren'ge* were denied opportunities to do so due to their status as concubines.

Compared to concubine administrators, concubine students were a more common phenomenon during this period, though probably only the most sensational or controversial incidents ended up in newspapers. In 1913, the same year as the Yao Wenyu episode, *Shibao* reported on another school incident. In an article titled: "Female Student Not Tolerated for Having Become a Concubine," the newspaper recounted a student in a woman's school in Henan Province becoming part of a "free-love marriage" (*ziyou jiehun*): the concubine of a man surnamed Liu. Her classmates learned of it and felt that she had violated the principle of monogamy, bringing "shame" to the entire "women's circle (*nüjie*)." They held a meeting on campus and planned to force her to divorce. But the school's more "moderate faction" began holding discussions of their own and expressed a belief that this was a matter of personal freedom that could not be forced. Though they could advise the student in question, they had to allow her room for a "personal realization." Eventually, plans to force her to divorce were abandoned.[9] It is noteworthy that in this case and Yao Wenyu's case, the concept of *ren'ge* was not invoked: Both incidents took place before the May Fourth New Culture Movement, when *ren'ge* as a modern term originated. However, they shared a similar focus on a woman's virtue and morality. The rationale in this case was that by becoming a concubine, the student brought shame to the entire women's circle, an idea that resembled the rationale for firing Yao Wenyu: She could no longer be a moral exemplar for the school's students. Both reveal a deep concern – what we might even term a moral panic – about a concubine's tainting influence on the other women of her community.

When a similar incident occurred at Xi'an Women's Normal School (Xi'an nüzi shifan xuexiao) in 1923, there was no moderate faction to champion the importance of personal freedom. According to a report in *Minguo ribao*, a male Chinese teacher used "insidious means" and "seduced" a female student into becoming his concubine, causing an "uproar" at the school. In the name of safeguarding their *ren'ge*, the entire student body decided to expel the teacher, who was said to have also "slandered" the leader of the Student Council. Meanwhile, the Student Council resolved to expel the girl from their organization for agreeing to become the teacher's concubine despite knowing that he had a wife. Facing expulsion, the teacher refused to leave. His supporters at the Shaanxi Provincial Assembly – of which he was a member – defended him. Students began boycotting classes, demanding that the Provincial Assembly and the local court punish the teacher so as to "restore students' reputations." Shaanxi's governor, Liu Zhenhua, visited the school in person to resolve the issue. The news report concludes by blaming the school for failing to provide proper education to its students on the importance of *ren'ge*. Had the school done so, the young woman would not have chosen to become a concubine.[10]

It is noteworthy that neither the students nor the press commented on the impropriety of the teacher–student relationship. As public school education for girls developed in early twentieth-century China, concerns arose among school leaders about the potential for improper relationships between teachers and students. To safeguard the reputations of female students, some school presidents decided to avoid hiring unmarried young male teachers, instead preferring to hire "married and older men" and closely monitoring student–teacher interactions beyond the classroom.[11] To their disappointment, this strategy did not entirely work: Some students became concubines of their teachers. Sometimes, the teacher and student involved refused to acknowledge that they were practicing concubinage. The famous progressive writer Lu Xun (1881–1936) and his student Xu Guangping (1898–1968) fell in love while Lu was teaching at Beijing Women's Normal College in 1925. Lu could not divorce his wife and did not want Xu to become a stigmatized concubine, so Xu moved in with him as his life partner without ceremony or procedure.[12] Public reactions to teacher–student relationships varied depending on a variety of factors. Certain cases generated social controversy; others were accepted. Shen Congwen (1902–1988), a well-known writer, fell in love with his student Zhang Zhaohe (1910–2003) while teaching at Zhongguo Gongxue (China College) in Shanghai. When Zhang reported his feelings to Hu Shi (1891–1962) – president of the college and a leading intellectual in the New Culture Movement – Hu offered to be a matchmaker for the couple. Hu was also a major advocate for free choice in love. He was probably taking on this role to express his views that love should be the best basis for marriage.[13] Shen and Zhang married in 1933 with the blessing of their families and friends.[14] The fact that Shen was single when they met and that their relationship had the support of the school's president likely made it broadly acceptable.

What agitated the students at Xi'an Women's Normal School was the concern that one degraded classmate could endanger the public reputation of the entire student body. Consequently, the larger community she belonged to was expected to take swift action: to punish and expel those involved, make their stance public, and cleanse the contamination threatening the moral standing of every student. To understand the extent to which female students becoming concubines was viewed as a shameful matter – not only for the women themselves, but also for the larger communities of which they were part – it is illustrative to discuss the Chen Hengzhe incident of 1936. Chen (1890–1976) was the first female professor in China and a pioneering writer of modern vernacular Chinese literature. Originally from Hunan Province, Chen was among the first group of Chinese women to be awarded a Boxer Indemnity Scholarship to study in the United States. She attended Vassar College and later the University of Chicago, where she received an MA in history in 1920. In February of the same year, Peking University hired Chen as its first female professor, teaching Western history. In September, she married Ren Hongjun (1886–1961), who had received an MA in chemistry from Columbia University and was also offered a professorship at Peking University.[15] In 1935, Ren, who was Sichuanese, received an appointment to serve as the president of Sichuan University. The couple decided to relocate, with their two children, from Beijing to Chengdu. The next year, in *Duli pinglun* (*Independent Critic*) – a liberal journal she co-founded with other leading New Culture Movement figures such as Hu Shi – Chen published a series of three essays describing her relocation experience and subsequent life in Chengdu.

Chen did not foresee that the scale of circulation for her essays – or the comments on them in various news media – would travel so far beyond the small intellectual circle for which she originally intended the work. "Miscellaneous Accounts of [our] Journey to Sichuan" was comprised of three "open letters" written for an audience of friends in different Chinese cities. The essays received little public attention until *Xinmin bao* (*New People*) in Nanjing reprinted her second piece in June 1936, adding in a large font the subtitle: "She Said Sichuan Female Students Were Not Ashamed of Becoming Concubines and Sichuan's Eggs Do Not Taste Like Eggs." The newspaper then reprinted Chen's other two pieces and published articles criticizing her, written chiefly by Sichuanese in Nanjing. By June 20th, the battlefield of critique had moved to Chengdu, and by early July, major local newspapers had all published pieces criticizing Chen. In response, *Xinxin xinwen* (*Latest News*), which had the largest local circulation, received almost 600 letters of complaint from readers. Many Sichuanese were indignant about Chen's "denigration" of Sichuan; in addition to the concubine issue, she brought to light social ills such as widespread opium smoking and the dominance of warlords. Before long, criticisms of Chen escalated into personal attacks, with many of her critics attributing Chen's account of

Sichuan's conservative social atmosphere and backward material conditions to her own overly Westernized and extravagant background, and consequently, an arrogant perspective.[16]

Throughout the incident, Chen's commentary on the phenomenon of Sichuan students becoming concubines was both the initial trigger and the subsequent center of critique. An author in *Xinxin xinwen* insisted Chen's suggestion that "a majority of Sichuan students are willing to become concubines" should be "testified to by the circle of Sichuan female students themselves."[17] A female student from a provincial technical school argued in the same newspaper that by claiming "a majority of Sichuan students are willing to become concubines, and many students do not feel ashamed to do so," Chen had committed "slander."[18] Many critics demanded that Chen present evidence. On July 8th, Huayang Women's Association (Huayang funü xiehui) held an emergency meeting that resulted in their insistence that Chen's letter had committed "the crime of defamation." The organization also sent letters to various county-level women's organizations and asked students to participate in lawsuits.[19]

But what exactly did Chen say? The original comment in her open letter reads as follows:

> As for concubinage, it is a naturally corrupt institution of China and is by no means exclusively a Sichuan phenomenon. However, the situation in Sichuan is different. In other regions, the social origins of concubines are nothing more than three: maidservants, prostitutes, and poor girls. However, in Sichuan, the so-called *taitai* of many wealthy men are female students, and some of these female students are not ashamed of becoming concubines (With regard to the extravagant hope of female students who are "willing to be the concubine of a general rather than the wife of a commoner," I have heard too many reports, and hence it can be said it is an undeniable truth. I hope that those excellent ones among Sichuan students can figure out a way to wash away this shame.).[20]

Chen was mistaken in believing that few female students chose to become concubines in other parts of China, but nowhere did she claim that "a majority of" Sichuan students were willing to become concubines. And only "some," by her reading, felt no shame. However, many readers had not seen the original text of Chen's letters and believed the words of her critics as they were reprinted and circulated in various newspapers. Later, Chen's husband published a response in *Duli pinglun* clarifying, among other matters, that Chen's original letters did not suggest "female students in Sichuan all love to become concubines of military men."[21] His response seems to have been too little, too late, and his efforts failed to quell the widespread anger Chen's comments had aroused. As her letters and their critiques were reprinted again and again by additional newspapers and seen by an ever-increasing readership, more and more people threatened to sue Chen for "insulting Sichuanese."[22] Meanwhile, local lawyers were collecting evidence from her open letters to prepare for litigation. Through it all, Chen remained silent. On July 9th, amid ever-intensifying attacks, she left Sichuan for Beijing. The next spring, her husband resigned from his post and left Sichuan as well.[23]

The issue of female students becoming concubines was the focal point of conflict and drew widespread public attention. Nobody participating in the debate disputed the idea that students becoming concubines was a shameful matter. The dispute concerned whether Chen had evidence to prove that Sichuan students did so and how widespread the phenomenon was. A consensus seemed to emerge that female students becoming concubines was not only a disgraceful matter to the women themselves but also to the reputation of the larger communities they belonged to. Otherwise, Chen's comment would not have aroused such widespread public anger (including the threat of lawsuits). This reputational concern for the larger community was explicitly articulated in 1922 by Zhu Caizhen, who argued in his journal *Fei qie hao* that a woman becoming a concubine, even if she did so for "love," mattered not only for "the woman's own personhood (*ren'ge*)," but had an impact on "the personhood of the entire women's circle."[24] Indeed, the most vigorous protests against Chen's comments came from Sichuan students and women's associations, women who probably felt they had the most to lose if their reputations were tarnished by association with the category of concubine. The same anxiety was shared by the students at Xi'an Women's Normal School. Their fear of reputation contamination by a concubine in their school was so strong that it overrode their concern about the improper nature of a teacher–student relationship: They boycotted classes to demand punishment for those involved and cleanse the reputation of their group. The same concern about protecting members' reputations prompted some progressive women's organizations to propose excluding concubines altogether.

CONCUBINES IN PROGRESSIVE WOMEN'S ORGANIZATIONS

Early twentieth-century China saw the establishment of numerous women's organizations, which grew in part out of an anxiety that the country's scarcity of civic groups was hindering its development. Compared to the elite women's organizations of the late imperial period, such as poetry societies, many of these new groups formed around an ideal or goal beyond a shared interest in literature, with particular attention paid to women's education and economic independence, nationalism, and political radicalism. Educated progressive women, most of whom came from wealthy families, found these gender-segregated groups to be ideal places to practice their leadership abilities and engage with the public sphere.

Concubines interested in the same progressive causes were eager to join. But they were often rejected from women's organizations, much like the women with bound feet who were denied admission to public schools despite their desire to learn: Though their origins and experiences differed, both categories of women were deemed socially backward.[25] Almost every woman's suffrage group in the Republican period included in its manifestos a call for the abolition of concubinage.[26] A religious civic organization, the YWCA (Young Women's Christian Association) also regarded itself as a progressive body and was, by the 1920s, the largest women's organization in China. Its leaders, most of whom were modern-/Western-educated Chinese women or foreigners, also opposed concubinage. The secretary conferences of 1913, 1916, and 1919 recommended that "secondary wives" (an English term that foreign secretaries preferred to use in reference to concubines, though concubines were not technically wives) not be granted membership.[27] At their National Convention in 1923, attended mostly by "first wives," the group's leaders decided that the YWCA "take a definite stand against the system of concubinage and that every member do all in her power to further this purpose."²⁸ The first wives likely had personal stakes in their efforts to eliminate concubines from their homes and the world.

Nonetheless, actual practices varied. In most cities, concubines were debarred from joining, but in some, they were admitted, indicating the difficulty of implementing the policy consistently across various branches nationwide. The organization's foreign secretaries frequently noted what they called "class loyalties": First wives were willing to work for concubines but not with them, suggesting that traditional class consciousness among these women remained strong, even in an international social service organization like the YWCA. Historian Nancy Boyd notes that "some local Associations excluded second wives; others discouraged first wives from attending meetings – their presence inhibited the second wives who were the more committed and active members."²⁹ In fact, we know little about concubines' engagements with the YWCA. Since the organization's official policy was against concubinage, local secretaries may have cautiously avoided mentioning the concubine status of some committed participants in their work reports.

The decision made by the Tianjin Chinese Women's Patriotic Association (Tianjin nüjie aiguo tongzhihui, TCWPA) to refuse admission to concubines resulted in social consequences that some members had to deal with personally. While traveling through China in the 1920s, Grace Seton learned that TCWPA members included "several hundred educated ladies and wives of the most intellectual families in the city." Their announcement that no concubines were eligible to join the organization "caused much discussion in Chinese society and has involved unpleasant consequences, as many of the concubines are personal friends, even relatives, of the members." Seton's account provides a useful reminder that many concubines existed in the same social circles as progressive women; rejecting them was not merely a matter of abstract principle, but could have serious repercussions for personal relationships. Still, Seton observed, the TCWPA was prepared to "stand by its decision and forgo the support of thousands and thousands of concubines who as a rule are wealthy and generous."³⁰

In defense of its controversial decision, the TCWPA publicized a detailed rationale in an influential Beijing-based newspaper, *Chenbao*

(*Morning News*), in August 1919.[31] I will print their justification in full, as it enables us to look closely at the concerns involved:

> Unless concubinage is abolished, our family system and finally our nation will be destroyed. We modern women cannot refrain from paying attention to this question. The result of our deliberation is the passing of a resolution excluding concubines from the membership of the association. We herewith give the detailed reasons why we have adopted this strong attitude:
>
> 1. Although the promoters of the association are teachers and students in girls' schools, they are more than pleased to have wives and members of reputable families join them so that they may be able to render greater service to the country. Why not take in concubines, who are also Chinese women and patriotic? We have been asked to answer this question. However, to allow concubines to be members would go against our first principle. Our object in organizing the association was to arouse our sisters to do something for their country. Our future plan is to reform the family, to reform society and to abolish any social system that is detrimental to Chinese women. The concubines who desire to join us will probably fail to understand the association's ultimate objectives. They would be offended should we in the future discuss the question of the abolition of concubinage. Such a disagreement of views will hinder the progress of the Association.
> 2. Such being our principle, we cannot admit the right of concubines to exist as part of society and consequently cannot allow them to become members; otherwise our task of uprooting the evil will be increased tenfold. However, we do not look down upon them or consider them not as ours. On the contrary, we are devising means for their salvation from their present deplorable state.
> 3. There are three classes of concubines in China. Some are ambitious women belonging to good families. Some are sold into slavery as a result of calamity or misfortune, some are women without principle, not knowing the sin they have committed, and are satisfied with worldly comforts and luxuries. Still others are prostitutes, who are impudent and proud of their degraded position. If we take in as our members any concubines at all, the good name of the association will surely be compromised. Furthermore, this is the first time that Chinese women

4 EXCLUDING CONCUBINES

have tried to do something for their country, and we are consequently passing a trying period.

4. Ninety-nine out of a hundred women in China are not free. We are now sending out eighty or ninety women to speak on public questions. These lecturers include teachers, students, matrons and young women. We have now completed our patriotic work inside the city and will continue our campaign outside it. We are grateful to our parents for their support and sympathy, which will be withdrawn if they discover that we are not living up to our principles. Our parents will dislike our association with degraded women. These are the four reasons why we exclude concubines from the association.[32]

Of the four reasons, three and four both concern the fear of concubines' contaminating influence on "reputable" women, a fear shared by the female students who tried to expel concubines from public schools. Although the leaders at TCWPA claimed not to "look down upon" the concubines or "consider them not as our equals," the statement twice refers to concubines as "degraded women." The declaration differentiates between three classes of concubines but makes no effort to suggest any varied treatment based on this distinction. All concubines were to be regarded as morally dubious, leaving other women activists – who sought, through virtuous behavior, proof of their qualification for political participation and civic engagement – vulnerable to the taint of proximity. The rationale also specifically points out that many of their lecturers had engaged in public speaking, and if some of them turned out to be concubines, the reputation of all would be endangered.

The decision to exclude concubines could be highly contentious and did not always prevail within an organization. The members of Guangdong United Women's Association (Guangdong nüjie lianhe hui, GUWA) provide one such example. Founded in December 1919, the group had a broad goal of promoting women's movements with specific agendas such as "instituting universal education for women," "striving to eliminate the suffering of oppressed women," and "developing women's morality." Later, it explicitly added women's suffrage to its agenda.[33] On January 20, 1920, the GUWA hosted a heated discussion about allowing concubines to become members. Their internal dispute attracted press attention, offering a glimpse into the proceedings. According to a report from *Minguo ribao*, Wu Zhimei, the organization's founder and a medical educator trained in the United States, proposed that the GUWA should be composed of women of "noble personhood" (*gaoshang ren'ge*). Concubines, who were believed to have lost their *ren'ge*, should not be allowed to join the association or should at least be deprived of the right to vote or be elected to any leadership roles.

Another GUWA member, Cheng Liqing, opposed Wu's proposal, arguing that women's liberation should help ordinary women regain their "original personhood" (*yuanren ren'ge*) and that all women should be liberated regardless of social class. (It was taken for granted that concubines belonged to a low social class, even though some had married wealthy husbands and received a modern education.) If the association rejected concubines, it would serve as merely a "wives and young ladies' association" (*furen xiaojie de lianhehui*) rather than a true women's association. Were Wu and her supporters suggesting that concubines were not women?, Cheng asked. The very existence of concubinage proved that women were not yet liberated, she argued; concubines needed sympathy and aid, not further oppression. More than twenty women supported Cheng's argument and expressed similar opinions. Wu's supporters, who numbered just ten, left the meeting angrily and early. With insufficient members present, the meeting was dismissed without an official outcome.[34] The question of concubine membership remained a divisive factor, causing internal tensions that threatened to fracture precisely the united women's liberation movement the GUWA championed.

What triggered this specific dispute among members of the GUWA was none other than the incident described earlier in this chapter: student protests against the appointment of He Zhifen, a concubine, as the president of Guangzhou Women's Normal School. GUWA members had gathered at a local girls' athletic school for a meeting. They began by discussing the student strike against He then occurring in their city. The chairwoman, Wu Zhimei, used the opportunity to propose banning concubines from becoming members of GUWA. Riding with the tide of protests against He's appointment, Wu might have thought her proposal would easily pass. However, a number of oppositional voices (including those of Cheng Liqing, a former Provisional Provincial Assembly member, and Li Lian, president of the girls' athletic school) made themselves heard, and the group could not reach an agreement. They decided to reconvene on another day.[35] Considering the two incidents together, it is notable that in Guangdong Province during the 1920s, concubines were active in both educational circles and the women's rights movements. Furthermore, there appears to have been an overlap in leadership between the women's rights groups and the circles of female educators. The fact that local girls' schools were sites where progressive women's organizations regularly gathered further demonstrates their connections.

The primary rationale used by Wu and her followers in the GUWA to exclude concubines was a familiar one: concubines do not possess *ren'ge*. This was the same rationale used by students at the Guangzhou Women's Normal School and Xi'an Women's Normal School to protest against their concubine members, whether a president or a schoolmate. Even members who supported concubines joining the GUWA did not refute this influential New Culturalist criteria, but merely insisted that concubines deserved their sympathy and needed to be liberated as well. In other words, it was a widely shared contemporary belief in progressive circles that the concubine, as a category, did not possess *ren'ge* and was thus morally dubious. This conviction can help us further understand why He Zhifen, in her resignation letter, did not argue about whether a concubine could be a school president.

A student from Peking University – the most renowned institution of higher education in the faraway capital city of Beijing – commented (perhaps after reading news reports in *Minguo ribao*) in the school's student journal on the GUWA's stance of "excluding concubines" (*paiqie*). Like both Wu Zhimei and Cheng Liqing, the Peking University student highlighted the importance of *ren'ge*, believing it a quality that all women who became concubines had lost. But the author also recognized that many women became concubines and that quite a few of them were equipped with "new vision" and "new intellect." If every concubine was flatly rejected, the organization was only partially liberating, for it failed to push beyond class boundaries. The author proposed that concubines with a "thorough consciousness" divorce their husbands and take back their "noble personhood." In this way, they could stand at the vanguard of the Anti-Concubinage Movement and encourage women's emancipation. But if a woman merely promoted liberation verbally while remaining a concubine, she was only half liberated. The author disapproved of a concubine joining the organization in this way.[36] In other words, as long as a woman remained a concubine, she did not have *ren'ge* and should not be allowed to become a member, despite the student's belief that the organization should transcend class boundaries.

The Peking University student had, however, made a distinction: Not all concubines were the same – some had "new vision" and "new intellect," much as the TCWPA announcement had conceded. This indicates that he/she was influenced by – or at least aware of – changes that concubinage underwent during this period and the fact that the category of concubine was not homogeneous. However, this understanding did not prevent the student from believing these women had lost their *ren'ge* by allowing themselves to degenerate into the tainted category – *qie*. By the Republican period, the low status of the category *qie* had more to do with social stigma than with social origin, since by then many concubines were not prostitutes or entertainers but merely from poor families. Regardless, in the student writer's eyes, concubines who had not first liberated themselves from such a low position were not qualified to join an organization dedicated to the broader cause of women's liberation. According to this reading, it was not the organization's fault for failing to transcend class boundaries, but the individual concubine's fault for failing to demonstrate her ability to liberate all women, since she had not first liberated herself. This line of thinking is reminiscent of the social critics who blamed individual female students' own moral deficiencies for becoming concubines rather than considering the lingering social and cultural legacies of the past (see Chapter 3).

Meanwhile, oppositional voices expressed their disapproval of excluding concubines from women's organizations. In a June 1921 "Random Thoughts" column, also in *Minguo ribao*, an author described having recently received a pamphlet circulated before a meeting of the Shanghai Women's Society (Shanghai funü hui), also to be held in a

4 EXCLUDING CONCUBINES

local girls' school. The pamphlet stipulated that no concubines would be allowed to join. The author wondered what this meant, asking:

> Do these women mean that concubines are too shameful to be human? Those concubines did not just willingly become concubines; they were forced by circumstances to live helplessly in such inhuman ways! You regard yourselves as educated, but want to exclude them? A certain lady wrote such lofty words in the announcement as "Chinese women's circle has been in darkness for thousands of years and could not invigorate itself. Chinese Women's Society was exactly established to promote women's rights, cultivate morality, build personhood, and maintain social welfare." However, she would not even show sympathy to the most pitiful concubines. I really feel shame for the words borrowed by these women – women's rights (*nüquan*), morality (*daode*), personhood (*ren'ge*), and public good (*gongyi*).³⁷

Unlike the progressive women who emphasized the concubine's loss of *ren'ge* and degrading influence, this author stressed concubines' lack of free will, arguing that they should be recognized as victims deserving of sympathy. The author also mocked progressive leaders' use of key terms, such as "*ren'ge*," to justify their decisions. By excluding concubines from joining the organization, the author maintained, elite women revealed their own hypocrisy, turning their seemingly lofty principles into little more than empty slogans.

Other voices opposed to excluding concubines explicitly argued that concubines did not necessarily have low *ren'ge*, directly challenging the discourse and rationale of Anti-Concubinage Movement activists. However, this type of argument was rarely expressed directly through opinion pieces in print media. The example that follows was inadvertently revealed in another incident of excluding concubines, reported by *Shibao* (*Eastern Times*), a major Shanghai daily newspaper. In March 1921, the Beijing United Women's Association (Beijing nüjie lianhe hui, BUWA) held a meeting to discuss the issue of charitable donations. Dozens of women attended. When the meeting was about to begin, a certain Ms. Wu proposed that the BUWA should be composed only of "noble" (*gaoshang*) women, with concubines denied membership. A number of women agreed with her, but two seated concubines – one of them married to a very wealthy man – began whispering to each other in indignation. A public dispute nearly erupted. Later, another attendee attempted to resolve the dispute by arguing that the principle of women's liberation is to help women regain their *ren'ge*. The institution of concubinage is a manifestation of women's lack of liberation. Therefore, the association should pity the concubines' situations and help rather than boycott them. The majority of those present agreed, but Ms. Wu and her followers did not believe concubines should be accepted into the organization. Angry, they abruptly left the room. Since the meeting could not reach a consensus, it had to be dismissed.

The reporter later heard that Ms. Wu intended to implement her proposal by calling another meeting on a future day to discuss detailed ways to bar concubines from membership, just as Wu Zhimei had attempted at GUWA. But those inclined to protect concubines preferred to mediate the dispute, and they articulated their rationale: China's historical records are replete with chaste and virtuous concubines. The behavior of so-called "free women" (*ziyou nü*) in the present might not necessarily be noble. Whether or not a woman's *ren'ge* is honorable depends on whether she has "self-respect" (*zi'ai*). The word "wife" or "concubine" was merely a superficial term that had no bearing on a woman's *ren'ge*. The reporter concluded that each side's argument had merits and that it was unclear which side would prevail.[38]

The initial argument that concubines could be victims of oppression and thus deserved help rather than rejection was shared by the oppositional voices discussed earlier in this chapter. But in this case, the pro-concubine side later added new rationales to make their argument more persuasive. First, they placed concubines within a long spectrum of Chinese history and pointed to ample evidence of "chaste and virtuous" concubines. Next, they brought up cases of contemporary "free women" for comparison, arguing that they might not all have noble *ren'ge*. This comparison was probably made in reference to the so-called Modern Girls, many of which were viewed as scandalous and superficial by their contemporaries, including leftists, nationalists, and even among different strands of feminists.[39] In this way, the pro-concubine side argued convincingly that it was unreasonable to use generalized categories or labels to judge an individual woman's morality. However, they never questioned the validity of *ren'ge* as the criteria for membership, either, similar to other women's civic organizations. This not only demonstrates the influence the newly created term had gained among progressive women's circles, but also highlights the high value these circles placed on women's morality as they defined it.

It should be noted that during this period, in nonprogressive women's organizations, the issue of concubine membership was hardly controversial. I have shown elsewhere that concubines participated actively in some conservative women's organizations, such as the women's branches of redemptive societies – the syncretic religious and philanthropic groups prevalent in Republican China. In the women's branches of Daoyuan (School of the Way), for example, the wives and concubines of male members often engaged in religious and charitable activities together. The nominal leadership position was typically given to a wife, whereas within the family, the younger and more energetic concubines often played a more active role. The organization's spiritual teaching drew from a reinterpreted version of Confucian gender doctrines that emphasized the importance of domestic harmony and the accumulation of religious merit, rather than asserting women's independent personhood. Consequently, little political strife or division surrounded the concubine issue within these women's organizations.[40]

CONCLUSION

New changes often bring new challenges. The category of concubine underwent significant changes in the Republican period. Some modern, educated concubines were eager to work in or study at public schools and participate in progressive women's organizations. These types of organizations were comprised mostly of elite women who could be sympathetic to poor women, factory women, and other members of classes that they regarded as beneath them but worthy of their benevolence. But they coexisted uneasily with concubines, some of whom had the money, leisure, and education to see themselves as the peers of elite women rather than merely subjects of their charity. In addition to their stated lofty ideals, the progressive women leaders who proposed to ban concubines were probably partly driven, consciously or unconsciously, by the age-old emotion of jealousy when considering the concubine membership issue. During the Republican era, the topic of jealousy among wives and concubines received frequent coverage in the press. Many incidents of domestic violence caused by wife or concubine jealousy were widely reported.[41] These women must be fully aware that it was men of their husbands' social classes who could afford to bring concubines into their homes and thus were determined to eliminate all concubines from their world. As members of various communities and social organizations struggled to reach a consensus on the issue, their heated debates not only caused internal conflicts but also drew media attention, which probably generated cynical views of and bad publicity for the women's groups and their collective feminist causes.

On the other hand, these cases also reveal the anxiety that many progressive women felt about their own reputations. In an era when respectable women were just beginning to step into public life, they faced battles against long-held assumptions that virtuous women should remain in the domestic sphere. Progressive women's groups took great pains to emphasize the good moral standing of their members, hoping to prove their qualification for political participation and civic engagement. However, their overemphasis on the importance of purity and virtue led to their outright intolerance and undifferentiated discrimination against an entire category of women. Fearful of being tainted by their public association with concubines, some of these women made a special point of demonstrating their respectability by seeking to exclude concubines from the same public institutions they regularly attended. Their persistence and insistence on this issue make us wonder whether some elite women leaders cared as much about their own reputation or social gains as they did about the collective cause of liberating all Chinese women.

Furthermore, the cases also show that concubines encountered widespread social discrimination and moral censure within progressive women's circles, often couched in lofty, elusive terms of the New Culture Movement, such as *ren'ge*. Remaining unchallenged as the membership eligibility criteria for progressive women's groups, be it a public school or a civic organization, *ren'ge* depersonalized concubines into an undifferentiated collective category – *qie* – that embodied sexual immorality, degraded social class, parasitic existence, and political backwardness. Consequently, regardless of whether an individual concubine had a "new intellect" and "new vision," her status as a concubine rendered her vulnerable to attacks and frequently prevented her from becoming a regular member of progressive women's groups. Unfortunately, it seems that concubines did not organize themselves into groups to fight for their interests and demand better treatment during this era. As a result, individual concubines, even well-educated ones like Yao Wenyu and He Zhifen, after voicing their indignation at the intolerance they encountered, still had to accept their forced expulsion or resignation. The exceptions seemed to be those who married very powerful officials, as seen in the cases of Li Benwei and Guo Dejie, who generally enjoyed public respect while their husbands were alive. This reminds us that concubines were not all equal and not all equally discriminated against. Previously, imperial concubines often came from elite families, and these women, even if they were concubines, were elevated above other women of their own class by the power of their husbands (such as the emperor).[42]

Finally, the cases of excluding concubines seen in this chapter suggest that more investigation is needed into the differences and divisions among progressive women in Republican China – whether suffragists, patriots, feminists, educators, or other activists. As we have seen, concubines sometimes moved in the same social networks as other progressive women – as family members, relatives, and friends. However, their social connections did not prevent them from being rejected when they wanted to join the women's groups dedicated to public causes. The key difference was class status rather than doctrinal disagreement. Other sources reveal instances of separate women's rights organizations in the same city refusing to merge into a united, single group due to "irreconcilable personal differences" between participants, which boiled down to "who was friends with whom." Personal social connections played a significant role in determining whether members were included or excluded. An extended critical engagement with the differences and divisions among progressive women could reveal hidden issues within Chinese women's movements, just as scholars have fruitfully revealed divisions within other social and political organizations such as the

CONCLUSION

Chinese Communist Party.[43] Other factors related to group politics may also have played a role. It appears that the demand to exclude concubines was primarily seen in women-only schools and organizations, rather than in coeducational schools or social groups that included both men and women. This might be because women controlled the leadership positions in women-only organizations and were able to act more forcefully, even radically.[44] It is also possible that in these women-only groups a stronger sense of community among women prevailed, raising the stakes for maintaining their collective virtuous reputation. Further research is needed to provide more comprehensive answers to these questions.

Epilogue

IN MANY RESPECTS, this is a book about contradictions. The new Republican civil code aimed to eliminate concubines. Instead, concubines not only flourished but also became highly visible and controversial players in China's rapidly evolving public sphere. Embodying both the country's modernity and its backwardness, the presence of these women at social occasions, in public schools, and in civic organizations demonstrates both the unprecedented privileges they gained but also the tensions, politics, and divisions they could cause. Progressive women's organizations proclaimed their goals to unite all Chinese women to fight for their liberation, but in reality, their leaders often refused to work with concubines and attempted to ban them from membership. Meanwhile, the *institution* of concubinage, despite having been legally abolished in the 1930s, did not die out quickly but showed a remarkable capacity for innovation and resilience, adapting to the new challenges of the early twentieth century. The types of women who became concubines changed: Some had had a modern education and were socially progressive, others did not have tainted social origins and became concubines willingly, in pursuit of the new ideal of "free love," and many had separate living arrangements from the main wives. Moreover, the social and public skills of concubines were increasingly valued by elite men, in some cases more so than their ability to produce male heirs, further contributing to their rising domestic status. Such important dimensions of the concubine issue manifested in the society of Republican China cannot be easily shoehorned into historiographies focused on progressive efforts to stamp out this "shameful" Chinese custom. The cases discussed in this book caution us that, despite our desire to see progress on gender issues as a linear process, we need to resist narratives that are too tidy, as they fail to capture the complexity and contradictions of lived history.

Seen from the perspective of individual concubines' lives, there were contradictions, too. On the one hand, some concubines were given new opportunities to participate in public life and to be treated with the respect nominally paid to wives. Domestically, some concubines carved out a space of their own owing to their modern education, social skills, youthful adaptability, and appearance or sense of style. Their separate living arrangements also made them less subject to the hierarchical rules and whims of the main wives. On the other hand, their public appearances sometimes left them vulnerable to social discrimination and contempt, expressed by those who viewed their very existence as a national disgrace or collective shame. Once their husbands died, most concubines lost their public platforms, their privileges, and their sources of support. Due to the lack of effective legal protections over their rights of inheritance, sonless concubines were sometimes driven out of their husbands' homes by their main wives or children and had to remarry for economic reasons or learn to make a living for themselves. Their status was complicated: They lived in a state of flux that cannot be easily summarized by an "overall" argument. Each woman's life was shaped by her specific situation and personal circumstances.

This study has also revealed a range of intertwined historical forces that existing literature on the efforts to abolish concubinage has largely overlooked. In this sense, the book is not merely about concubines, but also about several broader historical issues that have been largely forgotten, yet helped shape modern China. By investigating concubines' public appearances with their husbands on social occasions and their memberships in progressive women's organizations and public schools, this book also sheds new light on the politics of gender and etiquette in late Qing diplomacy and international relations, the newly emerged role of the "social wife," the innovations to concubinage in Republican China, the growing importance of women's social and public skills in elite socialization and networking, and the tensions and divisions within progressive women's circles and Chinese women's liberation movements.

By focusing on the emergence and rise of the social wife role, as exemplified by concubines, I have highlighted the increasing visibility and influence of women in urban, public, and social spheres, a topic deserving further study. Most scholars have examined how being a "modern" woman in China meant becoming professional, politically active, or revolutionary, resisting feudal traditions or patriarchal oppression. These are important topics, to be sure. However, for many Chinese women, becoming modern meant learning the etiquette and skills necessary to properly socialize in public settings, especially when male strangers were also present. This territory has received less attention; as a result, we still have an inadequate understanding of women's changing social and public lives in the course of China's modernization beyond the discursive shift from valuing domestic seclusion to celebrating public engagement.

This topic is significant for several reasons. First, women were clearly playing an increasingly important role in elite social and political networking. The high-profile assistance that Guo Dejie provided to her husband's vice-presidential campaign is a prime example. In addition to socializing and campaigning for Li's career advancement, Guo also projected a positive image of an attractive woman with a modern education in her role as Madame Li Zongren. Madame Li was also active in women's education and charitable causes, which helped improve and soften public perceptions of her husband as a mere military man, a point raised by Kate Merkel-Hess in her case study of Li Dequan (1896–1972) and her warlord husband Feng Yuxiang (1882–1948), and some other women who married warlords.[1] Moreover, in the first half of the twentieth century, concubines' public skills had a direct impact on their domestic status, especially in elite urban households. Concubines such as Li Benwei, who were adept at playing the role of the social wife, were increasingly valued by elite men because they could do what the men's old-fashioned main wives could not. The new cross-gender mingling social culture in urban Republican China provided unprecedented opportunities for women who were traditionally regarded as inferior; a concubine who seized this moment could demonstrate her worth, shake up the domestic hierarchy, and improve her lot.

Admittedly, from a long-term perspective, the twentieth century would see concubines gradually replaced by wives in public functions and occasions. As concubinage was attacked and eventually outlawed, the public presence of concubines became increasingly controversial and regarded as "backward." Eventually, the Communists effectively ended concubinage by defining it as bigamy, thereby rendering it illegal – a decisive action that the Nationalists were reluctant to take. Meanwhile, new generations of Chinese women educated in modern public schools had grown up, becoming the principal (in many cases, only) wives of officials and other elite men. Such women had far less difficulty playing the role of the modern social wife themselves.

The most notable example of a Republican official's wife playing an active public role was Song Meiling, who enjoyed a high profile as Madame Chiang Kai-shek. From a powerful, wealthy, and respected family, she was educated in the US and spoke fluent English. Due to her family's Christian beliefs, Chiang had to cut ties with his three previous wives and concubines to formally make her his only wife in 1927. After her marriage, Madame Chiang Kai-shek was often seen with her husband on public occasions, serving as his English interpreter, assistant, hostess, and public companion. On February 18, 1943, as the First Lady of the Republic of China, she became the first Chinese national and the second woman to address both houses of the United States Congress. Later that year, she accompanied Chiang to the Cairo Conference to discuss the progress of the war against Japan and the future of Asia.[2] Although she had no children with her husband, no one questioned whether she should be considered a member of the Chiang family after he died in 1975. Although concubines gradually ceased playing the role of social wives, the presence of women at public occasions increased substantially. As the First Lady of the Nationalist government, Song was only the most visible case. To better understand the growing importance of women in elite socialization and political networking in twentieth-century China will require creatively unearthing the relevant sources to carry out more comprehensive studies.

It is noteworthy that, despite the revolutionary upheavals of the Mao years (1949–1976), what some Chinese historians refer to as "wife diplomacy" (*furen waijiao*) largely continued, albeit with some resistance.[3] Scholars have noted that many of the wives of Communist diplomats and officials in the early 1950s resisted merely assisting their husbands in diplomatic and public functions – a practice, the women argued, that contradicted the principles of gender equality and women's liberation.

Instead, they believed it important to have careers of their own.[4] The nature of serving as the social wives of their husbands in public was believed to have a strong bourgeois flavor at odds with the values of the revolution. Their protests prompted Premier Zhou Enlai (1898–1976) to send his wife, Deng Yingchao (1904–1992), to talk with them. Deng emphasized the unique advantage of women in diplomacy by pointing out that in foreign countries, the wives of diplomats and officials not only enjoyed a high status, but their pillow talk could influence their husbands, thereby helping steer the nation's path forward. Later, Zhou himself would stress the significance and indispensability of wife diplomacy. Consequently, more officials' wives willingly accepted government training in foreign languages and etiquette to better play their public roles. Since the late 1950s, the most prominent officials' wives with high public profiles have been the wife of President Liu Shaoqi (1898–1969), Wang Guangmei (1921–2006), and the wife of Minister of Foreign Affairs Chen Yi (1901–1972), Zhang Qian (1922–1974). Both accompanied their husbands on important diplomatic occasions.[5] Wang particularly stood out for her beauty, elegance, and sophistication on the public stage, inciting jealousy from Jiang Qing (1914–1991), the wife of Chairman Mao Zedong (1893–1976). By the early 1960s, after Mao finally gave his permission, Jiang began to participate more actively in "wife diplomacy." On September 24, 1962, when Hartini, the second wife of Indonesian President Sukarno (1901–1970), visited China, Mao personally received her in Beijing at a reception in the grandest possible style. Jiang, together with Wang Guangmei, Deng Yingchao, Zhang Qian, and some other leading officials' wives, attended the event.[6] During the Cultural Revolution (1966–1976), the Western origins of wife diplomacy made it vulnerable to the criticism that it was a residue of the bourgeoisie, and it was halted temporarily.[7] Soon after Liu was purged by Mao due to their political differences, Jiang maneuvered to have Wang publicly humiliated for her "bourgeois" crimes: In 1967, Wang was paraded onto a public stage in Beijing wearing "a form-fitting dress festooned with a garland of ping-pong balls to mock the elegant silk *qipao* and pearl necklace ensemble that she had worn" while accompanying her husband on a state visit to Indonesia in 1959.[8] In this way, Jiang was finally able to punish Wang for outshining Jiang in wife diplomacy.

However, once China moved beyond the Mao period and began its path of opening and reform, wife diplomacy resumed. Since 2013, many Chinese have praised the public appearances of Peng Liyuan (b. 1962), the wife of President Xi Jinping (b. 1953), when she joins him on visits to foreign countries. These observers believe that the glamor and sense of fashion displayed by Peng, who was also a famous folk singer, promote a positive image of China on the international stage.[9] However, few people know that a number of the earliest, most daring social wives in China's history were, in fact, concubines. Those pioneers deserve to be recognized for playing roles with no precedent, for the social criticism, contempt, and discrimination they faced, and for the suffering that many of them endured living as embodied subjects of China's polygynous, patriarchal hierarchy.

Moreover, in the post-Mao era, as China opened its borders and initiated market-oriented reforms, businessmen from Hong Kong and Taiwan who arrived in China for extended stays began setting up separate households with "secondary wives" (*er nai*). With the rapid improvement of domestic living standards, wealthy urban Chinese men were able to follow the same practice. These men considered their possession of *er nai* and ability to provide these women with apartments and other forms of remuneration to be markers of social status,[10] not so different from the symbolism of concubine possession in the imperial period. What is different in the post-Mao era is that the women they supported technically could not be called concubines, as their relationships were never legally recognized as marriages.[11] Still, the fact that these women were often nicknamed "secondary wives" suggests that, in popular perceptions, their living arrangements represented a kind of remnant of concubinage; either way, their presence certainly caught the public's attention.[12]

Finally, during the Mao era, former concubines resurfaced in public and politics, though this time primarily as targets of reeducation, political struggle, and persecution. The extremely limited and fragmentary sources suggest that despite their humble class origins, these women often became victims of radical political persecution, due in part to their connections with men of "evil" social classes, whether bourgeoisie "reactionary capitalists" or "reactionary military officials." Although former concubines rarely wrote about their experiences, we occasionally get a glimpse of their lives in other people's life histories. In his biography of Wang Xiulan (b. 1932), a star of Pu opera (*puju*, a type of Shanxi opera), the author (a playwright who worked closely with Wang over the years) recorded an interview with another Pu singer, Fu Xiuyun (1930–2011), who expressed gratitude for the help Wang had once provided her. The singers had come to know one another around the Anti-Rightist Campaign (roughly June 1957 to the following summer), during a political movement billed as "Surrendering Your Heart to the Party" (Xiang dang jiaoxin), which required anyone harboring non-Socialist thoughts to report the details of their wrongdoings to higher-level party leaders.[13] Wang, then Vice Deputy Head of Southern Shanxi Opera Troupe and a party cadre, was assigned Fu's case for thought reform. After Wang's "thought work" and encouragement, Fu "tearfully" confessed to Wang that she was a former concubine of a "reactionary Nationalist military official" (*fandong junguan*) who was in charge of defending the city of Linfen, a key military stronghold in the southwest of Shanxi province, against attack from the People's Liberation Army (PLA). After being defeated, the Nationalist official fled to Taiwan with his wife, children, and remaining wealth, leaving her behind.[14]

Fu's confession reads like a formulaic narrative of oppression: Her emphasis on the lack of free will involved in her wrongdoings prompts a historian to take the veracity of its details with a grain of salt. Fu described herself as being from a poor but "good and clean" family whose poverty forced them to sell her into a local performance troupe when she was young. In attendance at one of her performances, the Nationalist official took a fancy to her and forced her to become his concubine. She was treated as a "plaything" and endured endless rounds of beatings from the official and his wife. When the PLA attacked Linfen (from March to May 1948), the official forced her at gunpoint to appear on the city wall and "shout propaganda" (*hanhua*) at PLA soldiers. She repeated whatever she was told, such as: "Do not attempt to conquer Linfen... It is an invincible iron bastion." Because the Nationalist Party had American support and would soon launch a full-scale counterattack, she declared (under orders) that it would be better for the PLA to surrender their guns immediately.[15]

It is difficult to know whether Fu's public appearance in front of soldiers on both sides of the city wall was truly coerced. When she confessed to Wang, a Communist Party loyalist during the Anti-Rightist Campaign, she had every reason to emphasize her subjugation: "If I don't shout, they will beat me with a belt."[16] Even if she was indeed coerced, it is worth asking why her then-husband wanted her to convey the propaganda rather than doing it himself or ordering his wife or other subordinates to do it. It is possible that he did not want to endanger himself by appearing publicly on the city wall. But it is also possible that Fu had some previous experience playing the role of a public wife and could, therefore, carry out the task with her composure intact. This may not have been her first time appearing in front of soldiers and giving a speech on behalf of her husband, as Li Benwei had for Li Yuanhong after the Wuchang Uprising. Even though Fu's words were directed at the PLA, her husband's troops must have been listening as well. If they could recognize her face as their military leader's public companion, they might be inclined to believe her and find some assurance amid anxious circumstances. We have no sources to either confirm or refute these speculations. Fu concluded her confession by apologizing to the Communist Party and the PLA for what she had done. She thanked the Party and Chairman Mao for sparing her life – giving her food, clothing, and a new profession as an opera singer in a local performance troupe. She swore to work tirelessly to repay her debt and show her gratitude to the Party.[17] It seems that the Party accepted Fu's story and did not force her to suffer further.

Fu later used her excellent performance skills and devotion to her work to demonstrate that she had indeed reformed, though it was not enough to save her from the new waves of political campaigns. With Wang's help, Fu "improved her political consciousness" and participated in various revolutionary operas. She became a beloved performer and won many awards. Still, sources suggest that at the height of her career she was unable to escape the turmoil of the Cultural Revolution. We know that she was persecuted – probably due to her time spent as the concubine of a reactionary Nationalist official – and that she was unable to perform on stage for a long time.[18] Sources suggest that she survived and lived into the post-Mao period.[19]

There were probably many former concubines who suffered like Fu, or even more severely, during the Mao years. To be sure, anyone with a pre-1949 past could be targeted in political campaigns during the Mao period, not just concubines. However, it is noteworthy that among the countless accusatory labels created in endless rounds of political campaigns to classify and weed out class enemies, concubines seem to have received their own labels, from "concubines of reactionary bureaucrats" (*fandong guanliao yitaitai*), to "concubines of reactionary military officials" (*fandong junguan yitaitai*) and "concubines of landlords" (*dizhu xiao laopo*).[20] The political labels specially designed for concubines drew their meanings from two sources simultaneously: First and foremost are the classes of men said to be evil and exploitive, with whom the women in question had once associated. In this sense, these concubine victims were often the byproducts of various political campaigns.

The second source these labels drew from was the long-running popular stereotype of the parasitic, conniving, and backward concubine. Lisa Tran has noted the polarizing stereotype of the concubine as either "a hapless victim" or "a conniving vixen" in both popular perceptions and literary portrayals.[21] In Mao's China, the perception that prevailed at a particular moment could be a matter of life or death for the woman in question, as the following case illustrates. According to an unpublished memoir written around 2001 by Li Yinxiang – a retired former PLA soldier at Qujing, Yunnan Province, during the Land Reform Movement that ran from March to May 1951 in Zhanyi County – an incident befell a concubine of the largest local landlord, Pan Zihu. In a public session waged against landlords and held in front of a local audience of 30,000–40,000 spectators, Pan was suffering from previous rounds of brutal struggle sessions, a type of denunciation rallies used to punish "class enemies" and enforce ideological conformity. Too weak to utter a word, he was unable to confess where he had hidden his money. Someone in the audience loudly suggested that his concubine be forced to reveal the location of the money and many others agreed. A young woman was hustled to the center of the stage. Facing the public, with her hands tied behind her back, the woman insisted that she did not know the location of Pan's money as he had never allowed her to manage his household. Several "radical elements" present at the session refused to believe her; one of them took out a knife and threatened to cut off one of her breasts if she did not confess. She cried and begged him for clemency, claiming that she truly did not know the money's whereabouts. Suddenly, a breast fell to the ground and blood spilled over the concubine's body. She fainted from the pain. As the session concluded, the People's Court announced the list of criminals they had sentenced to death. Though the initial list included forty-two individuals who were condemned to die, forty-three people were ultimately shot and killed: The concubine was added to the list ad hoc. According to Li Yinxiang, who was on the stage observing as the leader of the local youth league, a county political commissar gave the order because he was afraid, as he told another county leader, that if she were allowed to live, the unplanned incident and her suffering would cause future controversy.[22]

Li himself felt that the killing of the concubine was a mistake, one of the many manifestations of leftist excesses exhibited by the Communist Land Reform Movement. He later learned that landlord Pan had two concubines: The woman who was killed that day had only lived with Pan for four or five years. She was around twenty-four years old, more than twenty years younger than Pan. Most importantly, she had received a middle-school education and was forced to become Pan's concubine as a way to pay the debt her family owed him. Li felt that she was, in fact, a victim of the landlord class and that it was unlikely Pan let her manage his family finances: The murdered girl would not have known where his money was.[23]

What Li did not reflect on in his memoir was *why*, when someone suggested hounding her, so many of the audience immediately agreed. No evidence was presented to indicate that she knew where the landlord's money could be found. Instead, the decision was likely based on assumptions and a stereotype deeply familiar to the audience: This parasitic, conniving vixen must be the partner in crime to an evil, exploitative landlord. Gripped by this image, those gathered rejected any thought of her innocence, leading to her torture and unjustified death.

The stories of the landlord's concubine and the opera singer Fu Xiuyun suggest that during the Mao era – allegedly a "post-liberation," Communist, new society – the past came back to haunt these women, their stigma becoming brutally relevant once again.[24] How, then, were their pasts recollected and reconstructed as political material to torment them during the upheavals of Mao's rule? In what scenarios would a concubine be treated merely as a hapless victim of the old "feudal" society and consequently saved from severe punishment, while another concubine be singled out as the scheming accomplice of her reactionary husband and judged to have played an active counterrevolutionary role? Who volunteered (or found themselves forced) to serve as witnesses to history in this process? In cases without solid evidence, where were the indispensable ingredients and sources found (or created) to reconstruct the women's life histories so as to fit into a new epistemological framework of class struggle and anti-imperialism and assign them damaging political labels? And to what extent did assumptions about a concubine's past hinge on moments of historical contingency, such as the volatile emotions of a mass audience in a particular struggle session?[25]

All of these questions await thorough investigation and detailed answers. For now, I can only hope that one day, if this period's history becomes less politically sensitive, historians will gain access to sources that will allow us to understand how a concubine's Republican past could be reinterpreted and translated into the dangerous politics of public memory during the decades of Mao's Communist rule.

Notes

INTRODUCTION

1. "E sheng nüjie xin choushi," *Shenbao*, January 16, 1913. This report refers to Yao as an accountant, but a later report (see note 2) formally refers to her as a general secretary, which probably was more accurate.
2. "Sui Hubei nüzi fazheng xuexiao xiaozhang Li Qimin shang jiaoyusi bing," *Shenbao*, March 1, 1913.
3. Gail Hershatter, "Modernizing Sex, Sexing Modernity: Prostitution in Early-Twentieth-Century Shanghai," in *Chinese Femininities, Chinese Masculinities: A Reader*, ed. Susan Brownell and Jeffrey Wasserstrom (Berkeley, CA: University of California Press, 2002), 199–221, at 205.
4. Kathryn Bernhardt, *Women and Property in China, 960–1949* (Stanford, CA: Stanford University Press, 1999), 161.
5. Wang Xiang, "Ru furen de fannao: zhongguo ershi shiji zaoqi youguan naqie de yiji, xushi yu xianshi," MA thesis, Shoudu shifan daxue, 2012, 12. Also see Beverly Bossler, *Courtesans, Concubines and the Cult of Female Fidelity* (Cambridge, MA: Harvard University Press, 2013) and Bernhardt, *Women and Property in China*.
6. Bernhardt, *Women and Property in China*, 163–78.
7. Bernhardt, *Women and Property in China*, 163–78.
8. The seven grounds included: failure to produce sons, adultery, incurable disease, disobedience to in-laws, jealousy, loquacity, and theft (from family members). See Lisa Tran, "The Concubine in Republican China: Social Perception and Legal Construction," *Etudes Chinoises* 28 (2009): 119–50, at 125.
9. Olivia Milburn, "Jealousy and Domestic Violence by Women in Early and Medieval China," *T'oung Pao* 107, no. 5 (2021): 555–81.
10. Shiau-Yun Chen, "Jealous and Violent: Constraining and Celebrating Wifely Jealousy in mid-to-late Ming China," *Ming Studies*, 2019, no. 79 (2019): 21–48.
11. For these accounts and some translated stories, see Yenna Wu, *The Chinese Virago: A Literary Theme* (Cambridge, MA: Council on East Asian Studies, Harvard University Press, 1995); Yenna Wu, *The Lioness Roars: Shrew Stories from Late Imperial China* (Ithaca, NY: East Asian Program, Cornell University, 1995); and Yenna Wu, "The Inversion of Marital Hierarchy: Shrewish Wives and Henpecked Husbands in

Seventeenth-Century Chinese Literature," *Harvard Journal of Asiatic Studies* 48, no. 2 (1988): 363–82.

12. Keith McMahon, *Polygamy and Sublime Passion: Sexuality in China on the Verge of Modernity* (Honolulu: University of Hawaii Press, 2009), 143–44.
13. Paul Ropp, "The Seeds of Change: Reflections on the Condition of Women in the Early and Mid Ch'ing," *Signs* 2, no. 1 (1976): 5–23, at 16–17.
14. Ruzhen Li and Tai-yi Lin, *Flowers in the Mirror* (Berkeley, CA: University of California Press, 1965), 173–75.
15. About missionaries' critique on concubinage in China, see Cheng Yu, *Qing zhi minguo xuqie xisu zhi bianqian* (Shanghai: Shanghai shiji chuban gufen youxian gongsi, 2006), 330–40.
16. Liang Qichao later took his wife's maid, Wang Guiquan, as his concubine. Although Wang eventually gave birth to six children for Liang, Liang always avoided mentioning the fact that Wang was his concubine. Even in his family letters to his children, he only referred to Wang as "Miss Wang" or "Aunt Wang." See Yu Hualin, *Nüxing de "chongshu": Minguo chengshi funü hunyin wenti yanjiu* (Beijing: Shangwu yinshuguan, 2009), 346–47. Also, after he had a concubine, even at the height of the Anti-Concubinage Movement in the 1920s, Liang seemed to avoid directly criticizing those who opposed abolishing concubinage. See Wang Zheng, "Wei xuqie wenti zhi Liang Rengong xiansheng," *Qinghua zhoukan* 24, no. 9 (1925): 9–12.
17. Yu, *Nüxing de "chongshu,"* 307.
18. Wong Shee Ping, *The Poison of Polygamy: A Social Novel*, trans. Ely Finch (Sydney: Sydney University Press, 2019), 27. In addition to concubinage, the novel also criticized many other aspects of traditional Chinese culture, such as footbinding, superstitions, and women's lack of education. Technically, the word polygyny (one man, many wives) is more accurate than polygamy (one individual, many spouses). In addition, both terms imply that multiple spouses are equal in status, which was not true with regard to the concubine's status in Chinese history.
19. Wong, *The Poison of Polygamy*, 27.
20. *Tung Wah Times*, December 24, 1904, supplement, quoted in Mei-fen Kuo and Michael Williams, "Why is Polygamy Poisonous? An Historical Context," in Wong, *The Poison of Polygamy*, 11–35, at 31, note 42.
21. Wong, *The Poison of Polygamy*, 80.
22. Jin Shiyin, "Ershi nian fuyun zhi yi da gongzuo – feiqie," *Funü gongming* 41 (1931): 6–14.
23. Yu, *Nüxing de "chongshu,"* 309–10.
24. Yu, *Nüxing de "chongshu,"* 314–15.
25. On the domestic labor of wife and concubines and the new hierarchy it produced among women, see Naifei Ding, "Wife-in-Monogamy and 'The Exaltation of Concubines,'" *Interventions* 9, no. 2 (2007): 219–37.
26. Guan Ruiwu, "Qie zhi yanjiu," *Shehui xue jie* 6 (June 1931): 87–121, at 92, 98.
27. Luo Dunwei, *Zhongguo zhi hunyin wenti* (Shanghai: Shanghai dadong shuju, 1931), 119.
28. Feng Mocun, "Cong shishi shang shuodao feiqie de biran xing," *Funü gongming* 2, no. 7 (June 1933): 37–41, at 38.
29. Yisheng, "Lun jinri quqie zhe zhi xinli ji suoyi jinzhi zhidao," *Funü zazhi* 5, no. 7 (July 1919): 6–8, at 8.

30. Zhao Zichen, "Qiebi zhidu de yinguo he chanchu de fangfa," *Jiefang yu gaizao* 1, no. 6 (November 15, 1919): 43–53, at 51.
31. Luo, *Zhongguo zhi hunyin wenti*, 120.
32. Lisa Tran, *Concubines in Court: Marriage and Monogamy in Twentieth-Century China* (Lanham, MD: Rowman & Littlefield, 2015).
33. Bernhardt, *Women and Property in China*, 178.
34. Tran, *Concubines in Court*, 73.
35. Lisa Tran, "Sex and Equality in Republican China: The Debate over the Adultery Law," *Modern China* 35, no. 2 (2009): 191–223.
36. Tran, "Sex and Equality in Republican China." For some estimates of the number of concubines in Republican China, see Cheng, *Qing zhi minguo xuqie xisu zhi bianqian*, 290–97. Considering that, socially, a concubine was still viewed as a minor wife in Republican China, in this book, I still mostly use the word "husband" to refer to the man to whom a concubine was "married." I will only use the word "master" when referring to the legal aspects of concubinage in Republican China.
37. Tran, *Concubines in Court*, 175–96.
38. For more on the complexity of concubinage's legal abolition, see Max W. L. Wong, *Chinese Marriage and Social Change: The Legal Abolition of Concubinage in Hong Kong* (Singapore: Springer, 2020).
39. Bernhardt, *Women and Property in China*; Margaret Kuo, *Intolerable Cruelty: Marriage, Law, and Society in Early Twentieth-Century China* (Lanham, MD: Rowman & Littlefield, 2012); and Tran, *Concubines in Court*.
40. Susan L. Glosser, *Chinese Visions of Family and State, 1915–1953* (Berkeley, CA: University of California Press, 2003); and Yu, *Nüxing de "chongshu."*
41. Cheng, *Qing zhi minguo xuqie*.
42. Susan Mann, *The Talented Women of the Zhang Family* (Berkeley, CA: University of California Press, 2007); Vincent Goossaert, "Irrepressible Female Piety: Late Imperial Bans on Women Visiting Temples," *Nan Nu* 10, no. 2 (2008): 212–41.
43. Catherine Vance Yeh, *Shanghai Love: Courtesans, Intellectuals, and Entertainment Culture, 1850–1910* (Seattle: University of Washington Press, 2006); and Mark Swislocki, *Culinary Nostalgia: Regional Food Culture and the Urban Experience in Shanghai* (Stanford, CA: Stanford University Press, 2013).
44. Andrew Field, "Selling Souls in Sin City: Shanghai Singing and Dancing Hostesses in Print, Film, and Politics, 1920–49," in *Cinema and Urban Culture in Shanghai, 1922–1943*, ed. Yingjin Zhang (Stanford, CA: Stanford University Press, 1999), 99–127, at 101.
45. Christian Henriot, "Chinese Courtesans in Late Qing and Early Republican Shanghai," *East Asian History*, no. 8 (December 1994): 33–52, at 41.
46. Elizabeth J. Remick, *Regulating Prostitution in China: Gender and Local Statebuilding, 1900–1937* (Stanford, CA: Stanford University Press, 2014).
47. Hershatter, "Modernizing Sex, Sexing Modernity."
48. Paul Bailey, "'Women Behaving Badly': Crime, Transgressive Behaviour and Gender in Early Twentieth Century China," *Nan Nü: Men, Women, and Gender in China* 8, no. 1 (2006): 156–97, at 194.

49. Zhang Yun, *Engendering the Woman Question: Men, Women, and Writing in China's Early Periodical Press* (Leiden: Brill, 2020), 166.
50. Shu Yang, *Untamed Shrews: Negotiating New Womanhood in Modern China* (Ithaca, NY: Cornell University Press, 2023), ch. 1.
51. Scholarships on different types of "new women," to name a few, are: Ye Weili, *Seeking Modernity in China's Name: Chinese Students in the United States, 1900–1927* (Stanford, CA: Stanford University Press, 2001); Paul Bailey, *Gender and Education in China: Gender Discourses and Women's Schooling in the Early Twentieth Century* (London: Routledge, 2007); Wang Zheng, *Women in the Chinese Enlightenment: Oral and Textual Histories* (Berkeley, CA: University of California Press, 1999); Lien Ling-ling, "Searching for the 'New Womanhood': Career Women in Shanghai, 1912–1945," PhD dissertation, University of California, Irvine, 2001; Louise Edwards, *Gender, Politics, and Democracy: Women's Suffrage in China* (Stanford, CA: Stanford University Press, 2008); Christina Gilmartin, *Engendering the Chinese Revolution: Radical Women, Communist Politics, and Mass Movements in the 1920s* (Berkeley, CA: University of California Press, 1995); Yan Haiping, *Chinese Women Writers and the Feminist Imagination, 1905–1948* (New York: Routledge, 2008); Ma Yuxin, *Women Journalists and Feminism in China, 1898–1937* (Amherst, NY: Cambria Press, 2010); and Hu Ying, *Tales of Translation: Composing the New Woman in China, 1899–1918* (Stanford, CA: Stanford University Press, 2000).
52. Xia Shi, *At Home in the World: Women and Charity in Late Qing and Early Republican China* (New York: Columbia University Press, 2018).
53. Liang Jinghe, "Lun wusi shiqi de 'nannü shejiao gongkai' sichao," *Shixue yuekan*, no. 1 (1998): 51–64.
54. Shao Ziling, "Lüelun xinwenhua yundong shiqi de nannü shejiao," *Harbin xueyuan xuebao* 26, no. 11 (November 2005): 105–09. About the importance of speechmaking in Republican China, see David Strand, "Citizens in the Audience and at the Podium," in *Changing Meanings of Citizenship in Modern China*, ed. Merle Goldman and Elizabeth J. Perry (Cambridge, MA: Harvard University Press, 2002), 44–70.
55. See, for example, Xiao Qing, "Changshi tanhua: oumei shejiao lijie," *Funü zazhi (Shanghai)* 7, no. 5 (1921): 83; Yü, "Oumei shejiao de changshi," *Guohuo yuekan (shanghai)*, no. 3 (1932): 29; Chen Suwen, "Xiaojie bidu de changshi keben: shejiao baojian," *Shishi xinbao wankan*, June 7, 1947; and Shao Ying, "Jiaojichang zhong de liyi yishu," *Funü zazhi* 13, no. 3 (1927): 8–10.
56. Various authors, "Shejiao teji," *Nüsheng* 3, no. 6 (1934): 11–23.
57. Qianjin, "Xiandai jiating bibei changshi: shejiao lijie xuzhi," *Jiating zhoukan* 138 (1937): 31–33.
58. Louise Edwards, "The Shanghai Modern Woman's American Dreams: Imagining America's Depravity to Produce China's 'Moderate Modernity,'" *Pacific Historical Review* 81, no. 4 (2012): 567–601.
59. Marie-Claire Bergère, *The Golden Age of the Chinese Bourgeoisie 1911–1937* (Cambridge: Cambridge University Press, 1989).
60. Ziling Shao, "Minguo nüzi shejiao shenghuo yu nüxing yishi yanjiu–yi dushi nüxing wei zhuti." MA thesis, Guangxi shifan daxue, 2006, 22.

61. Field, "Selling Souls in Sin City," 109.
62. Field, "Selling Souls in Sin City," 105–06.
63. Xiao Hongsong and Chen Nana, "Ershi shiji ersanshi niandai Beiping jiaojiwu de sanbo yu shehui fengshang shanbian," *Hebei daxue xuebao* 40, no.1 (2015): 96–102, at 99. Also see Shao, "Minguo nüzi shejiao shenghuo," 24.
64. Tang Xiaobing, "Xiangyata yu bailemen: Minguo Shanghai daxuesheng 'jinwu' shijian kaoshu," *Kaifang shidai*, May 10, 2007. Also see Field, "Selling Souls in Sin City," 106.
65. For example, see Ping, "Jiaojihua Tang Ying shang yinmu," *Qingchun dianying* 2, no. 5 (1935): 1; "Hu jiaoji hua Tang Ying fumei," *Funü yuebao* 1, no. 12 (1936): 14. On a study of newspaper reports on Tang Ying, see Li Meng, "Zhongwai jindai meiti dui 'jiaojihua' baodao de nüxing zhuyi yanjiu: yi Shenbao he Beihua jiebao dui Tang Ying de baodao weili," *Haiwai Yingyu*, no. 9 (April 2015): 158–66. As for reports on Lu Xiaoman, see, for example, Huang Meisheng, "Xu Zhimo furen Lu Xiaoman nüshi xinying," *Lianyi zhiyou*, no. 115 (1929).
66. One such prominent example is the character of Chen Bailu, created by Cao Yu (1910–1996) in his play *Sunrise* (*Richu*), written around 1936. A former student from an educated family in Tianjin, the beautiful and intelligent Chen became a *jiaoji hua* after her father's death and her family's subsequent fall into poverty. Surrounded and chased after by men of power and wealth, she lived a decadent life in a luxurious hotel. Later, when her sugar daddy, a banker over thirty years older than her, went bankrupt and stopped giving her economic support, she ran into debt, grew despondent, and eventually committed suicide at the age of twenty-three. For more analysis on Chen Bailu and the role of *jiaoji hua* in Chinese plays in the 1930s, see Wang Guimei, "Cong Chen Bailu dao Yin Xueyan: dui jiaojihua de butong shenmei shuxie," *Jingdian youyue*, no. 1 (2007): 23–28; and Xing Jie, "Dushi, xingbie, biaoyan: yi ershi shiji sanshi niandai zhongguo huaju zhong de jiaojihua wei kaocha duixiang," *Hangzhou shifan daxue xuebao*, no. 4 (July 2011): 83–88.
67. Laura Tyson Li, *Madame Chiang Kai-Shek: China's Eternal First Lady* (New York: Grove Press, 2007), 81.
68. Lin Zhaoqi, "Guo Songling yu tiaowu," *Shenbao*, May 18, 1927.
69. Lin, "Guo Songling yu tiaowu."
70. Shao, "Minguo nüzi shejiao shenghuo," 24–25.
71. Rachel Tamar Van, "The 'Woman Pigeon': Gendered Bonds and Barriers in the Anglo-American Commercial Community in Canton and Macao, 1800–1849," *Pacific Historical Review* 83, no. 4 (November 2014): 561–91.
72. John D. Wong, "Fidelity and Sacrifice: The Gender Discourse of Traders in Pre- and Post-Opium War Canton," *Frontiers of History in China* 14, no. 4 (2020): 473–507.
73. Van, "The 'Woman Pigeon,'" 591.
74. Elisabeth Croll, *Wise Daughters from Foreign Lands: European Women Writers in China* (London: Pandora, 1989), 110.
75. See, for example, "Jiaotongbu you kai tiaowuhui," *Shenbao*, February 16, 1914; and "Zhang Shizhang fufu juxing chawuhui," *Xinwen bao*, October 30, 1930.
76. See, for example, "Yu Fengzhi zhuban xiezhenhui," *Shenbao*, September 15, 1931; "Gu Weijun Furen xiaoying (tupian)," *Shenbao*, April 17, 1921; and "Gu furen kai tiaowu hui," *Dagong Bao* (Tianjin), February 8, 1927.

77. Glosser, *Chinese Visions of Family and State*, 73. Glosser's conclusion was mostly based on two surveys conducted by two Chinese sociologists in the 1920s. The respondents were mostly relatively affluent, well-educated male urbanites in the Jiangnan area between the ages of seventeen and twenty-eight, and more than half were unmarried. She thinks that although they were not a representative sample of China as a whole, they were "an accurate profile of those interested in family reform."
78. Daria Berg, "Cultural Discourse on Xue Susu: A Courtesan in Late Ming China," *International Journal of Asian Studies* 6, no. 2 (2009): 171–200, at 175. About the cult of *qing*, see, for example, Kang-i Sun Chang, *The Late-Ming Poet Ch'en Tzu-Lung: Crises of Love and Loyalism* (New Haven, CT: Yale University Press, 1991), 9–18; Dorothy Ko, *Teachers of the Inner Chambers: Women and Culture in Seventeenth-Century China* (Stanford, CA: Stanford University Press, 1995), 68–112; and Richard Wang, "The Cult of *Qing*: Romanticism in the Late Ming Period and in the Novel *Jiao hong ji*,'" *Ming Studies*, 1994, no. 1 (1994): 12–55.
79. Bossler, *Courtesans, Concubines, and the Cult of Female Fidelity*.
80. Molly Wood, "Diplomatic Wives: The Politics of Domesticity and the 'Social Game' in the US Foreign Service, 1905–1941," *Journal of Women's History* 17, no. 2 (2015): 142–65.
81. Xia Shi, "'Madame Wellington Koo': A Diplomatic Wife and a Peranakan Representing and Socializing for Republican China," *International Journal of Asian Studies* 21, no. 1 (January 2024): 109–27.
82. "E sheng nüjie xin choushi."
83. Cheng, *Qing zhi minguo xuqie*, 319.
84. Wang, "Ru furen de fannao," 7.
85. Cheng, *Qing zhi minguo xuqie*, 327. According to Matthew Sommer, in imperial China, the legal term *jian min* included a variety of hereditary laborers, such as slaves, serfs, bondservants, and *yue hu* (those who worked in "music households," including prostitutes and others involved in entertainment services). The defining factor in debased-status stigma was sexual immorality. The opposite of the debased category was *liang min* (free common people). The guiding principle for regulation of sexuality from the Tang dynasty (618–907) until the early Qing was status performance – the assumption that one must perform the role conferred by a particular legal status – rather than according to a single standard across classes. In 1723, the Yongzheng emperor "expunged the debased status of the key groups associated with prostitution." This, Sommer argues, in effect, "extended a commoner standard of morality and criminal liability to all" rather than brought assumed emancipation or liberation of the oppressed people. See Matthew Sommer, *Sex, Law, and Society in Late Imperial China* (Stanford, CA: Stanford University Press, 2002), 6, 211, 264–70.
86. Tani Barlow, *The Question of Women in Chinese Feminism* (Durham, NC: Duke University Press, 2004), 114.
87. Barlow, *The Question of Women in Chinese Feminism*, 126.
88. Bryna Goodman, "The Vocational Woman and the Elusiveness of 'Personhood' in Early Republican China," in *Gender in Motion: Divisions of Labor and Cultural Change*

in Late Imperial and Modern China, ed. Bryna Goodman and Wendy Larson (Lanham, MD: Rowman & Littlefield, 2005), 265–86.
89. Du Yaquan, "Lun xuqie," *Dongfang zazhi* 8, no. 4 (1911): 15–19, at 15.
90. Mei Lü, "Fei qie tan," *Rensheng zazhi*, no. 3 (1924): 13–16.
91. Qiu Ying, "Qie shi zunao renlei jinhua de zhangai wu," in *Fei qie hao*, ed. Zhu Caizhen (Hangzhou: Zhejiang shuju, 1922), 30.
92. Cheng, *Qing zhi minguo xuqie*, 327.
93. Cheng, *Qing zhi minguo xuqie*, 327–28.
94. Yi Wei, "Chao yitai zhidu," *Nüsheng* 1, no. 1 (1932): 4–5.
95. Cheng, *Qing zhi minguo xuqie*, 322–23.
96. The fifth concubine of "Warlord" Zhang Zuolin (1875–1928), Zhang Shouyi (1890–1966), is a good example. See Xia Shi, *At Home in the World*, 178–79.
97. Rubie S. Watson, "Wives, Concubines, and Maids, Servitude, and Kinship in the Hong Kong Region, 1900–1940," in *Marriage and Inequality in Chinese Society*, ed. Rubie Watson and Patricia Buckley Ebrey (Berkeley, CA: University of California Press, 1991), 231–255, at 247.
98. McMahon, *Polygamy and Sublime Passion*, 2.
99. Yu, *Nüxing de "chongshu,"* 353.
100. Zhu, *Fei qie hao*, 1–2. Translation (with slight modification) quoted from Bryna Goodman, "'A World of Concubines': Fissures in the Category of 'Woman' in Republican China," *Journal of Women's History* 32, no. 1 (2020): 85–110, at 86.
101. Sidney Gamble, *Peking: A Social Survey* (Beijing: George Doran Company, 1921), 259–60.
102. Yu, *Nüxing de "chongshu,"* 308.
103. Goodman, "A World of Concubines," 93.
104. Cheng, *Qing zhi minguo xuqie*, 349–50.
105. Harald Fuess, *Divorce in Japan: Family, Gender, and the State, 1600–2000* (Stanford, CA: Stanford University Press, 2004), 55–56.
106. Wang Chaoran, "Qie de wenti," *Funü zazhi* 4, no. 3 (1928): 24–25.
107. Qi, "Yitaitai Hu Shi," *Zhenglun xunkan* 1, no. 16 (1935): 3–4.
108. A good example is how various print media depicted "Warlord" Zhang Zongchang (1882–1932) as the epitome of an evil warlord with numerous concubines. For some of these depictions, see Wang, "Ru furen de fannao," 58–60.
109. About Gu Hongming, see Du Chunmei, *Gu Hongming's Eccentric Chinese Odyssey* (Philadelphia: University of Pennsylvania Press, 2019).
110. Wang, "Ru furen de fannao," 38.
111. Zhang Xicheng, "Feiqie lun de qianbo," *Chenbao liu zhounian zengkan*, no. 12 (1924): 59–64.
112. Zhang, "Feiqie lun de qianbo."
113. Chen Bainian, "Yifu duoqi de xin hufu," *Xiandai pinglun* 1, no. 14 (1925): 6–8, at 6. The term *Yifu duoqi* (one husband, multiple wives) is technically incorrect since the primary model in China only allowed for one wife for each man; the other women a man married were his concubines, who were strictly of lower status.

114. Jun Ping, "Xin xing daode yu yifu duoqi," *Funü zhoukan*," no. 26 (1925): 2–6, at 2; and Yanwu Xu, Huiying, and Changlin Jiang, "Du xin xing daode hao," *Funü zazhi* 11, no. 4 (1925): 632–40.
115. Zhang Xichen and Zhou Jianren, *Xin xing daode taolun ji* (Shanghai: Kaiming chubanshe, 1926).
116. Cai Zhen, "Bianjizhe de yusheng," in Zhu, *Fei qie hao*, 5–6.
117. Yu, *Nüxing de "chongshu,"* 336.
118. Cheng, *Qing zhi minguo xuqie*, 354.
119. Te-kong Tong and Li Tsung-jen, *The Memoirs of Li Tsung-jen* (Boulder, CO: Westview Press, 1979), 167, 620.
120. Leo Ou-fan Lee and Andrew J. Nathan, "The Beginnings of Mass Culture: Journalism and Fiction in the Late Ch'ing and Beyond," in *Popular Culture in Late Imperial China*, ed. Andrew J. Nathan, David Johnson, and Evelyn S. Rawski (Berkeley and Los Angeles, CA: University of California Press, 1985), 360–98, at 361.
121. Perry Link, *Mandarin Ducks and Butterfly: Popular Fiction in Early Twentieth-Century Chinese Cities* (Berkeley: University of California Press, 1981), 10.
122. Joan Judge, Barbara Mittler, and Michel Hockx, eds., *Women and the Periodical Press in China's Long Twentieth Century: A Space of Their Own?* (Cambridge: Cambridge University Press, 2018), "Introduction," 3.
123. Yun Zhang, *Engendering the Woman Question*.
124. The central issue of these debates was whether Jürgen Habermas's concept of the public sphere could be applied to China. For a summary of these debates, see Frederic Wakeman, "The Civil Society and Public Sphere Debate: Western Reflections on Chinese Political Culture," *Modern China* 19, no. 2 (1993): 108–38. Later, scholars also explored the multiplicity of "publics" in Republican China. See Eugenia Lean, *Public Passions: The Trial of Shi Jianqiao and the Rise of Popular Sympathy in Republican China* (Berkeley, CA: University of California Press, 2007) and Haiyan Lee, "All the Feelings that are Fit to Print: The Community of Sentiment and the Literary Public Sphere in China, 1900–1918," *Modern China* 27, no. 3 (July 2001): 291–327.
125. These scholars have concentrated their research on the gap between the Chinese rhetorical *nei/wai* (inner/out) dichotomy and actual practice in late imperial China. For example, see Ko, *Teachers of the Inner Chambers*, and Susan Mann, *Precious Records: Women in China's Long Eighteenth Century* (Stanford, CA: Stanford University Press, 1997).

CHAPTER 1: THE EMERGENCE OF THE SOCIAL WIFE IN LATE QING DIPLOMACY

1. Robert Bickers, ed., *Ritual and Diplomacy: The Macartney Mission to China 1792–1794: Papers Presented at the 1992 Conference of the British Association for Chinese Studies Marking the Bicentenary of the Macartney Mission to China* (London: Wellsweep Press, 1993); and James Hevia, *Cherishing Men from Afar: Qing Guest Ritual and the Macartney Embassy of 1793* (Durham, NC: Duke University Press, 2005).
2. George Macartney, *An Embassy to China: Being the Journal Kept by Lord Macartney during His Embassy to the Emperor Ch'ien-Lung, 1793–1794* (London: Longmans, 1963), 223.

3. Macartney, *An Embassy to China*, 223.
4. Beverly Bossler, "Shifting Identities: Courtesans and Literati in Song China," *Harvard Journal of Asiatic Studies* 62, no. 1 (June 2002): 5–37; and Harriet Zurndorfer, "Prostitutes and Courtesans in the Confucian Moral Universe of Late Ming China (1550–1644)," *International Review of Social History* 56, no. 19 (2011): 197–216.
5. About Zongli Yamen, see Jennifer Rudolph, *Negotiated Power in Late Imperial China: The Zongli Yamen and the Politics of Reform* (Ithaca, NY: East Asia Program, Cornell University, 2008).
6. You Shujun, *Binli dao libin: waishi jinjian yu wanqing shewai tizhi de bianhua* (Beijing: Shehui kexue wenxian chubanshe, 2013); He Xinhua, *Weiyi tianxia: Qingdai waijiao liyi jiqi biange* (Shanghai: Shanghai shehui kexueyuan chubanshe, 2011); Wang Kaixi, *Qingdai waijiao liyi de jiaoshe yu lunzheng* (Beijing: Renmin chubanshe, 2009); and Tseng-Tsai Wang, "The Audience Question: Foreign Representatives and the Emperor of China, 1858–1873," *The Historical Journal* 14, no. 3 (September 1971): 622.
7. On Cixi's gendered diplomacy, see Daniel Barish, *Learning to Rule: Court Education and the Remaking of the Qing State, 1861–1912* (New York: Columbia University Press, 2022), ch. 4.
8. Helen McCarthy and James Southern, "Women, Gender, and Diplomacy: A Historical Survey," in *Gender and Diplomacy*, ed. Jennifer Cassidy (London; New York: Routledge, 2017), 15–31, at 23.
9. Glenda Sluga, "Women, Diplomacy, and International Politics before and after the Congress of Vienna," in *Women, Diplomacy and International Politics since 1500*, ed. Glenda Sluga and Carolyn James (London; New York: Routledge), 2016, 120–36.
10. For an introduction of *chahui* (also called *chayan*) in the Tang and Song dynasties, see Chen Gangjun, "Songdai chayan shulun," *Nongye kaogu*, no. 5 (2016): 68–71.
11. Liu Xihong, *Yingyao siji* (Changsha: Yuelu shushe, 1986), 79.
12. Guo Songtao, *Lundun yu bali riji* (Changsha: Yuelu shushe, 1985), 563.
13. Zeng Jize, *Zeng Jize riji*, vol. 1 (Changsha: Yuelu shushe, 1998), 842.
14. For more about Cai Jun, see Zhang Xiaochuan, "Bingdang xuzhang shebian: Cai Jun yu wanqing difang duiwai jiaoshe," *Zhonghua wenshi luncong* 138, no. 2 (2020): 117–46.
15. For more on Cai Jun's publication of *Chu shi xu zhi*, see Quan Hexiu, "Wanqing zhongguo yu xibanya guanxi de yibu hanjian shiliao," *Shehui kexue yanjiu*, no. 3 (2012): 154–62.
16. Chen Siyi and Mu Yi, eds., *Cai Jun chuyang suoji* (Changsha: Yuelu shushe, 2016), 79.
17. Chen and Mu, eds., *Cai Jun chuyang suoji*, 80.
18. Chen and Mu, eds., *Cai Jun chuyang suoji*, 81.
19. Chen and Mu, eds., *Cai Jun chuyang suoji*, 83.
20. Chen and Mu, eds., *Cai Jun chuyang suoji*, 80; translation quoted from David Arkush and Leo Ou-fan Lee, *Land without Ghosts: Chinese Impressions of America from the Mid-Nineteenth Century to the Present* (Berkeley, CA: University of California Press, 1993), 56.
21. Ji Manhong and Lin Guangrong, "Guo Songtao yu 'furen waijiao,'" *Jiangxi shehui kexue*, no. 7 (2008): 123. On American diplomats' wives and their roles in the mid twentieth century, see Arlie Hochschild, "The Role of the Ambassador's Wife: An Exploratory Study," *Journal of Marriage and Family* 31, no. 1 (1969): 73–87.
22. Ji and Lin, "Guo Songtao yu 'furen waijiao.'"

23. Owen Hong-hin Wong, *A New Profile in Sino-Western Diplomacy: The First Chinese Minister to Great Britain* (Hong Kong: Chung Hwa Book, 1987), 134.
24. Jiang Ming, *Qiufeng baojian guchen lei: wan Qing de zhengju he renwu xubian* (Hong Kong: Xianggang zhonghe chuban gongsi, 2016), 215.
25. J. D. Frodsham, Sung-t'ao Kuo, Hsi-hung Liu, and Te-yi Chang, *The First Chinese Embassy to the West: The Journals of Kuo Sung-T'ao, Liu Hsi-Hung and Chang Te-Yi* (Oxford: Clarendon Press, 1974), xlviii.
26. Frodsham et al., *The First Chinese Embassy to the West*, xlviii.
27. Zhang Deyi, *Suishi ying'e ji* (Changsha: Yuelu shushe, 1985), 540.
28. Originally from the *Illustrated London News*, February 24, 1877, 171, quoted in Frodsham et al., *The First Chinese Embassy to the West*, xlviii.
29. "To the Tottering Lily," *Punch*, February 17, 1877, quoted in Frodsham et al., *The First Chinese Embassy to the West*, lxiv–lxv.
30. Originally from *The Special of the Standard* (quoted in the *London and China Express*, January 26, 1877), quoted in Wong, *A New Profile in Sino-Western Diplomacy*, 134.
31. Guo, *Lundun yu bali riji*, 810–11.
32. Qingsheng Tong, "Guo Songtao in London: An Unaccomplished Mission of Discovery," in *China Abroad: Travels, Subjects, Spaces*, ed. Elaine Yee Lin Ho and Julia Kuehn (Hong Kong: Hong Kong University Press, 2009), 45–62, at 53.
33. According to Guo's family members' recollection, in 1934 they celebrated concubine Liang's eightieth birthday. This means that she was about twenty-four years old in 1878. See Wang Huan and Zou Rui, "Guo Songtao houdai jiangsu jiazu wangshi," https://read01.com/zxeAEK.html#.Y5JXGC-B0UQ, accessed December 8, 2022.
34. Guo, *Lundun yu bali riji*, 100, 105, 135.
35. Frodsham et al., *The First Chinese Embassy to the West*, xlviii.
36. September 4, 1877, from Liu Xihong's journal, English translation quoted from Frodsham et al., *The First Chinese Embassy to the West*, 148–49.
37. Undated, from Zhang Deyi's journal, English translation quoted from Frodsham et al., *The First Chinese Embassy to the West*, 171–72.
38. Frodsham et al., *The First Chinese Embassy to the West*, 148–49.
39. Joan Perkin, *Women and Marriage in Nineteenth-Century England* (New York: Routledge, 2014).
40. Zhang, *Suishi ying'e ji*, 560.
41. For the details on how Guo Songtao and Liu Xihong's relationship quickly deteriorated, see Zhang Yuquan, "Wanqing waijiao shi shang de yidian yiwen: Lun Guo Songtao yu Liu Xihong de guanxi," *Shekewang*, November 2010, 5–10, at 9, www.sinoss.net/uploadfile/2010/1130/4913.pdf, accessed December 8, 2022.
42. Zhang, "Wanqing waijiao shi shang de yidian yiwen," 9.
43. Zhang, *Suishi ying'e ji*, 8.
44. "The Chinese Legation," *The Times (of London)*, June 20, 1878, 9; emphasis added.
45. "Qinshi yanke," *Shenbao*, August 6, 1878.
46. "Lun libie nannü," *Shenbao*, August 9, 1878.
47. "Nannü xiangjian lijie bian," *Shenbao*, November 15, 1878. For a discussion about the conflict between *Shenbao* and Guo Songtao, see Rudolf Wagner, "The *Shenbao* in

Crisis: The International Environment and the Conflict between Guo Songtao and the *Shenbao*," *Late Imperial China* 20, no. 1 (1999): 107–43.
48. Lily Xiao Hong Lee, Clara Lau, and A. D. Stefanowska, *Biographical Dictionary of Chinese Women: The Qing Period, 1644–1911* (New York, NY: Routledge, 2015), 182–84. On the construction of the images of Sai Jinhua, see Shengqing Wu, "Gendering the Nation: The Proliferation of Images of Zhen Fei (1876–1900) and Sai Jinhua (1872–1936) in Late Qing and Republican China," *Nan Nü* 11 (2009): 1–64.
49. Zhong Shuhe, "Sai Jinhua zai Bolin," *Luxun yanjiu yuekan*, no. 11 (2002): 76–77.
50. Ellen Widmer, "Gentility in Transition: Travels, Novels, and the New Guixiu," in *The Quest for Gentility in China: Negotiations beyond Gender and Class*, ed. Daria Berg and Chloë F. Starr (New York: Routledge, 2007), 21–44, at 24.
51. Hu Ying, "Re-configuring Nei/Wai: Writing the Woman Traveler in the Late Qing," *Late Imperial China* 18, no. 1 (1997): 77.
52. Quoted in Hu, "Re-configuring Nei/Wai," 78.
53. Quoted in Hu, "Re-configuring Nei/Wai," 78.
54. Guo, *Lundun yu bali riji*, 563, 565, 571.
55. Zeng, *Zeng Jize riji*, 841–42.
56. Zeng, *Zeng Jize riji*, 841–42.
57. Zeng, *Zeng Jize riji*, 984.
58. Lin Weihong, "Miandui xifang wenhua de zhongguo nüxing: cong Zeng Jize riji kan Zeng shi funü zai ouzhou," *Zhejiang xuekan*, no. 4 (2007): 213.
59. Zeng, *Zeng Jize riji*, 803–4.
60. Zeng, *Zeng Jize riji*, 812–13.
61. Zeng, *Zeng Jize riji*, 1319–20.
62. Zeng, *Zeng Jize riji*, 1086–298.
63. Zeng, *Zeng Jize riji*, 963.
64. Zeng, *Zeng Jize riji*, 993.
65. Zeng, *Zeng Jize riji*, 1258.
66. Lin, "Miandui xifang wenhua de zhongguo nüxing," 212. Lin Weihong suggests that the Zeng women's encounters with Western cultures and societies were not only frequent but also more comprehensive than we might expect. Lin points out that before he headed to Europe, Zeng tried to familiarize his family members with Western social etiquette and cultures with the help of the female family members of his Western friends to get them better prepared for the trip. As a very "family-oriented" man, Zeng, Lin shows, while in Europe, also liked to take his family out to visit parks, zoos, museums, circuses, beaches, and other public places for sightseeing when possible (he still tried to pick days when there were fewer people in these places). This is not to mention that the Zeng family members frequently needed the treatment of Western doctors, most of whom were men. On all of these occasions, they also learned more about common people's lives in the West.
67. Hu, "Re-configuring Nei/Wai," 90–91. About Shan's travel, also see Widmer, "Gentility in Transition"; and Hu Ying, "'Would That I Were Marco Polo': The Travel Writing of Shan Shili (1856–1943)," *Journeys: Special Issue on East Asian Travel Writing* 5, no. 1 (2004): 119–41.

68. Wang Kaixi, "Lüelun 'renchen wu waijiao' sixiang zai jindai zhongguo de lishi mingyun," *Beijing Shifan Daxue xuebao (shehui kexueban)* 215, no. 5 (2009): 62–70.
69. Wang, "Lüelun 'renchen wu waijiao' sixiang," 66; Wang, "The Audience Question."
70. Wang, "Lüelun 'renchen wu waijiao' sixiang," 67–68.
71. "The Taotai's Ball," *The North-China Herald and Supreme Court &Consular Gazette*, November 12, 1897, 871.
72. "The Taotai's Ball," 871.
73. "The Taotai's Ball," 871.
74. "Prince Henry of Prussia in Shanghai," *The North-China Herald*, April 25, 1898, 718.
75. "Ji Mei gongzi guanju shi," *Shenbao*, May 22, 1879.
76. Xiong Yuezhi, "Daike zhidao: cong waishi huodong kan Shanghai huajie yu zujie guanxi," *Xueshu yuekan*, no. 7 (2004): 54.
77. "Secretary Taft's Visit to Shanghai," *Journal of the American Association of China*, November 1907, 12.
78. "Step in Women's Emancipation," *New York Times*, October 9, 1907, 1.
79. Paul Bailey, *Gender and Education in China: Gender Discourses and Women's Schooling in the Early Twentieth Century* (New York: Routledge, 2007), 21.
80. A more recent exception is Jenny Huangfu Day's book, *Qing Travellers to the Far West: Diplomacy and the Information Order in Late Imperial China* (New York: Cambridge University Press, 2018). It examines how the process of Qing envoys establishing legations in the West created a new type of information order since these diplomats had to navigate through the conceptual and physical spaces of a geographical region that is unexplored in Chinese intellectual tradition. However, this book is not focused on diplomatic socialization, such as the importance of *chahui* and the role of the social wife.

CHAPTER 2: FROM COURTESAN TO SOCIAL WIFE

1. Patrick Fuliang Shan, "Unveiling China's Relinquished Marital Mode: A Study of Yuan Shikai's Polygamous Household," *Frontiers of History in China* 14, no. 2 (2019): 185–211.
2. Liu Yunxing, "Yuan Shikai de yiqi jiuqie," in *Xiangcheng wenshi ziliao*, vol. 8, ed. Cui Chenglie and Jiang Debian (Xiangcheng Xian: Zhongguo renmin zhengzhi xieshang huiyi Xiangcheng Xian weiyuanhui, 2000), 89–95, at 90. Also see Hou Yijie, *Yuan Shikai quanzhuan* (Beijing: Qunzhong chubanshe, 2013), 452.
3. Janey Sheau Yueh Chao and Kachuen Yuan Gee, "Early Life of Yuan Shikai and the Formation of Yuan Family," paper presented at the 5th International Conference of Institutes and Libraries for Chinese Overseas Studies, CUNY, New York, 2012, 21, https://academicworks.cuny.edu/cgi/viewcontent.cgi?article=1011&context=bb_pubs, accessed December 8, 2022.
4. Elisabeth Croll, *Wise Daughters from Foreign Lands: European Women Writers in China* (London: Pandora, 1989), 111.
5. Xia Shi, *At Home in the World: Women and Charity in Late Qing and Early Republican China* (New York: Columbia University Press, 2018), 80.

6. Wang Shaoxi, *Xiao qie shi* (Shanghai: Shanghai wenyi chubanshe, 1995), 144–45.
7. Madame Wellington Koo and Mary Van Rensselaer Thayer, *Hui-Lan Koo: An Autobiography* (New York: Dial Press, 1943), 182.
8. Grace Gallatin Seton, *Chinese Lanterns* (New York: Dodd, Mead, 1924), 118.
9. Seton, *Chinese Lanterns*, 129.
10. According to Li's eldest daughter, Benwei was purchased for 3,000 *yuan* by Li. See Li Shaofen, "Wo de fuqin Li Yuanhong," in *Minguo dazongtong Li Yuanhong*, ed. Quanguo zhengxie wenshi ziliao weiyuanhui (Beijing: Zhongguo wenshi chubanshe, 1991), 32–33.
11. Zhang Yaojie, *Hongfen minguo: Zhengxue liangjie de nüquan chuanqi* (Taibei: Xinrui wenchuang, 2013), 39–49.
12. Zhang, *Hongfen minguo*, 43.
13. About Xu Zonghan, see Li Yu-ning, "Hsu Tsung-Han: Tradition and Revolution," *Republican China* 10, no. 1 (November, 1984): 13–28.
14. Liu Chongxi, "Huainian zufumu Liu Gong Liu Yi," *Shijixing*, no. 8 (2011): 34–37; also see Zhang, *Hongfen minguo*, 43–44.
15. Zhang, *Hongfen minguo*, 44–45.
16. "Li fu zongtong juanshu ji shuguan beishangji," *Shenbao*, December 17, 1913.
17. Zhang, *Hongfen minguo*, 45.
18. Zhang, *Hongfen minguo*, 46.
19. Cheng Yu, *Qing zhi minguo xuqie xisu zhi bianqian* (Shanghai: Shanghai shiji chuban gufen youxian gongsi, 2006), 325.
20. Wanshi, "Beijing teyue tongxin," *Shenbao*, June 17, 1923.
21. "Li Huangpo zuori fangyang dongdu," *Shenbao*, November 9, 1923.
22. Li, "Wo de fuqin," 33.
23. Su Quanyou and Wang Shichao, "Xin shiliao de faxian yu Zhou Ziqi yanjiu de shenhua," *Nanyang ligong xueyuan xuebao* 8, no. 1 (January 2016): 89–94.
24. Zhou Shunqin was the name that Zhou Ziqi gave her after she became his concubine, adopting his surname. It is unclear what her previous name was.
25. Cheng, *Qing zhi minguo*, 325–26.
26. Cheng, *Qing zhi minguo*, 325–26.
27. "Zhou Ziqi zhi qie," *Shibao tuhua zhoukan*, no. 92, 1922.
28. Koo and Thayer, *Hui-Lan Koo*, 146.
29. Madame Wellington Koo and Isabella Taves, *No Feasts Last Forever* (New York: Quadrangle, 1975), 217.
30. Koo and Thayer, *Hui-Lan Koo* and Koo and Taves, *No Feasts Last Forever*.
31. For more on Madame Koo's role as a diplomatic wife, see Xia Shi, "'Madame Wellington Koo': A 'Diplomatic Wife' and a Peranakan Representing and Socializing for Republican China," *International Journal of Asian Studies* 21, no. 1 (January 2024): 109–27.
32. Seton, *Chinese Lanterns*, 221.
33. Seton, *Chinese Lanterns*, 202–03.
34. Zhou Zheng, "Zhou Ziqi aiqi," http://blog.sina.com.cn/s/blog_ec5d43bc0102vmwt.html, accessed February 1, 2022.

35. Seton, *Chinese Lanterns*, 203.
36. "Chinese Lanterns: Minguo nüxing renwu zaji," https://kknews.cc/history/5la58jk.html, accessed December 10, 2022. About Lun Qianru, also see "Lun Qianru baoshihou, yangbing faguo yiyuan," *Yishibao* (Tianjin ban), September 30, 1948.
37. Croll, *Wise Daughters from Foreign Lands*, 10.
38. Croll, *Wise Daughters from Foreign Lands*, 10.
39. Seton, *Chinese Lanterns*, 192.
40. Seton, *Chinese Lanterns*, 193.
41. Seton, *Chinese Lanterns*, 193.
42. For more about Sai Jinhua, see Paola Zamperini, "But I Never Learned to Waltz: The 'Real' and Imagined Education of a Courtesan in the Late Qing," *Nan Nü* 1, no. 1 (1999): 107–44, at 125.
43. Lisa Tran, *Concubines in Court: Marriage and Monogamy in Twentieth-Century China* (Lanham, MD: Rowman & Littlefield, 2015), 68–75; Kathryn Bernhardt, *Women and Property in China, 960–1949* (Stanford, CA: Stanford University Press, 1999), 188–95.
44. Tran, *Concubines in Court*, 35–41.
45. "Li Yuanhong zhi yichan jiufen," *Shenbao*, July 10, 1932; and "Li Yuanhong qie Wei Wenxiu tuoli jiating," *Shenbao*, September 2, 1934.
46. "Li Yuanhong zhi yichan jiufen." This article also included the other side of the story: Li's eldest son, Li Shaoji, explained that this was because Li Yuanhong had debts when he was alive. After his death, the Li family had no cash, just properties and some stocks that could not be converted to money.
47. "Li Yuanhong qie Wei Wenxiu tuoli jiating."
48. "Aishu zaijia kuzhong," *Shenbao*, January 17, 1935.
49. "Lu Diping zuochen shishi," *Shenbao*, February 1, 1935.
50. "Lu Diping zuo dalian," *Shenbao*, February 2, 1935.
51. See Sanmu, "Yiwei guomindang shengzhuxi de yiwai cusi," *Jiancha fengyun*, no. 4 (2007): 66–68; and Gao Feng, "Ansha Lu Diping de xiongshou shishui," *Wenshi chunqiu*, no. 1 (2008): 12–15.
52. "Lu Diping zhi ru furen shashi zisha," *Funü gongming yuekan* 4, no. 2 (1935): 58.
53. Wufa, "Wei Wenxiu zajia Wang Kuixuan," *Shenbao*, January 21, 1935.
54. "Lingjiu you jin di han," *Shenbao*, April 13, 1933.
55. For example, see "Li gu zongtong lingjiu dihan," *Tuhua Zhonghua zazhi* (Shanghai), no. 18 (1933): 5; and "Qian gu zongtong Li Yuanhong shi jiqi furen zhi lingjiu benyue yunjin anzang," *Liangyou* 76 (1933): 12.
56. Zhang Rongsheng, "Xianwei renzhi de Li Yuanhong zangli," *Wenshi chunqiu*, no. 3 (1999): 79.
57. Ming, "Qingdao shi quzhu Li Benwei," *Zhengzhi pinglun*, no. 140 (1935): 325.
58. Wang Chengbin et al., eds., *Minguo gaoji jiangling liezhuan*, vol. 5 (Beijing: Jiefang jun chubanshe, 1996), 322.
59. Wang et al., *Minguo gaoji jiangling liezhuan*, 322.
60. "Qing dangju xianling chujing," *Shenbao*, January 30, 1935.
61. "Zai qu yu gaijia," *Shenbao*, February 22, 1935.

62. Zhang, *Hongfen minguo*, 34.
63. Yi, "Sanlao xinhun," *Shenbao*, March 2, 1935.
64. "Funü tuanti zuo kaihui-yuanzhu Wei Wenxiu zaijiao an," *Shenbao*, February 18, 1935.
65. "Nanjingshi funü wenhua cujinhui dianwei Wei Wenxiu," *Funü gongming* 4, no. 2 (February 1935): 57.
66. It seems that Wei lived at least until the early Communist period, for records suggest that she was once interviewed by someone from the Chinese People's Political Consultative Conference and recounted her recollection of the story of Cao Kun intercepting the train for the presidential seals and her own involvement in this. See Li Benwei, "Cao Kun lanche jieyin chouju," in *Minguo dazongtong Li Yuanhong*, ed. Quanguo zhengxie wenshi ziliao weiyuanhui, 281–84.

CHAPTER 3: FROM "FEMALE STUDENT" TO CONCUBINE

1. Paul Bailey, *Gender and Education in China: Gender Discourses and Women's Schooling in the Early Twentieth Century* (New York: Routledge, 2007). Fabio Lanza has also pointed out that the political category of "student" was produced through the May Fourth Movement in 1919. Fabio Lanza, *Behind the Gate: Inventing Students in Beijing* (New York: Columbia University Press, 2010).
2. Ping-chen Hsiung, *A Tender Voyage: Children and Childhood in Late Imperial China* (Stanford, CA: Stanford University Press, 2005), 186–93, 205–17. As Hsiung has noted, in addition to womanly skills, girls were expected to learn texts exclusively written for women, such as Ban Zhao's *Nüjie* (*Admonitions to Women*) and Liu Xiang's *Lie nüzhuan* (*Biographies of Exemplary Women*). On female education in traditional China, also see John Cleverley, *The Schooling of China: Tradition and Modernity in Chinese Education* (Sydney: Allen & Unwin, 1985), 26–28, 39–40, 47. On talented elite women during the Qing dynasty, see Susan Mann, *The Talented Women of the Zhang Family* (Berkeley, CA: University of California Press, 2007).
3. Bailey, *Gender and Education in China*, 6.
4. Bailey, *Gender and Education in China*, 21.
5. Bailey, *Gender and Education in China*, 6.
6. Bailey, *Gender and Education in China*, 2.
7. Paul Bailey, *Women and Gender in Twentieth-Century China* (London: Palgrave Macmillan, 2012), 56.
8. Bailey, *Women and Gender in Twentieth-Century China*, 56.
9. Xiaoping Cong, *Teachers' Schools and the Making of the Modern Chinese Nation-State 1897–1937* (Vancouver: University of British Columbia Press, 2007), 17.
10. Bailey, *Gender and Education in China*, 122; Qin Fang, *"Nüjie" zhi xingqi: wan Qing Tianjin nüzi jiaoyu yu nüxing xingxiang jiangou* (Beijing: Zhonghua shuju, 2009), and Yun Zhang, *Engendering the Woman Question: Men, Women, and Writing in China's Early Periodical Press* (Leiden: Brill, 2020), 150.
11. Bailey, *Gender and Education in China*, 122.
12. Joan Judge, *The Precious Raft of History: The Past, the West, and the Woman Question in China* (Stanford, CA: Stanford University Press, 2008), 4.

13. Bailey, *Gender and Education in China*, 57–58.
14. For more on policing Chinese female students through discursive regulation, see Zhang, *Engendering the Woman Question*, ch. 5.
15. On the Modern Girl, see Madeleine Yue Dong, "Who Is Afraid of the Chinese Modern Girl?" in *The Modern Girl around the World: Consumption Modernity and Globalization*, ed. Weinbaum Alys Eve and Modern Girl Around the World Research Group (Durham, NC: Duke University Press, 2008), 194–219. On the Modern Woman, see Louise Edwards, "Policing the Modern Woman in Republican China," *Modern China* 26, no. 2 (2000): 115–47.
16. Zeng Yue, "Minguo shiqi nüxuesheng de xingxiang kunjing," *Shehui kexuejia*, no. 5 (2014): 144–47.
17. Lin Meijing, "Yeqie zhilu," in *Fei qie hao*, ed. Zhu Caizhen (Hangzhou: Zhejiang shuju, 1922), 33–34.
18. "Lian jian zuo xiaoxing: nü xuesheng zigan xiajian," *Xiaoduo* 130, June 8, 1917.
19. Zhang Genghua, *Renlei de xiangrui: Lü Simian zhuan* (Shanghai: Huadong shifan daxue chubanshe, 1998), 81.
20. Zhang, *Renlei de xiangrui*.
21. Zhu, *Fei qie hao*, 1.
22. Xuedu, "Pian nüxuesheng zuoqie," *Shijie chenbao*, December 18, 1931. For more examples, see "Jian xiani, nü xuesheng shizhi qieteng," *Xinwen bao*, December 6, 1931; "Nü xuesheng beiyou weiqie," *Beijing qianshuo huabao*, no. 890 (1911): 4. For more, see Yu Hualin, *Nüxing de "chongsu": Minguo chengshi funü hunyin wenti yanjiu* (Beijing: Shangwu yinshuguan, 2009), 358–59.
23. "Xinniang jiao songshi shangmen, nü xuesheng buyuan zuoqie zisha," *Dagong bao* (Tianjin), December 9, 1923.
24. "Nü xuesheng buyuan weiqie," *Shibao*, March 1, 1926.
25. "Nü xuesheng tancai shishen," *Minguo ribao*, February 29, 1924.
26. Guo Youqi, "Shehui wenti yu jiaoyu zhuanxing: shi lun minguo shiqi de xuesheng jiuye kunnan (1912–1937)," *Jiaoyu Lilun Yanjiu*, no. 4 (2011): 271–310. Also see Chen Jiaohua, "Minguo nüsheng de zhiye chulu tansuo: jiyu Mengke and Diyi luxiang de yanjiu," *Zhonghua nüzi xueyuan xuebao*, no. 4 (2018): 68–75.
27. Relu, "Ziyuan zuoqie zhi nü xuesheng," *Xinwen bao*, March 14, 1924.
28. Haiyan Lee, *Revolution of the Heart: A Genealogy of Love in China, 1900–1950* (Stanford, CA: Stanford University Press, 2010), 5.
29. To name a few, see "Zhouzhuang shisheng lian'an an, juanhao nü xuesheng Tao Suzhen ganzuo tengqie," *Tiebao*, October 11, 1935; "Nü xuesheng jieshi junguan quju tengqie diwei," *Shibao*, July 18, 1933; Tianzhu, "Nü xuesheng ganzuo xiaoxing, san yitaitai zisha," *Guanghua ribao*, April 24, 1945; and "Nü xuesheng ganzuo xiaoxing," *Shibao*, October 14, 1930.
30. Zhu, *Fei qie hao*, preface, 3; translation cited from Bryna Goodman, "'A World of Concubines': Fissures in the Category of 'Woman' in Republican China," *Journal of Women's History* 32, no. 1 (2020): 85–110, at 101.
31. Xu Helin, "Hanghu suxining de funü," *Funü zazhi* (Shanghai) 13, no. 5 (1927): 5–11, at 6.

32. Mei Lü, "Fei qie tan," *Rensheng zazhi*, no. 3 (1924): 13–16, at 14, translation cited from Goodman, "'A World of Concubines,'" 97.
33. Goodman, "'A World of Concubines,'" 97.
34. This is according to a keyword search in the database of Quanguo baokan suoyin (National Index to Chinese Newspapers and Periodicals), which provides access to over 50,000 types of newspapers and periodicals, with more than 50 million entries published from 1833 to 1992. I have only found one article that called her "*ru furen*" rather than *furen* to indicate her concubine status. But the point of the article is it was a miracle in modern Chinese history that a poor girl originally from the countryside, after almost thirty years' experience, eventually became the second lady of China and a news figure. There seemed to be no public reactions in the press to her concubine status after this article mentioned it. See Miershi, "Guo Dejie hexing you jinri," *Zhongguo renwu*, no. 12 (1949): 6.
35. Li Xiuwen and Tan Ming, *Wo yu Li Zongren* (Guilin: Lijiang chubanshe, 2018), 117.
36. "Renwu: Fu zongtong furen Guo Dejie sumiao," *Dagang zhoukan* 2, no. 20 (1948): 6.
37. About civilized weddings' popularity among female students, see Bailey, *Gender and Education in China*, 74.
38. Lisa Tran, "Ceremony and the Definition of Marriage under Republican Law," in *Research from Archival Case Records: Law, Society, and Culture in China*, ed. Philip Huang and Kathryn Bernhardt (Leiden: Brill, 2014): 348–53.
39. Li and Tan, *Wo yu Li Zongren*, 33.
40. He Wangfang, "Li Zongren yu Guo Dejie," *Shilin manbu*, no. 1 (2004): 40–41; also see Su Lili, "Li Zongren rongru yugong de qizi Guo Dejie," in *Guilin wenshi ziliao*, vol. 24: *Li Zongren jiashi*, ed. Wei Hualing (Guilin: Lijiang chubanshe, 1993), 89–91. On how Li and Guo met, Li's own memoir briefly records the following: "Kuo Te-chieh [Guo Dejie], a student in the local public school. We were introduced by a mutual friend and married in the winter of 1923. The simple wedding was the beginning of a long and happy family life. I was then thirty-two and she sixteen." However, this does not clarify whether, when Li met Guo, Guo was attending college or not, since "local public school" was a broad category. See Te-kong Tong and Li Tsung-jen, *The Memoirs of Li Tsung-jen* (Boulder, CO: Westview Press, 1979), 104.
41. "Song Meiling nüshi di'er: Li furen Guo Dejie nüshi yinxiang ji," *Dadi tuwen xunkan* 1, no. 10 (1938): 182–83; and "Renwu: Fu zongtong furen Guo Dejie sumiao," 6.
42. Su, "Li Zongren rongru yugong de qizi Guo Dejie," 91.
43. Li and Tan, *Wo yu Li Zongren*, 42.
44. Li and Tan, *Wo yu Li Zongren*, 56.
45. Li and Tan, *Wo yu Li Zongren*, 142. Li Zhisheng, born in 1937, was their adopted son.
46. Li and Tan, *Wo yu Li Zongren*, 39.
47. Li and Tan, *Wo yu Li Zongren*, 43.
48. Li and Tan, *Wo yu Li Zongren*, 44.
49. Li and Tan, *Wo yu Li Zongren*, 43.
50. Li and Tan, *Wo yu Li Zongren*, 43.
51. Li and Tan, *Wo yu Li Zongren*, 42.
52. Li and Tan, *Wo yu Li Zongren*, 99.

53. Li and Tan, *Wo yu Li Zongren*, 224–26.
54. This conclusion is derived from a keyword search in the database Quanguo baokan suoyin.
55. "Zhuima zhongshang shishi," *Shenbao*, July 10, 1935.
56. Yao Ming, "Guo Dejie secai xianming," *Xinwen tiandi*, no. 64 (1949): 19; and "Li Zongren dangxuan fu zongtong, Guo Dejie gonglao bushao," *Zhujiang bao*, no. 52 (1949): 4.
57. Tong and Li, *The Memoirs of Li Tsung-jen*, 167. Consisting of over 100 female students, under the leadership of Guo Dejie, this corps worked on the front lines during the Northern Expedition. Thus, Li Zongren boasted that his army included the largest contingent of women, whereas other armies tended to avoid putting their female personnel on the front lines. See Christina Kelley Gilmartin, *Engendering the Chinese Revolution: Radical Women, Communist Politics, and Mass Movements in the 1920s* (Berkeley, CA: University of California Press, 1995), 176.
58. On women's wartime mobilization and networking power as part of the New Life Movement, see Federica Ferlanti, "Women's Activism and Mobilization in Wartime China: Cadre Training, National Economic Production, and Workers' Literacy (1937–1945)," *Journal of Chinese History* 9, no. 1 (2023): 1–22; Vivienne Xiangwei Guo, "Forging a Women's United Front: Chinese Elite Women's Networks for National Salvation and Resistance, 1932–1938," *Modern Asian Studies* 53, no. 2 (2019): 483–511; Harriet T. Zundorfer, "Wartime Refugee Relief in Chinese Cities and Women's Political Activism, 1937–1940," in *New Narratives of Urban Space in Republican Chinese Cities*, ed. Billy K. L. So and Madeleine Zelin (Leiden: Brill, 2013), 65–94; and Helen M. Schneider, "Mobilising Women: The Women's Advisory Council, Resistance and Reconstruction during China's War with Japan," *European Journal of East Asian Studies* 11, no. 2 (2012): 213–36.
59. "Li Zongren furen juanxian jinshi," *Shenbao*, October 4, 1937.
60. "Renwu: Fu zongtong furen Guo Dejie sumiao," 6.
61. Kate Merkel-Hess, *Women and Their Warlords: Domesticating Militarism in Modern China* (Chicago, IL: University of Chicago Press, 2024), ch. 2.
62. Merkel-Hess, *Women and Their Warlords*, 69.
63. "Renwu: Fu zongtong furen Guo Dejie sumiao," 6; Ouyang Sujuan, "Fu zongtong furen Guo Dejie," *Zhujiang bao*, no. 165 (1949): 1–2.
64. As the only son of Sun Yat-sen, the renowned revolutionary and father of the nation, Sun Ke, a top Nationalist official himself, dared not to take any concubines, fearing tarnishing the reputations of both his late father and himself. So his mistress, Lan Ni (1912–1996), was never given any official status, despite the fact that she gave birth to his daughter. For details on Lan Ni's relationship with Sun Ke, see Tang Naikang, "Wo suo zhidao de Lan Ni hunlian ji jiating (shang)," *Shiji*, no. 5 (2018): 66–69 and Tang Naikang, "Wo suo zhidao de Lan Ni hunlian ji jiating (xia)," *Shiji*, no. 6 (2018): 62–65.
65. "Fu zongtong jingxuan de qundaifeng: chuxian zai shoudu de funüjie de huixing Li Guo Dejie," *Xinwen zazhi*, no. 2 (1948): 5–6.
66. Shangguan Liangxiang, "Li Zongren Guo Dejie lian'ai shi," *Neimu xinwen*, no. 4 (1948): 16.

67. Li and Tan, *Wo yu Li Zongren.*
68. See, for example, Minzi, "Nü xuesheng yu rufuren," *Renmin zhoubao* 80, no. 2 (1933): 12–13, and Nutao, "Duanping: Tichang guohuo qi zhong de zhang'aiwu: Yitaitai, xiaojie, nü xuesheng," *Shengsheng* 3, no. 6 (1935): 2.

CHAPTER 4: EXCLUDING CONCUBINES

1. Zhang Genghua, *Renlei de xiangrui: Lü Simian zhuan* (Shanghai: Huadong shifan daxue chubanshe, 1998), 81.
2. Grace Thompson Seton, *Chinese Lanterns* (New York: Dodd, Mead and Company, 1924), 193.
3. Bryna Goodman, "'A World of Concubines': Fissures in the Category of 'Woman' in Republican China," *Journal of Women's History* 32, no. 1 (2020): 85–110, at 93.
4. See, for example, "Nü jiaoyuan ganxin zuoqie, lü shi de shi fengliu," *Daobao* (Shanghai), August 24, 1938.
5. "Nüzi shifan xuexiao yi you xuechao fasheng," *Dagong bao,* January 12, 1920.
6. "Guangzhou sanxiao fengchao zhi yubo," *Minguo ribao,* March 10, 1920.
7. Bryna Goodman, "The Vocational Woman and the Elusiveness of 'Personhood' in Early Republican China," in *Gender in Motion: Divisions of Labor and Cultural Change in Late Imperial and Modern China,* ed. Bryna Goodman and Wendy Larson (Lanham, MD: Rowman & Littlefield, 2005), 265–86.
8. Goodman, "The Vocational Woman and the Elusiveness of 'Personhood.'"
9. "Nü xuesheng burong zuoqie," *Shibao,* June 19, 1913.
10. Lü Yi, "Shanxi nüshi zhi ren'ge ziwei," *Minguo ribao,* November 17, 1923.
11. Ni Haoran, "Xiaoyuan lian yu jiemei Qing: richang shenghuo shijiao xia de minguo nü xuesheng," in *Funü yu xingbie shi yanjiu,* vol. 5, ed. Yin Yaping and Yi Zhaoyin (Shanghai: Shanghai sanlian shudian, 2021), 103–16, at 116.
12. Bonnie S. McDougall, *Love-Letters and Privacy in Modern China: The Intimate Lives of Lu Xun and Xu Guangping* (Oxford: Oxford University Press, 2002).
13. Selena Orly and Louise Edwards, "Chastity, Foreign Theories, and National Heritage Reorganization: Hu Shi (1892–1962) Addresses 'The Woman Problem,'" *Nan Nü* 23, no. 2 (2021): 272–300.
14. Zhang Yunhe, *Qu zhong ren busan: Zhang Yunhe zi shu wenlu* (Wuhan: Hubei renmin chubanshe, 2009).
15. Denise Gimpel, *Chen Hengzhe: A Life between Orthodoxies* (Lanham, MD: Lexington Books, 2015), 23.
16. Wang Dongjie, "Difang guannian he guojia guannian de chongtu yu huzhu: 1936 nian chuanxing suoji fengbo," *Sichuan daxue xuebao (Zhesheban),* no. 1 (2004): 76–86.
17. Xiangbeilao, "Zai changchang Chen Hengzhe nüshi de yaowei," *Xinxin xinwen,* July 6, 1936, cited in Zhang Jing, "Chen Hengzhe zhi sanjin sichuan: jianlun 'Chuanxing suoji shijian,'" in *Zhongguo shehui kexueyuan jindaishi yanjiusuo qingnian xueshu luntan wenji* (Beijing: Shehui kexue wenxian chubanshe, 2007), 515–36, at 534.
18. Hu Jishan, "Jingzhi Chen Hengzhe nüshi," *Xinxin xinwen,* July 2, 1936, cited in Zhang, "Chen Hengzhe zhi sanjin Sichuan," 534.

19. Wang, "Difang guannian," 77.
20. Chen Hengzhe, "Chuanxing suoji: yifeng gei pengyoumen de gongxin," *Duli pinglun* 195 (April 5, 1936): 14–20, at 17.
21. Shuyong, "Guanyu 'Chuanxing suoji' de jijuhua," *Duli pinglun* 215 (August 16, 1936): 10–12, at 12.
22. Three of the newspapers that circulated and discussed Chen's comments were *Fuxing ribao*, *Xin Wanbao*, and *Xin Minbao*. For more details on the newspaper reports, see Wang, "Difang guannian."
23. Zhang, "Chen Hengzhe zhi sanjin Sichuan," 535–36.
24. Zhu Caizhen, *Fei qie hao* (Hangzhou: Zhejiang shuju, 1922), preface, 4.
25. Xia Shi, *At Home in the World: Women and Charity in Late Qing and Early Republican China* (New York: Columbia University Press, 2018), 11, 121–22.
26. Louise Edwards, *Gender, Politics, and Democracy: Women's Suffrage in China* (Stanford, CA: Stanford University Press, 2008), 99.
27. Tsai Kuei and Lily K. Haass, "A Study of the YWCA of China, 1890–1930," 14, Box 325, The YWCA of the USA Records, Sophia Smith Collection, Smith College, 17.
28. Young Women's Christian Association of China, First National Convention, October 19–25, 1923, 30–31, The YWCA of the USA Records.
29. Nancy Boyd, *Emissaries, the Overseas Work of the American YWCA 1895–1970* (New York: Woman's Press, 1986), 250.
30. Seton, *Chinese Lanterns*, 225.
31. "Tianjin nüjie aiguo tongzhi hui jujue rufuren ruhui zhi liyoushu," *Chenbao*, August 15, 1919.
32. "Tianjin nüjie aiguo tongzhi hui," translation quoted from Tyau Min-ch'ien, *China Awakened* (New York: Macmillan, 1922), 61–62.
33. Edwards, *Gender, Politics, and Democracy*, 114.
34. "Yue nüjie zhi paiqie huiyi," *Minguo ribao*, January 31, 1920; also see "Nüjie lianhehui zhi paiqie sheng," *Shishi xinbao*, February 2, 1920.
35. "Nüjie duiyu qie zhi wenti zhi zhengyi," *Dahan gongbao*, March 19, 1920.
36. Wo Sheng, "Jinshi piping: paiqie," *Beijing daxue xuesheng zhoukan*, no. 7 (1920): 14.
37. Kejiu, "Sui ganlu: Wo zhen ti zhexie zi kexi," *Minguo ribao*, June 13, 1921, 4.
38. Song, "Beijing nüjie paiqie zhi huiyi," *Shibao*, March 14, 1921, 11.
39. Madeleine Yue Dong, "Who Is Afraid of the Chinese Modern Girl?" in *The Modern Girl Around the World: Consumption Modernity and Globalization*, ed. Weinbaum Alys Eve and Modern Girl Around the World Research Group (Durham, NC: Duke University Press, 2008), 194–219, at 214.
40. Shi, *At Home in the World*, Part III.
41. For an example of how the *Yishi Bao* (*Social Welfare*), a major newspaper in Tianjin, covered the incidents caused by wife and concubine jealousy, see Zhao Xiuli, *Tiaoshi yu Yingdui: Tianzhu jiao hunyin jiating lunli zaihua chujing yanjiu: yi Tianjin "Yishi Bao" wei zhongxin de kaocha (1915–1937)* (Beijing: Zongjiao wenhua chubanshe, 2017), 93–98.
42. About imperial concubines, see Keith McMahon, *Women Shall Not Rule: Imperial Wives and Concubines in China from Han to Liao* (Lanham, MD: Rowman & Littlefield, 2013),

and Keith McMahon, *Celestial Women: Imperial Wives and Concubines in China from Song to Qing* (Lanham, MD: Rowman & Littlefield, 2016).

43. For an excellent study of the history of gender politics and the impact of feminist ideals on the Chinese Community Party during its formative years in the 1920s, see Christina Gilmartin, *Engendering the Chinese Revolution: Radical Women, Communist Politics, and Mass Movements in the 1920s* (Berkeley, CA: University of California Press, 1995).

44. During the Cultural Revolution (1966–1976), according to Emily Honig, it was the girls at girls' schools, rather than girls in coed schools, who tended to be the most radical Red Guards who committed violence toward their teachers and the principals. Some Chinese who had first-hand experience on this further observed that "once students from all-girl schools joined coed Red Guard units, they suddenly – almost automatically – assumed roles subservient to the male leaders." See Emily Honig, "Maoist Mappings of Gender: Reassessing the Red Guards," in *Chinese Femininities, Chinese Masculinities: A Reader*, ed. Susan Brownell and Jeffrey Wasserstrom (Berkeley, CA: University of California Press, 2002), 258–62, 265.

EPILOGUE

1. Kate Merkel-Hess, "A New Woman and Her Warlord: Li Dequan, Feng Yuxiang, and the Politics of Intimacy in Twentieth-Century China," *Frontiers of History in China* 11, no. 3 (2016): 431–57; and Kate Merkel-Hess, *Women and Their Warlords: Domesticating Militarism in Modern China* (Chicago: University of Chicago Press, 2024).
2. Laura Tyson Li, *Madame Chiang Kai-Shek: China's Eternal First Lady* (New York: Grove Press, 2007), 243.
3. For example, see Wang Falong, "Guoji zhengzhi wutaishang 'furen waijiao' de zhongguo shijiao," *Zhonggong Jinan shiwei dangxiao xuebao*, no. 5 (2013): 71–74; Zheng Leqiang, "Xin zhongguo diyi furen waijiao zhineng tanxi," *Caijing zhengfa zixun*, no. 6 (2015): 40–45; and Jiang Huajie, "Geming waijiao de zhangli: guanyu xin zhongguo furen waijiao de lishi kaocha (1950–1965)," *Zhonggong dangshi yanjiu*, no. 5 (2016): 35–46.
4. Jiang, "Geming waijiao de zhangli," 37.
5. Jiang, "Geming waijiao de zhangli," 36, 41–43, 45.
6. Jiang, "Geming waijiao de zhangli," 42.
7. Jiang, "Geming waijiao de zhangli," 37.
8. Elizabeth Perry, "The 1960s: Wang Guangmei and Peach Garden Experience," in *The Chinese Communist Party: A Century in Ten Lives*, ed. Timothy Cheek, Klaus Muhlhahn, and Hans van de Ven (Cambridge: Cambridge University Press, 2021), 91–124, at 91.
9. Zhou Jiali, "'Diyi furen' waijiao jiazhi yu Peng Liyuan de gonggong waijiao tese," *Chifeng xueyuan xuebao (Hanwen zhexue shehui kexueban)* 37, no. 1 (2016): 144–46.
10. Harriet Zurndorfer, "Polygamy and Masculinity in China: Past and Present," in *Changing Chinese Masculinities: From Imperial Pillars of State to Global Real Men*, ed. Kam Louie (Hong Kong: Hong Kong University Press, 2016), 13–33.
11. Deborah Davis and Sara Friedman, eds., *Wives, Husbands, and Lovers: Marriage and Sexuality in Hong Kong, Taiwan, and Urban China* (Stanford, CA: Stanford University Press, 2014).

12. See, for example, Pueng Tongs, "China's New Concubines: The Kept Can Be Keepers, Too," *Pacific News Service*, January 22, 2004, https://shorturl.at/poN0o, accessed January 6, 2023.
13. Scholars have traditionally viewed the Surrendering Your Heart to the Party Movement as part of the Anti-Rightist Campaign. However, recently, some have argued that the two political movements were separate, though with considerable overlaps in reality. See Ni Chunna, "Jiaoxin yundong yu fanyou yudong bianxi," *Zhongnan daxue xuebao (shehui kexue ban)* 18, no. 2 (April 2012): 55–59.
14. Yang Yuhuan, *Wang Xiulan* (Jinan: Shandong jiaoyu chubanshe, 2001), 117.
15. Yang, *Wang Xiulan*, 118.
16. Yang, *Wang Xiulan*, 118.
17. Yang, *Wang Xiulan*, 118.
18. "Puyun liusheng: Puju 'yige zhiyuanjun de weihunqi,' Fu Xiuyun," www.sohu.com/a/417750044_257554, accessed January 6, 2023.
19. "Puju lao changpian: Fu Xiuyun Dan Hequ," www.sohu.com/a/392637193_120066939, accessed January 6, 2023.
20. It is still forbidden to discuss many of these political labels in formal publications. We can only get a glimpse of some as circulated on the internet. For a catalog of crimes against the Chinese people in the Mao Era, see Laoqiao 2, "Mao shidai guoren zuiming lu," http://jevons.blog.caixin.com/archives/80526, accessed January 6, 2023.
21. Lisa Tran, "The Concubine in Republican China: Social Perception and Legal Construction," *Etudes Chinoises* 28 (2009): 119–50, at 120.
22. Li Yinxiang, "Kulü jishi: wo yisheng de suantian kula," unpublished memoir, written around 2001, 138–41. Some sections of this memoir have been circulated on the internet. For this story on the torture and killing of landlord Pan's concubine, see https://avoidharmony.blogspot.com/2012/02/2012-02-21-123306-1951-57-11.html, accessed January 6, 2023. On May 22, 2014, Li himself also answered some questions from netizens about his memoir on his blog: http://blog.sina.com.cn/s/blog_12b1272b40101hohj.html, accessed March 1, 2021.
23. Li, "Kulü jishi," 138–41.
24. For a discussion of how the 1949 Communist Revolution was discursively celebrated and interpreted as a "liberation" for Chinese women, see Harriet Evans, "The Language of Liberation: Gender and *Jiefang* in Early Chinese Communist Party Discourse," in *Twentieth-Century China: New Approaches*, ed. Jeffrey Wasserstrom (London: Routledge, 2003), 193–220.
25. For the important role of "emotion work" as part of a conscious strategy of psychological engineering in Communist mobilization and mass campaigns, see Elizabeth Perry, "Moving the Masses: Emotion Work in the Chinese Revolution," *Mobilization: An International Quarterly* 7, no. 2 (2002): 111–28.

Glossary of Chinese Names and Terms

Bai Chongxi 白崇禧
Beijing nüjie lianhe hui 北京女界聯合會
Beiping xingyuan zhuren 北平行轅主任
boniang 伯娘
Cai Jun 蔡鈞
Cai Yuanpei 蔡元培
Cao Kun 曹錕
chahuahui 茶話會
chaonei chahui 朝內茶會
Chen Bainian 陳百年
Chen Hengzhe 陳衡哲
Chen Yi 陈毅
Cheng Liqing 程立卿
Chiang Kai-shek 蔣介石
Chushi xuzhi 出使須知
Cong Xiaoping 丛小平
da furen 大夫人
Daliyuan 大理院
daode 道德
Daotai 道台
Daoyuan 道院
Deng Yingchao 邓颖超
dizhu xiao laopo 地主小老婆
Duan Qirui 段祺瑞
Duo qi du 多妻毒
Er nai 二奶

fandong guanliao yitaitai 反动官僚姨太太
fandong junguan 反动军官
fei qie yundong 廢妾運動
Feng Yuxiang 馮玉祥
Fu Caiyun 傅彩雲
Fu Xiuyun 傅秀云
furen waijiao 夫人外交
furen xiaojie de lianhehui 夫人小姐的聯合會
furen 夫人
gaoshang ren'ge 高尚人格
Gaozhou 高州
Gongjin hui 共進會
gongwu 公務
gongyi 公益
Gu Hongming 辜鴻銘
Gu Weijun (also Wellington Koo) 顧維鈞
guanchang yingchou 官場應酬
Guangdong nüjie lianhe hui 廣東女界聯合會
Guangxi funü kangdi houyuanhui 廣西婦女抗敵後援會
Guimao lüxing ji 癸卯旅行記
Guiping nüzi shifan xuexiao 桂平女子師範學校
Guiqian Ji 歸潛記
Guo daren 郭大人
Guo Dejie 郭德潔
Guo sao 郭嫂
Guo Songling 郭松齡
Guo Songtao 郭嵩燾
guoji shejiao 國際社交
guoru 國辱
hanhua 喊话
Hanyu wailaizi cidian 汉语外来字大辞典
He Zhifen 何智芬
Hong Jun 洪鈞
Hu Shi 胡適
Huang Shaohong 黄紹竑
Huang Xing 黃興

Huayang funü xiehui 華陽婦女協會
Hubei nüzi fazheng xuexiao 湖北女子法政學校
hufu 護符
Jiangning 江寧
Jiang Qing 江青
Jianmin 賤民
jiaoji chang 交際場
jiaoji hua 交際花
jiaoji jia 交際家
Jiaxing 嘉興
Jin de hui 進德會
Jin Wenqing 金雯青
Jinghua yuan 鏡花緣
jishi 姬侍
jiu sao 九嫂
jiuniang 舅娘
Kui Jun 奎俊
Lan Ni 藍妮
Li Benwei 黎本危
Li Dequan 李德全
Lifan yuan 理藩院
Li Lian 李蓮
Li Ruzhen 李汝珍
Li Xiuwen 李秀文
Li Yinxiang 李蔭祥
Li Youlin 李幼林
Li Yuanhong 黎元洪
Li Zhisheng 李志聖
Li Ziqing 李子清
Li Zongren 李宗仁
Liang Shiyi 梁士詒
Liang Shi 梁氏
Liangmin 良民
Linfen 臨汾
Linglong 玲瓏
Liu Gong 刘公

GLOSSARY OF CHINESE NAMES AND TERMS

Liu Xihong 劉錫鴻
Liu Yi 刘一
Liu Zhenhua 劉鎮華
Lu Diping 魯滌平
Lu Rongting 陸榮廷
Lü Simian 呂思勉
Lu Xiaoman 陸小曼
Lu Xun 魯迅
Lun Qianru 掄倩如
Lüqing hubei tongxianghui 旅青湖北同鄉會
Ma Geli (Halliday Macartney) 馬格理
ma-dan 馬單
Mao Yanwen 毛彥文
Mao Zedong 毛澤東
minguo diyi rufuren 民國第一如夫人
mofan 模範
Nanjing shi funü wenhua cujinhui 南京市婦女文化促進會
nengli 能力
Nie Jigui 聶緝槼
Niehai hua 孽海花
nü xuesheng 女學生
nüjie 女界
nüquan 女權
Nüsheng 女聲
Nüzi beifa dui 女子北伐隊
Nüzi canzheng tongmenghui 女子參政同盟會
Oei Hui-lan (Mme. Wellington Koo) 黃蕙蘭
paiqie 排妾
Pan Zihu 潘子笏
Peng Liyuan 彭丽媛
pingqi 平妻
puju 蒲剧
qi 妻
Qian Xun 钱恂
qie 妾
qing 情

GLOSSARY OF CHINESE NAMES AND TERMS

qingzhi 情質
Ren Hongjun 任鴻雋
ren'ge 人格
renchen wu waijiao 人臣無外交
ru furen 如夫人
Sai Jinhua 賽金花
Shan Shili 單士厘
Shanghai funü hui 上海婦女會
shejiao diwei 社交地位
shejiao gongkai 社交公開
shejiao lijie 社交禮節
Shen Congwen 沈從文
Shen Honglie 沈鴻烈
Shenbao 申報
Shi Liangcai 史量才
shifan sheng 師範生
shouzhang 壽幛
shuwu zhang 庶務長
Song Meiling 宋美齡
Su Fengwen 蘇鳳文
Sun Ke 孫科
Sun Yat-Sen 孫中山
taidou 泰鬥
taitai 太太
Tan Ming 譚明
Tan Sitong 譚嗣同
Tang Kangyu 唐康玉
Tang Ying 唐瑛
tezheng 特徵
Tianjin nüjie aiguo tongzhihui 天津女界愛國同志會
Tianzu hui 天足會
tongsu hua 通俗化
tu po 土婆
Wang Guiquan 王桂荃
Wang Kuixuan 王葵軒
Wang Shaoxi 王紹璽

Wang Tao 王韜
Wang Xiulan 王秀兰
Wei Hongbao 危紅寶
Wei Wenxiu 危文繡
Wenming jiehun 文明結婚
Wong Shee Ping 黃樹屏
Wu Jingjun 吳敬君
Wu Zhimei 伍智梅
Xi Jinping 习近平
Xi Shangzhen 席上珍
Xi'an nüzi shifan xuexiao 西安女子師範學校
xiang dang jiaoxin 向党交心
xiangxia po 鄉下婆
xiaoqi 小妻
xin nüxing 新女性
xin xing daode 新性道德
xingge 性格
xinshi de qie 新式的妾
Xiong Xiling 熊希齡
Xu Guangping 許廣平
Xu Shichang 徐世昌
Xu Zonghan 徐宗漢
xunjie 殉節
xuqie 蓄妾
yan 宴
Yang Qusheng 楊渠生
Yao Wenyu 姚溫玉
yi niang 姨娘
yi taitai 姨太太
yifu duoqi zhi 一夫多妻制
Yishi bao 益世报
Yu Fengzhi 于鳳至
Yu Hualin 余华林
Yu Zhengxie 俞正燮
Yuan Shikai 袁世凱
yuanren ren'ge 原人人格

Yuehu 樂戶
Zai Lun 載掄
Zeng Guofan 曾國藩
Zeng Jize 曾紀澤
Zhang Deyi 張德彝
Zhang Peilun 張佩綸
Zhang Qian 张茜
Zhang Xichen 章錫琛
Zhang Xueliang 張學良
Zhang Zhaohe 張兆和
Zhang Zhidong 張之洞
Zhanyi 沾益
Zhongguo gongxue 中國公學
Zhongguo nü xuetang 中國女學堂
Zhou Enlai 周恩來
Zhou Jianren 周建人
Zhou Shunqin 周顺勤
Zhou Ziqi 周自齊
Zhu Caizhen 朱采真
Zhu Qihui 朱其慧
zi'ai 自愛
ziyou jiehun 自由結婚
ziyou lian'ai 自由恋爱
ziyou nü 自由女
Zongli Yamen 總理衙門

Works Cited

COMMONLY CITED NEWSPAPER, JOURNALS, AND MAGAZINES

Beijing daxue xuesheng zhoukan (*Peking University Students' Weekly*)
Beijing qianshuo huabao (*Beijing Elementary Pictorial*)
Beiping chenbao (*Peiping Morning News*)
Beiyang huabao (*Beiyang Pictorial*)
Chenbao (*Morning News*)
Chenbao liu zhounian zengkan (*Morning News's Additional Issue of Sixth Years Anniversary*)
Ciyou yuekan (*Child Welfare Monthly*)
Dadi tuwen xunkan (*The Earth Ten-day Periodical*)
Dahan gongbao (*The Chinese Times*)
Daobao (Shanghai) (*Leader Newspaper*)
Dagang zhoukan (*Dagang Weekly*)
Dagong bao (Tianjin) (*L'Impartial*)
Dongfang zazhi (*The Eastern Miscellany*)
Duli pinglun (*Independent Critic*)
Funü gongming (*Women's Resonance*)
Funü gongming yuekan (*Women's Resonance Monthly*)
Funü yuebao (*Women's Monthly*)
Funü zazhi (Shanghai) (*Ladies' Journal*)
Funü zhoukan (*Women's Weekly*)
Guanghua ribao (*Guanghua Daily*)
Guohuo yuekan (Shanghai) (*National Goods Monthly*)
Jiating zhoukan (*Family Weekly*)
Jiefang yu gaizao (*Liberation and Reform*)
Journal of the American Association of China
Liangyou (*Young Companion*)
Lianyi zhiyou (*Connected Companion*)
Minguo ribao (*Republican Daily*)
Neimu xinwen (*Inside News*)
Nüsheng (*Women's Voices*)
Qingchun dianying (*Youth Film*)

Renmin zhoubao (*People's Weekly*)
Rensheng zazhi (*Life Magazine*)
Shehui xue jie (*Sociology*)
Shenbao (*Shanghai News*)
Shibao (*The Eastern Times*)
Shibao tuhua zhoukan (*Pictorial Weekly of The Eastern Times*)
Shijie chenbao (*World Morning News*)
Shishi xinbao (*The China Times*)
Shishi xinbao wankan (*The China Times Evening News*)
The New York Times, 1907
The North-China Herald and Supreme Court &Consular Gazette, 1897, 1898
The Times (of London), 1878
Tiebao (*Iron Newspaper*)
Time Magazine
Tuhua Zhonghua Zazhi (*Pictorial China Magazine*)
Xiandai pinglun (*Modern Critique*)
Xiao ribao (*Small Daily*)
Xiaoduo (*Little Bell*)
Xinmin bao (*The New People*)
Xinwen bao (*News Press*)
Xinwen tiandi (*News World*)
Xinwen zazhi (*News Magazine*)
Xinxin xinwen (*Latest News*)
Yishibao (Tianjin) (*Social Welfare*)
Zhejiang minbao (*Zhejiang People's Daily*)
Zhenglun xunkan (*Righteous Discussion Ten-day Periodical*)
Zhengzhi pinglun (*Political Commentary*)
Zhongguo renwu (*Chinese Characters*)
Zhonghua (*China*)
Zhujiang bao (*Pearl River News*)

ANONYMOUS SOURCES

"Aishu zaijia kuzhong" (Sadly narrating difficult reasons to remarry). *Shenbao*, January 17, 1935.

"Chinese Lanterns: Minguo nüxing renwu zaji" (Chinese Lanterns: A miscellaneous account of women in Republican China), accessed December 10, 2022, https://kknews.cc/history/5la58jk.html.

"E sheng nüjie xin choushi" (A new scandal among women's circles of Hubei province). *Shenbao*, January 16, 1913.

"Fu zongtong jingxuan de qundaifeng: chuxian zai shoudu de funüjie de huixing Li Guo Dejie" (The wind of skirt in Vice President election: A comet appearing in the women's circle in the capital Li Guo Dejie). *Xinwen zazhi*, no. 2 (1948): 6.

"Funü tuanti zuo kaihui-yuanzhu Wei Wenxiu zaijiao an" (The case of women's organizations having a meeting to support Wei Wenxiu's remarriage). *Shenbao*, February 18, 1935.

"General Grant in Shanghai," *The North-China Herald*, May 27, 1879.

"Gu furen kai tiaowu hui" (Madame Gu held a dance party). *Dagong Bao* (Tianjin), February 8, 1927.

"Gu Weijun Furen xiaoying (tupian)." (A portrait of Madame Gu Weijun). *Shenbao*, April 17, 1921.

"Guangzhou sanxiao fengchao zhi yubo" (The aftermaths of the strikes at three schools in Guangzhou). *Minguo ribao*. March 10, 1920.

"Hu jiaojihua Tang Ying fumei" (Shanghai social butterfly Tang Ying went to the US), *Funü yuebao* 1, no. 12 (1936):14.

"Ji Mei gongzi guanju shi" (An account of American President Grant's children watching opera). *Shenbao*, May 22, 1879.

"Jian xiani, nü xuesheng shizhi qieteng" (Seeing inappropriate intimacy, female student finally learned she was deceived to be a concubine). *Xinwen bao*, December 6, 1931.

"Jiaotongbu you kai tiaowuhui" (Ministry of Transportation and Communications held a dance party again). *Shenbao*, February 16, 1914.

"Li fu zongtong juanshu ji shuguan beishangji" (Recording Vice President Li's family and affiliates' journey to the North). *Shenbao*, December 17, 1913.

"Li gu zongtong lingjiu dihan" (The coffin of the deceased President Li arrived Hankou). *Tuhua Zhonghua Zazhi* (Shanghai), no. 18 (1933): 5.

"Li Huangpo zuori fangyang dongdu" (Li Yuanhong set off traveling overseas yesterday). *Shenbao*, November 9, 1923.

"Li Yuanhong qie Wei Wenxiu tuoli jiating" (Li Yuanhong's concubine Wei Wenxiu severed her ties from the Li family). *Shenbao*, September 2, 1934.

"Li Yuanhong zhi yichan jiufen" (Li Yuanhong's inheritance dispute). *Shenbao*, July 10, 1932.

"Li Zongren dangxuan fu zongtong, Guo Dejie gonglao bushao" (Li Zongren was elected Vice President, which attributed a lot to Guo Dejie). *Zhujiang bao*, no. 52 (1949): 4.

"Li Zongren furen juanxian jinshi" (A true record of Madame Li Zongren's donation). *Shenbao*, October 4, 1937.

"Lian jian zuo xiaoxing: nü xuesheng zigan xiajian" (Seduced to be concubine: female student willingly debased herself). *Xiaoduo* 130, June 8, 1917.

"Lingjiu you jin di han" (Li's coffins arrived Hankou from Tianjin). *Shenbao*, April 13, 1933.

"Lu Diping zhi ru furen shashi zisha" (Lu Diping's concubine surnamed Sha committed suicide). *Funü gongming yuekan* 4, no. 2 (1935): 57.

"Lu Diping zuo dalian" (Lu Diping's encoffining ceremony was held yesterday). *Shenbao*, February 2, 1935.

"Lu Diping zuochen shishi" (Lu Diping passed away yesterday morning). *Shenbao*, February 1, 1935.

"Lun libie nannü" (On the Ritual Rule of Separating Men and Women). *Shenbao*, August 9, 1878.

"Lun Qianru baoshihou, yangbing faguo yiyuan" (After being released on bail, Lun Qianru is recuperating in a French hospital). *Yishibao* (Tianjin ban), September 30, 1948.

"Nanjingshi funü wenhua cujinhui dianwei Wei Wenxiu" (Women's Culture Promotion Society in Nanjing telegraphed to comfort Wei Wenxiu). *Funü gongming* 4, no. 2 (February 1935): 57.

"Nannü xiangjian lijie bian," *Shenbao*, November 15, 1878.

"Nü jiaoyuan ganxin zuoqie, lü shi de shi fengliu (Female teacher willing to become a concubine; the lawyer involved is licentious)." *Daobao* (Shanghai), August 24, 1938.

"Nü xuesheng beiyou weiqie" (Female student seduced to be concubine). *Beijing qianshuo huabao*, no. 890 (1911): 4.

"Nü xuesheng burong zuoqie" (A female student was not tolerated for becoming a concubine). *Shibao*, June 19, 1913.

"Nü xuesheng buyuan weiqie" (A female student refused to become a concubine). *Shibao*, March 1, 1926.

"Nü xuesheng ganzuo xiaoxing" (A female student voluntarily became a concubine). *Shibao*, October 14, 1930.

"Nü xuesheng jieshi junguan quju tengqie diwei" (A female student got acquainted with an officer and was forced to become his concubine). *Shibao*, July 18, 1933.

"Nü xuesheng tancai shishen" (Female student being greedy and losing her virginity). *Minguo ribao*, February 29, 1924.

"Nüjie duiyu qie zhi wenti zhi zhengyi (The dispute among women's circles on the concubine issue). *Dahan gongbao*, March 19, 1920.

"Nüjie lianhehui zhi paiqie sheng" (The voice to exclude concubines within Guangdong United Women's Association). *Shishi xinbao*, February 2, 1920.

"Nüzi shifan xuexiao yi you xuechao fasheng" (Student protests also happened at a Women's Normal School). *Dagong bao*. January 12, 1920.

"Prince Henry of Prussia in Shanghai," *The North-China Herald*, April 25, 1898, 718.

"Puju lao changpian: Fu Xiuyun Dan Hequ" (Old records of Pu opera: Fu Xiuyuan's *Sound of Dan River*). www.sohu.com/a/392637193_120066939, accessed January 6, 2023.

"Puyun liusheng: Puju 'yige zhiyuanjun de weihunqi,' Fu Xiuyun" (The lingering sound of Pu opera: *A Volunteer Soldier's Fiancée* by Fu Xiuyun). www.sohu.com/a/417750044_257554, accessed January 6, 2023.

"Qian gu zongtong Li Yuanhong shi jiqi furen zhi lingjiu benyue yunjin anzang" (The coffins of former President Li Yuanhong and his wife are about to be buried this month). *Liangyou* 76, (1933): 12.

"Qing dangju xianling chujing" (The government of Qingdao ordered Li Benwei to leave). *Shenbao*, January 30, 1935.

"Qinshi yanke" (Imperial Envoy hosting banquet). *Shenbao*, August 6, 1878.

"Renwu: Fu zongtong furen Guo Dejie sumiao" (People: A sketch on Madame Vice President Guo Dejie). *Dagang zhoukan* 2, no. 20 (1948): 6.

"Secretary Taft's Visit to Shanghai," *Journal of the American Association of China*, November 1907, 12.

"Song Meiling nüshi di'er: Li furen Guo Dejie nüshi yinxiang ji" (Madame Song Meiling the second: My impression of Madame Li Zongren Guo Dejie). *Dadi tuwen xunkan* 1, no. 10 (1938): 182–83.

"Step in Women's Emancipation," The *New York Times*, October 9, 1907, 1.

"Sui Hubei nüzi fazheng xuexiao xiaozhang Li Qimin shang jiaoyusi bing" (Following the report of the president of Hubei Women's School of Law and Politics Li Qimin to the Ministry of Education). *Shenbao*, March 1, 1913.

"The Chinese Legation." *The Times (of London)*, June 20, 1878, 9.

"The Taotai's Ball." *The North-China Herald and Supreme Court &Consular Gazette*, November 12, 1897, 871.

"Tianjin nüjie aiguo tongzhi hui jujue rufuren ruhui zhi liyoushu" (A statement from The Tianjin Chinese Women's Patriotic Association on why concubines were banned from becoming members). *Chenbao*, August 15, 1919.

"Wuhui jisheng" (An account of a splendid dance ball). *Shenbao*, May 23, 1879.

"Xinniang jiao songshi shangmen, nü xuesheng buyuan zuoqie zisha" (Bridal sedan chair carried over a corpse, female student committed suicide for refusing to become a concubine). *Dagong bao* (Tianjin), December 9, 1923.

"Yu Fengzhi zhuban xiezhenhui" (Yu Fengzhi organized a disaster relief committee). *Shenbao*, September 15, 1931.

"Yue nüjie zhi paiqie huiyi" (A meeting within Guangdong women's circle to exclude concubines). *Minguo ribao*, January 31, 1920.

"Zai qu yu gaijia" (Man's remarrying and woman's remarrying). *Shenbao*, February 22, 1935.

"Zhang Shizhang fufu juxing chawuhui" (Zhang Shizhang couple held a dancing party). *Xinwen bao*, October 30, 1930.

"Zhou Ziqi zhi qie" (Zhou Ziqi's concubine). *Shibao tuhua zhoukan* 92, 1922.

"Zhouzhuang shisheng lian'an an, juanhao nü xuesheng Tao Suzhen ganzuo tengqie" (A case of student and teacher falling in love: a fair female student Tao Suzhen willingly became a concubine). *Tiebao*, October 11, 1935.

"Zhuima zhongshang shishi" (Passing away due to a fall from a horse and being heavily injured). *Shenbao*, July 10, 1935.

NON-ANONYMOUS SOURCES

Arkush, David R. and Leo Ou-fan Lee. *Land without Ghosts: Chinese Impressions of America from the Mid-Nineteenth Century to the Present.* Berkeley, CA: University of California Press, 1993.

Bailey, Paul. "'Women Behaving Badly': Crime, Transgressive Behaviour and Gender in Early Twentieth Century China." *Nan Nü: Men, Women, and Gender in China* 8, no.1 (2006), 156–97.

Bailey, Paul. *Gender and Education in China: Gender Discourses and Women's Schooling in the Early Twentieth Century*. New York, NY: Routledge, 2007.

Bailey, Paul. *Women and Gender in Twentieth-Century China*. London: Palgrave Macmillan, 2012.

Barish, Daniel. *Learning to Rule: Court Education and the Remaking of the Qing State, 1861–1912*. New York, NY: Columbia University Press, 2022.

Barlow, Tani. *The Question of Women in Chinese Feminism*. Durham, NC: Duke University Press, 2004.

Berg, Daria. "Cultural Discourse on Xue Susu: A Courtesan in Late Ming China." *International Journal of Asian Studies* 6, no. 2 (2009): 171–200.

Bergère, Marie-Claire. *The Golden Age of the Chinese Bourgeoisie 1911–1937*. Cambridge: Cambridge University Press, 1989.

Bernhart, Kathryn. *Women and Property in China, 960–1949*. Stanford, CA: Stanford University Press, 1999.

Bickers, Robert ed. *Ritual & Diplomacy: The Macartney Mission to China 1792–1794: Papers Presented at the 1992 Conference of the British Association for Chinese Studies Marking the Bicentenary of the Macartney Mission to China*. London: Wellsweep Press, 1993.

Binchun. *Chengcuo biji* (Jottings on travels). Changsha: Yuelu shushe, 1985.

Bossler, Beverly. "Shifting Identities: Courtesans and Literati in Song China." *Harvard Journal of Asiatic Studies* 62, no. 1 (June 2002): 5–37.

Bossler, Beverly. *Courtesans, Concubines, and the Cult of Female Fidelity*. Cambridge, MA: Harvard University Asia Center, 2016.

Boulger, Demetrius Charles. *The Life of Sir Halliday Macartney K.C.M.G.: Commander of Li Hung Chang's Trained Force in the Taeping Rebellion, Founder of the First Chinese Arsenals, for Thirty Years Councillor and Secretary to the Chinese Legation in London*. London: John Lane the Bodley Head, 1908.

Boyd, Nancy. *Emissaries, the Overseas Work of the American YWCA 1895–1970*. New York, NY: Woman's Press, 1986.

Brownell, Susan and Jeffrey Wasserstrom eds. "Modernizing Sex, Sexing Modernity: Prostitution in Early-Twentieth-Century Shanghai." In *Chinese Femininities, Chinese Masculinities: A Reader*, 199–221. Berkeley, CA: University of California Press, 2002.

Cai Zhen. "Bianjizhe de yusheng" (A call from the editor). In *Fei qie hao* (Abolish Concubinage), edited by Zhu Caizhen, 5–6. Hangzhou: Zhejiang shuju, 1922.

Chang, Kang-i Sun. *The Late-Ming Poet Ch'en Tzu-Lung: Crises of Love and Loyalism*. New Haven, CT: Yale University Press, 1991.

Chao, Janey Sheau Yueh and Kachuen Yuan Gee. "Early Life of Yuan Shikai and the Formation of Yuan Family," paper presented at the 5th International Conference of Institutes and Libraries for Chinese Overseas Studies, CUNY, New York, 2012, 21, accessed January 26, 2021, https://academicworks.cuny.edu/cgi/viewcontent.cgi?article=1011&context=bb_pubs.

Chen, Bainian. "Yifu duoqi de xin hufu" (A New Talisman for One Husband and Multiple Wives). *Xiandai pinglun* 1, no. 14 (1925).

Chen, Gangjun. "Songdai chayan shulun" (A Review of Tea Party in the Song Dynasty). *Nongye kaogu,* no. 5 (2016): 68–71.
Chen, Hengzhe. "Chuanxing suoji: yifeng gei pengyoumen de gongxin" (Miscellaneous Notes of My Journey to Sichuan: An Open Letter to My Friends). *Duli pinglun,* no. 195 (April 5, 1936): 14–20.
Chen, Jiaohua. "Minguo nüsheng de zhiye chulu tansuo – jiyu Mengke and Diyi luxiang de yanjiu" (Exploration of Female Students' Career Development in Republican China: A Study Based on Mengke and The First Stove Incense). *Zhonghua nüzi xueyuan xuebao (Journal of China Women's University),* no. 4 (2018): 68–75.
Chen, Shiau-Yun. "Jealous and Violent: Constraining and Celebrating Wifely Jealousy in mid-to-late Ming China." *Ming Studies,* no. 79 (2019): 21–48.
Chen, Siyi and Mu Yi eds. *Cai Jun chuyang suoji* (A memoir of Cai Jun's journey abroad). Changsha: Yuelu shushe, 2016.
Chen, Suwen. "Xiaojie bidu de changshi keben: shejiao baojian" (A Textbook on General Knowledge for Misses: Treasured Mirror of Social Intercourse). *Shishi xinbao wankan,* June 7, 1947.
Cheng, Yu. *Qing zhi minguo xuqie xisu zhi bianqian* (The Change of Concubinage Custom from Qing to Republican China). Shanghai: Shanghai shiji chuban gufen youxian gongsi, 2006.
Cleverley, John. *The Schooling of China: Tradition and Modernity in Chinese Education.* Sydney: Allen & Unwin, 1985.
Cong, Xiaoping. *Teachers' Schools and the Making of the Modern Chinese Nation-State 1897–1937.* Vancouver: University of British Columbia Press, 2007.
Croll, Elisabeth. *Wise Daughters from Foreign Lands: European Women Writers in China.* London: Pandora, 1989.
Davis, Deborah and Sara Friedman eds. *Wives, Husbands, and Lovers: Marriage and Sexuality in Hong Kong, Taiwan, and Urban China.* Stanford, CA: Stanford University Press, 2014.
Day, Jenny Huangfu. *Qing Travellers to the Far West: Diplomacy and the Information Order in Late Imperial China.* New York, NY: Cambridge University Press, 2018.
Ding, Naifei. "Wife-in-monogamy and 'the exaltation of concubines.'" *Interventions* 9, no. 2 (2007): 219–37.
Dong, Madeleine Yue. "Who Is Afraid of the Chinese Modern Girl?" In *The Modern Girl Around the World: Consumption Modernity and Globalization,* edited by Weinbaum Alys Eve and Modern Girl Around the World Research Group, 194–219. Durham, NC: Duke University Press, 2008.
Du, Chunmei. *Gu Hongming's Eccentric Chinese Odyssey.* Philadelphia, PA: University of Pennsylvania Press, 2019.
Du, Yaquan. "Lun xuqie." *Dongfang zazhi* (A discussion on keeping concubines), 8, no. 4 (1911): 15–19.
Ebrey, Patricia Buckley. *The Inner Quarters: Marriage and the Lives of Chinese Women in the Sung Period.* Berkeley, CA: University of California Press, 1993.

Edwards, Louise. "Policing the Modern Woman in Republican China." *Modern China* 26, no. 2 (2000): 115–47.

Edwards, Louise. *Gender, Politics, and Democracy: Women's Suffrage in China.* Stanford, CA: Stanford University Press, 2008.

Edwards, Louise. "The Shanghai Modern Woman's American Dreams: Imagining America's Depravity to Produce China's 'Moderate Modernity.'" *Pacific Historical Review* 81, no. 4 (2012): 567–601.

Evans, Harriet. "The Language of Liberation: Gender and *Jiefang* in Early Chinese Communist Party Discourse." In *Twentieth-century China: New Approaches*, edited by Jeffrey Wasserstrom, 193–220. London: Routledge, 2003.

Feng, Mocun. "Cong shishi shang shuodao feiqie de biran xing" (A discussion of the inevitability of abolishing concubinage based on facts). *Funü gongming* 2, no. 7 (June 1933).

Ferlanti, Federica. "Women's Activism and Mobilization in Wartime China: Cadre Training, National Economic Production, and Workers' Literacy (1937–1945)." *Journal of Chinese History* (2023): 1–22.

Field, Andrew. "Selling Souls in Sin City: Shanghai Singing and Dancing Hostesses in Print, Film, and Politics, 1920–1949." In *Cinema and Urban Culture in Shanghai, 1922–1943*, edited by Yingjin Zhang, 99–127. Stanford, CA: Stanford University Press, 1999.

Frodsham, J. D., Sung-t'ao Kuo, Hsi-hung Liu, and Te-yi Chang. *The First Chinese Embassy to the West: The Journals of Kuo Sung-T'ao, Liu Hsi-Hung and Chang Te-Yi.* Oxford: Clarendon Press, 1974.

Fuess, Harald. *Divorce in Japan: Family, Gender, and the State, 1600–2000.* Stanford, CA: Stanford University Press, 2004.

Gamble, Sidney. *Peking: A Social Survey.* Beijing: George Doran Company, 1921.

Gao, Feng. "Ansha Lu Diping de xiongshou shishui" (Who Was the Assassin of Lu Diping?) *Wenshi chunqiu*, no. 1 (2008): 12–15.

Gilmartin, Christina. *Engendering the Chinese Revolution: Radical Women, Communist Politics, and Mass Movements in the 1920s.* Berkeley, CA: University of California Press, 1995.

Gimpel, Denise. *Chen Hengzhe: A Life between Orthodoxies.* Lanham, MD: Lexington Books, 2015.

Glosser, Susan. *Chinese Visions of Family and State, 1915–1953.* Berkeley, CA: University of California Press, 2003.

Goodman, Bryna. "'A World of Concubines': Fissures in the Category of 'Woman' in Republican China." *Journal of Women's History* 32, no. 1 (2020): 85–110.

Goodman, Bryna and Wendy Larson eds. "The Vocational Woman and the Elusiveness of 'Personhood' in Early Republican China." In *Gender in Motion: Divisions of Labor and Cultural Change in Late Imperial and Modern*, 265–86. Lanham, MD: Rowman &Littlefield, 2005.

Goodman, Bryna and Wendy Larson eds. *The Suicide of Miss Xi: Democracy and Disenchantment in the Chinese Republic.* Cambridge, MA: Harvard University Press, 2021.

Goossaert, Vincent. "Irrepressible Female Piety: Late Imperial Bans on Women Visiting Temples." *Nan Nu* 10, no.2 (2008): 212–41.

Guan, Ruiwu. "Qie zhi yanjiu" (A study on concubinage). *Shehui xue jie* 6 (1931): 87–121.

Guo, Songtao. *Lundun yu bali riji* (Diary from London and Paris). Changsha: Yuelu shushe, 1985.

Guo, Vivienne Xiangwei. "Forging a Women's United Front: Chinese Elite Women's Networks for National Salvation and Resistance, 1932–1938." *Modern Asian Studies* 53, no.2 (2019): 483–511.

Guo, Youqi. "Shehui wenti yu jiaoyu zhuanxing – shi lun minguo shiqi de xuesheng jiuye kunnan (1912–1937)" (Social Problem and Educational Transformation: The Difficulty in Graduates' Employment in the Period of Republic of China, 1912–1937). *Jiaoyu Lilun Yanjiu (Theory Research)*, no. 4 (2011): 271–310.

He, Wangfang. "Li Zongren yu Guo Dejie" (Li Zongren and Guo Dejie). *Shilin manbu*, no. 1 (2004): 40–41.

He, Xinhua. *Weiyi tianxia: Qingdai waijiao liyi jiqi bianqe* (Majestic presence over the whole country: diplomatic rituals and their evolution during the Qing Dynasty). Shanghai: Shanghai shehui kexueyuan chubanshe, 2011.

Henriot, Christian. "Chinese Courtesans in Late Qing and Early Republican Shanghai." *East Asian History*, no. 8 (1994): 33–52.

Hershatter, Gail. "Making the Visible Invisible: The Fate of 'the Private' in Revolutionary China." In *Going Public: Feminism and the Shifting Boundaries of the Private Sphere*, edited by Joan Scott and Debra Keates, 309–29. Urbana, IL: University of Illinois Press, 2005.

Hershatter, Gail. "Modernizing Sex, Sexing Modernity: Prostitution in Early-Twentieth-Century Shanghai." In *Chinese Femininities, Chinese Masculinities. A Reader*, edited by Susan Brownell and Jeffrey Wasserstrom, 199–221. Berkeley, CA: University of California Press, 2002.

Hershatter, Gail. *Dangerous Pleasures: Prostitution and Modernity in Twentieth-Century Shanghai*. Berkeley, CA: University of California Press, 1999.

Hevia, James. *Cherishing Men from Afar: Qing Guest Ritual and the Macartney Embassy of 1793*. Durham, NC: Duke University Press, 2005.

Hochschild, Arlie. "The Role of the Ambassador's Wife: An Exploratory Study." *Journal of Marriage and Family* 31, no.1 (1969): 73–87.

Honig, Emily. "Maoist Mappings of Gender: Reassessing the Red Guards." In *Chinese Femininities, Chinese Masculinities: A Reader*, edited by Susan Brownell and Jeffrey Wasserstrom, 255–68. Berkeley, CA: University of California Press, 2002.

Hou, Yijie. *Yuan Shikai quanzhuan* (A complete biography of Yuan Shikai). Beijing: Qunzhong chubanshe, 2013.

Hsiung, Ping-chen. *A Tender Voyage: Children and Childhood in Late Imperial China*. Stanford, CA: Stanford University Press, 2005.

Hu, Jishan. "Jingzhi Chen Hengzhe nüshi" (Respectfully to Lady Chen Hengzhe). *Xinxin xinwen*, July 2, 1936.

Hu, Ying. "'Would That I Were Marco Polo': The Travel Writing of Shan Shili (1856–1943)." *Journeys: Special Issue on East Asian Travel Writing* 5, no. 1 (2004): 119–41.

Hu, Ying. "Re-Configuring Nei/Wai: Writing the Woman Traveler in the Late Qing." *Late Imperial China* 18, no.1 (1997): 72–99.

Hu, Ying. *Tales of Translation: Composing the New Woman in China, 1899–1918.* Stanford, CA: Stanford University Press, 2000.

Huan, Wang and Zou Rui. "Guo Songtao houdai jiangsu jiazu wangshi" (Guo Songtao's descendants recounting their family history). https://read01.com/zxeAEK.html#.Y5JXGC-B0UQ, accessed December 8, 2022.

Huang, Meisheng. "Xu Zhimo furen Lu Xiaoman nüshi xinying" (New Photo of Mrs. Xu Zhimo Lu Xiaoman). *Lianyi zhiyou*, no. 115 (1929).

Jaschok, Maria. *Concubines and Bondservants: A Social History.* London: Zed Books, 1988.

Ji, Manhong and Lin Guangrong. "Guo Songtao yu 'furen waijiao'" (Guo Songtao and wife diplomacy). *Jiangxi shehui kexue*, no. 7 (2008): 122–26.

Jiang, Huajie. "Geming waijiao de zhangli: guanyu xin zhongguo furen waijiao de lishi kaocha (1950–1965)" (Tensions of revolutionary diplomacy: A historical examination of PRC Wife Diplomacy (1950–1965)). *Zhonggong dangshi yanjiu*, no. 5 (2016): 35–46.

Jiang, Ming. *Qiufeng baojian guchen lei: wan Qing de zhengju he renwu xubian* (Autumn wind, sword, and tears of former officials: A sequel to political situations and figures of the late Qing). Hong Kong: Xianggang zhonghe chuban gongsi, 2016.

Jin, Shiyin. "Ershi nian fuyun zhi yi da gongzuo – feiqie" (A major work of women's movements during the past twenty years – abolishing concubinage). *Funü gongming* 41 (1931): 6–14.

Judge, Joan. *The Precious Raft of History: The Past, the West, and the Woman Question in China.* Stanford, CA: Stanford University Press, 2008.

Judge, Joan, Barbara Mittler, and Michel Hockx eds. *Women and the Periodical Press in China's Long Twentieth Century: A Space of Their Own?* Cambridge: Cambridge University Press, 2018.

Kejiu. "Sui ganlu: Wo zhen ti zhexie zi kexi" (Random thoughts: I truly feel pity for these words). *Minguo ribao*, June 13, 1921, 4.

Ko, Dorothy. *Teachers of the Inner Chambers: Women and Culture in Seventeenth-Century China.* Stanford, CA: Stanford University Press, 1995.

Koo, Madame Wellington and Isabella Taves. *No Feasts Last Forever.* New York, NY: Quadrangle, 1975.

Koo, Madame Wellington and Mary Van Rensselaer Thayer. *Hui-Lan Koo: An Autobiography.* New York, NY: Dial Press, 1943.

Kuei, Tsai and Lily K. Haass. "A Study of the YWCA of China, 1890–1930." Box 325. The YWCA of the USA. Records, Sophia Smith Collection, Smith College, Northampton, MA.

Kuo, Margaret. *Intolerable Cruelty: Marriage, Law, and Society in Early Twentieth-Century China.* Lanham, MD: Rowman & Littlefield, 2012.

Kuo, Mei-fen and Michael Williams. "Why is Polygamy Poisonous? An Historical Context." In *The Poison of Polygamy: A Social Novel.* Sydney: Sydney University Press 2019, 11–35.

Lanza, Fabio. *Behind the Gate: Inventing Students in Beijing.* New York, NY: Columbia University Press, 2010.

Laoqiao 2. "Mao shidai guoren zuiming lu" (A list of Chinese people's charges of accusations during Mao's era). http://jevons.blog.caixin.com/archives/80526, accessed January 6, 2023.

Lean, Eugenia. *Public Passions: The Trial of Shi Jianqiao and the Rise of Popular Sympathy in Republican China.* Berkeley, CA: University of California Press, 2007.

Lee, Haiyan. "All the Feelings that are Fit to Print: The Community of Sentiment and the Literary Public Sphere in China, 1900–1918." *Modern China* 27, no. 3 (2001): 291–327.

Lee, Haiyan. *Revolution of the Heart: A Genealogy of Love in China, 1900–1950.* Stanford, CA: Stanford University Press, 2010.

Lee, Lily Xiao Hong, Clara Lau, and A. D. Stefanowska. *Biographical Dictionary of Chinese Women: The Qing Period, 1644–1911.* New York, NY: Routledge, 2015.

Lewis, D. J. "A Requiem for Chinese Customary Law in Hong Kong." *The International and Comparative Law Quarterly* 32, no. 2 (1983): 347–379.

Li, Benwei. "Cao Kun lanche jieyin chouju" (The scandal of Cao Kun stopping a train to intercept a presidential seal). In *Minguo dazongtong Li Yuanhong* (The President of Republican China Li Yuanhong), edited by Quanguo zhengxie wenshi ziliao weiyuanhui, 281–84. Beijing: Zhongguo wenshi chubanshe, 1991.

Li, Laura Tyson. *Madame Chiang Kai-Shek: China's Eternal First Lady.* New York, NY: Grove Press, 2007.

Li, Meng. "Zhongwai jindai meiti dui 'jiaojihua' baodao de nüxing zhuyi yanjiu–yi Shenbao he Beihua jiebao dui Tang Ying de baodao weili" (A feminist study on the modern Chinese and foreign media reports on the social butterfly – using the case of Shenbao and North China Herald's reports on Tang Ying). *Haiwai Yingyu*, no. 9 (2015): 158–166.

Li, Ruzhen, and Tai-yi Lin. *Flowers in the Mirror.* Berkeley, CA: University of California Press, 1965.

Li, Shaofen. "Wo de fuqin Li Yuanhong" (My father Li Yuanhong). In *Minguo dazongtong Li Yuanhong* (The President of Republican China Li Yuanhong), edited by Quanguo zhengxie wenshi ziliao weiyuanhui, 32–33. Beijing: Zhongguo wenshi chubanshe, 1991.

Li, Xiuwen and Tan Ming. *Wo yu Li Zongren* (Li Zongren and I). Guilin: Lijiang chubanshe, 2018.

Li, Yinxiang. "Kulü jishi: wo yisheng de suantian kula" (A truthful account of a journey of hardship: the ups and downs of my life), unpublished memoir, written around 2001.

Li, Yu-ning. "Hsu Tsung-Han – Tradition and Revolution." *Republican China* 10, no. 1 (November, 1984): 13–28.

Liang, Jinghe. "Lun wusi shiqi de 'nannü shejiao gongkai' sichao" (A study on the intellectual trend of 'open social intercourse between men and women' during the May Fourth period). *Shixue yuekan*, no. 1 (1998): 51–64.

Lien, Ling-ling. "Searching for the 'New Womanhood': Career Women in Shanghai, 1912–1945." PhD thesis, University of California, Irvine, 2001.

Lin, Meijing. "Yeqie zhilu" (Concubine-smelting furnace). In *Fei qie hao* (Abolish Concubinage), edited by Zhu Caizhen, 33–34. Hangzhou: Zhejiang shuju, 1922.

Lin, Weihong. "Miandui xifang wenhua de zhongguo nüxing: cong Zeng Jize riji kan Zeng shi funü zai ouzhou" (The Chinese women facing Western culture: The Zeng women in Europe as seen through Zeng Jize's journal). *Zhejiang xuekan*, no. 4 (2007): 211–19.

Lin, Zhaoqi. "Guo Songling yu tiaowu" (Guo Songling and dancing). *Shenbao*, May 18, 1927.

Link, Perry. *Mandarin Ducks and Butterfly: Popular Fiction in Early Twentieth-Century Chinese Cities.* Berkeley, CA: University of California Press, 1981.

Liu, Chongxi. "Huainian zufumu Liu Gong Liu Yi" (Commemorating my grandfather Liu Gong and grandmother Liu Yi), *Shijixing*, no. 8 (2011): 34–37.

Liu, Xihong. *Yingyao siji* (A private account of the mission to England). Changsha: Yuelu shushe, 1986.

Liu, Yunxing. "Yuan Shikai de yiqi jiuqie" (Yuan Shikai's one wife and nine concubines), In *Xiangcheng wenshi ziliao 8*, edited by Cui Chenglie and Jiang Debian, 89–95. Xiangcheng Xian: Zhongguo renmin zhengzhi xieshang huiyi Xiangcheng Xian weiyuanhui, 2000.

Lü, Mei. "Fei qie tan" (A discussion on abolishing concubinage). *Rensheng zazhi*, no. 3 (1924): 13–16.

Luo, Dunwei. *Zhongguo zhi hunyin wenti* (The issue of marriage in China). Shanghai: Shanghai dadong shuju, 1931.

Ma, Yuxin. *Women Journalists and Feminism in China, 1898–1937.* Amherst, NY: Cambria Press, 2010.

Macartney, George. *An Embassy to China: Being the Journal Kept by Lord Macartney During His Embassy to the Emperor Ch'ien-Lung, 1793–1794.* London: Longmans, 1963.

Mann, Susan. *Precious Records: Women in China's Long Eighteenth Century.* Stanford, CA: Stanford University Press, 1997.

Mann, Susan. *The Talented Women of the Zhang Family.* Berkeley, BA: University of California Press, 2007.

McCarthy, Helen, and James Southern. "Women, Gender, and Diplomacy: A Historical Survey." In *Gender and Diplomacy*, edited by Jennifer Cassidy, 15–31. London: Routledge, 2017.

McDougall, Bonnie and Anders Hansson eds. *Chinese Concepts of Privacy.* Leiden: Brill, 2002.

McDougall, Bonnie S. *Love-Letters and Privacy in Modern China: The Intimate Lives of Lu Xun and Xu Guangping.* Oxford: Oxford University Press, 2002.

McDougall, Bonnie S. "Privacy in Modern China." *History Compass* 2, no. 1 (2004): 1–8.
McMahon, Keith. *Polygamy and Sublime Passion: Sexuality in China on the Verge of Modernity.* Honolulu, HI: University of Hawai'i Press, 2009.
McMahon, Keith. *Women Shall Not Rule: Imperial Wives and Concubines in China from Han to Liao.* Lanham, MD: Rowman and Littlefield, 2013.
McMahon, Keith. *Celestial Women: Imperial Wives and Concubines in China from Song to Qing.* Lanham, MD: Rowman & Littlefield, 2016.
Merkel-Hess, Kate. "A New Woman and Her Warlord: Li Dequan, Feng Yuxiang, and the Politics of Intimacy in Twentieth-Century China." *Frontiers of History in China* 11, no.3 (2016): 431–57.
Merkel-Hess, Kate. *Women and Their Warlords: Domesticating Militarism in Modern China.* Chicago, IL: University of Chicago Press, 2024.
Miershi. "Guo Dejie hexing you jinri" (How fortunate Guo Dejie is today). *Zhongguo renwu*, no. 12 (1949): 6.
Milburn, Olivia. "Jealousy and Domestic Violence by Women in Early and Medieval China." *T'oung Pao* 107, no. 5 (2021): 555–81.
Ming. "Qingdao shi quzhu Li Benwei" (The city of Qingdao expelled Li Benwei). *Zhengzhi pinglun* 140 (1935): 325.
Minzi. "Nü xuesheng yu rufuren" (Female student and concubine). *Renmin zhoubao* 80, no. 2 (1933): 12–13.
Ni, Chunna. "Jiaoxin yundong yu fanyou yudong bianxi" (A differentiating analysis on Surrendering Your Heart to the Party Movement and Anti-Rightist Campaign). *Zhongnan daxue xuebao (shehui kexue ban)* 18, no. 2 (2012): 55–59.
Ni, Haoran. "Xiaoyuan lian yu jiemei Qing: richang shenghuo shijiao xia de minguo nü xuesheng" (Campus love and sisterhood feelings: Female students under the perspective of daily life in Republican China). In *Funü yu xingbie shi yanjiu* (A study of Women and Gender history) vol 5, 103–116, edited by Yin Yaping and Yi Zhaoyin (Shanghai: Shanghai sanlian shudian, 2021).
Nutao. "Duanping: Tichang guohuo qi zhong de zhang'aiwu: Yitaitai, xiaojie, nü xuesheng" (Short comment: Obstacles for promoting national products: Concubines, misses, and female students). *Shengsheng* 3, no. 6 (1935): 1.
Orly, Selena, and Louise Edwards. "Chastity, Foreign Theories, and National Heritage Reorganization: Hu Shi (1892–1962) Addresses 'The Woman Problem.'" *Nan Nü* 23, no. 2 (2021): 272–300.
Ou-fan Lee, Leo, and Andrew J. Nathan. "The Beginnings of Mass Culture: Journalism and Fiction in the Late Ch'ing and Beyond." In *Popular Culture in Late Imperial China*, edited by Andrew J. Nathan, David Johnson, and Evelyn S. Rawski, 360–98. Berkeley, CA: University of California Press, 1985.
Perkin, Joan. *Women and Marriage in Nineteenth-Century England.* New York, NY: Routledge, 2014.
Perry, Elizabeth. "Moving the Masses: Emotion Work in The Chinese Revolution." *Mobilization: An International Quarterly* 7, no. 2 (2002): 111–28.

Perry, Elizabeth. "The 1960s: Wang Guangmei and Peach Garden Experience." In *The Chinese Communist Party: A Century in Ten Lives*, edited by Timothy Cheek, Klaus Muhlhahn, and Hans van de Ven. Cambridge: Cambridge University Press, 2021, 91–124.

Ping. "Jiaojihua Tang Ying shang yinmu" (Social butterfly Tang Ying went on screen). *Qingchun dianying* 2, no. 5 (1935).

Ping, Jun "Xin xing daode yu yifu duoqi" (The new sexual morality and one husband and multiple wives). *Funü zhoukan*, no. 26 (1925): 2–6.

Pueng Tongs. "China's New Concubines: The Kept Can Be Keepers, Too." *Pacific News Service*, Jan 22, 2004, https://archive.ph/20051230225928/http://news.pacificnews.org/news/view_article.html?article_id=9f82750676b9ab92a2a2b7b558cc3b0e#selection-245.0-245.52, accessed on January 6, 2023.

Qi. "Yitaitai Hu Shi" (Concubine and Hu Shi), *Zhenglun xunkan* 1, no. 16 (1935): 3–4.

Qianjin. "Xiandai jiating bibei changshi: shejiao lijie xuzhi" (The essential knowledge of modern family: points for attention on social etiquette). *Jiating zhoukan* 138 (1937): 31–33.

Qin, Fang. *'Nüjie' zhi xingqi: wan Qing Tianjin nüzi jiaoyu yu nüxing xingxiang jiangou* (The emergence of women's circle: women's education in late Qing Tianjin and the construction of women's images). Beijing: Zhonghua shuju, 2009.

Quan, Hexiu. "Wanqing zhongguo yu xibanya guanxi de yibu hanjian shiliao" (A rare historical record on late Qing China's relationship with Spain). *Shehui kexue yanjiu*, no. 3 (2012): 154–62.

Remick, Elizabeth J. *Regulating Prostitution in China: Gender and Local Statebuilding, 1900–1937*. Stanford, CA: Stanford University Press, 2014.

Relu. "Ziyuan zuoqie zhi nü xuesheng" (A female student willingly became a concubine). *Xinwen bao*, March 14, 1924.

Ropp, Paul. "The Seeds of Change: Reflections on the Condition of Women in the Early and Mid Ch'ing." *Signs* 2, no. 1 (1976): 5–23.

Rudolph, Jennifer M. *Negotiated Power in Late Imperial China: The Zongli Yamen and the Politics of Reform*. Ithaca, NY: East Asia Program, Cornell University, 2008.

Sanmu. "Yiwei guomindang shengzhuxi de yiwai cusi" (A Nationalist provincial governor's sudden death). *Jiancha fengyun*, no. 4 (2007): 66–68.

Schneider, Helen M. "Mobilising Women: The Women's Advisory Council, Resistance and Reconstruction during China's War with Japan." *European Journal of East Asian Studies* 11, no.2 (2012): 213–36.

Seton, Grace Thompson. *Chinese Lanterns*. New York, NY: Dodd, Mead and Company, 1924.

Shan, Patrick Fuliang. "Unveiling China's Relinquished Marital Mode: A Study of Yuan Shikai's Polygamous Household." *Frontiers of History in China* 14, no. 2 (2019): 185–211.

Shangguan Liangxiang. "Li Zongren Guo Dejie lian'ai shi" (A love history of Li Zongren and Guo Dejie). *Neimu xinwen*, no. 4 (1948): 14.

Sujuan, Ouyang "Fu zongtong furen Guo Dejie" (Madame Vice President Guo Dejie). *Zhujiang bao*, no. 165 (1949): 1–2.

Shao, Ziling. "Lüelun xinwenhua yundong shiqi de nannü shejiao" (A brief study on social intercourse between men and women during the New Culture Movement). *Harbin xueyuan xuebao* 26, no. 11 (2005): 105–109.

Shao, Ziling. "Minguo nüzi shejiao shenghuo yu nüxing yishi yanjiu–yi dushi nüxing wei zhuti" (The social life of women and a study on female conciousness in Republican China – using urban women as subjects). MA thesis, Guangxi shifan daxue, Guilin, 2006.

Shi, Xia. *At Home in the World: Women and Charity in Late Qing and Early Republican China*. New York, NY: Columbia University Press, 2018.

Shi, Xia. "Just Like a 'Modern' Wife? Concubines on the Public Stage in Early Republican China." *Social History* 43, no. 2 (2018): 211–33.

Shi, Xia. "The Gendered Politics of Socializing and the Emergence of the 'Public Wife' in Late Qing Diplomacy." *Research on Women in Modern Chinese History* 37 (June 2021): 139–94.

Shi, Xia. "'Madame Wellington Koo': A Diplomatic Wife and A Peranakan Representing and Socializing for Republican China." *International Journal of Asian Studies* 21, no. 1 (2024): 109–27.

Shuyong. "Guanyu 'Chuanxing suoji' de jijuhua" (Some comments on Miscellaneous Notes of My Journey to Sichuan). *Duli pinglun* 215, (1936): 10–12.

Sluga, Glenda and Carolyn James, eds. *Women, Diplomacy and International Politics since 1500*. London: Routledge, 2016.

Sommer, Matthew. *Sex, Law, and Society in Late Imperial China*. Stanford, CA: Stanford University Press, 2002.

Song. "Beijing nüjie paiqie zhi huiyi" (Beijing women's circle held a meeting to discuss excluding concubines). *Shibao*, March 14, 1921, 11.

Strand, David. "Citizens in the Audience and at the Podium." In *Changing Meanings of Citizenship in Modern China*, edited by Merle Goldman and Elizabeth J. Perry, 44–69. Cambridge, MA: Harvard University Press, 2002.

Su, Lili. "Li Zongren rongru yugong de qizi Guo Dejie" (Li Zongren's wife Guo Dejie who shared weal and woe with him). In *Guilin wenshi ziliao* (*Guilin cultural and historical sources*) vol. 24, Li Zongren jiashi (Li Zongren's family history), edited by Wei Hualing, 89–109. Guilin: Lijiang chubanshe, 1993.

Su, Quanyou and Wang Shichao. "Xin shiliao de faxian yu Zhou Ziqi yanjiu de shenhua" (The discovery of new historical materials and the deepening of the study on Zhou Ziqi). *Nanyang ligong xueyuan xuebao* 8, no. 1 (2016): 89–94.

Swislocki, Mark. *Culinary Nostalgia: Regional Food Culture and the Urban Experience in Shanghai*. Stanford, CA: Stanford University Press, 2013.

Tang Naikang. "wo suo zhidao de Lan Ni hunlian ji jiating (shang)" (The Love, Marriage, and Family of Lan Ni as I know, Part I), *Shiji*, no. 5 (2018): 66–69.

Tang Naikang. "wo suo zhidao de Lan Ni hunlian ji jiating (xia)" (The Love, Marriage, and Family of Lan Ni as I know, Part II), *Shiji*, no. 6 (2018): 62–65.

Tang, Xiaobing. "Xiangyata yu bailemen: Minguo Shanghai daxuesheng 'jinwu' shijian kaoshu" (Ivory tower and Paramount: A study on the time of banning social dancing among college students in Shanghai during Republican China). *Kaifang shidai*, May 10, 2007.

Tianzhu. "Nü xuesheng ganzuo xiaoxing, san yitaitai zisha" (A female student voluntarily became a concubine, and the third concubine committed suicide). *Guanghua ribao*, April 24, 1945.

Tong, Qingsheng. "Guo Songtao in London: An Unaccomplished Mission of Discovery." In *China Abroad: Travels, Subjects, Spaces*, edited by Elaine Yee Lin Ho and Julia Kuehn, 45–62. Hong Kong: Hong Kong University Press, 2009.

Tong, Te-kong and Li Tsung-jen. *The Memoirs of Li Tsung-jen*. Boulder, CO: Westview Press, 1979.

Tran, Lisa. "Ceremony and the Definition of Marriage under Republican Law." In *Research from Archival Case Records: Law, Society, and Culture in China*, edited by Philip Huang and Kathryn Bernhardt, 348–53. Leiden: Brill, 2014.

Tran, Lisa. "Sex and Equality in Republican China: The Debate over the Adultery Law." *Modern China* 35, no. 2 (2009): 191–22.

Tran, Lisa. "The Concubine in Republican China: Social Perception and Legal Construction." *Etudes Chinoises* 28 (2009): 119–50.

Tran, Lisa. *Concubines in Court: Marriage and Monogamy in Twentieth-Century China*. Lanham, MD: Rowman et Littlefield, 2015.

Tyau, Min-ch'ien. *China Awakened*. New York, NY: Macmillan, 1922.

Van, Rachel Tamar. "The 'Woman Pigeon': Gendered Bonds and Barriers in the Anglo-American Commercial Community in Canton and Macao, 1800–1849." *Pacific Historical Review* 83, no. 4 (2014): 561–91.

Various authors, "Shejiao teji" (A special issue on social intercourse), *Nüsheng* 3, no. 6 (1934): 11–23.

Wagner, Rudolf. "The *Shenbao* in Crisis: The International Environment and the Conflict Between Guo Songtao and the *Shenbao*." *Late Imperial China* 20, no. 1 (1999): 107–43.

Wakeman, Frederic. "The Civil Society and Public Sphere Debate: Western Reflections on Chinese Political Culture." *Modern China* 19, no. 2 (1993): 108–38.

Wang, Chaoran. "Qie de wenti" (The problem of concubine). *Funü zazhi* 4, no. 3 (1928): 24–25.

Wang, Chengbin et al eds. *Minguo gaoji jiangling liezhuan* (The high ranking military officials of Republican China), Vol 5. Beijing: Jiefang jun chubanshe, 1996.

Wang, Dongjie. "Difang guannian he guojia guannian de chongtu yu huzhu: 1936 nian chuanxing suoji fengbo" (Conflict and Mutual Support between Local Consciousness and National Consciousness: Disturbance on Chuan Xing Suo Ji in 1936). *Sichuan daxue xuebao (Zhesheban)*, no. 1 (2004): 76–86.

Wang, Falong. "Guoji zhengzhi wutaishang 'furen waijiao' de zhongguo shijiao" (The Chinese perspective of the 'Wife Diplomacy' on international political stage). *Zhonggong Jinan shiwei dangxiao xuebao*, no. 5 (2013): 71–74.

Wang, Guimei. "Cong Chen Bailu dao Yin Xueyan–dui jiaojihua de butong shenmei shuxie" (From Chen Bailu to Yin Xueyan – the different asethetic writings on social butterfly). *Jingdian youyue*, no. 1 (2007): 23–28.

Wang, Kaixi. "Lüelun 'renchen wu waijiao' sixiang zai jindai zhongguo de lishi mingyun" (The Fate of The Policy of "never downgrading to a subordinate country that has no diplomatic power" in Modern Chinese History). *Beijing Shifan Daxue xuebao (shehui kexueban)* 215, no. 5 (2009): 62–70.

Wang, Kaixi. *Qingdai waijiao liyi de jiaoshe yu lunzheng* (Negotiations and debates on the diplomatic rituals in the Qing). Beijing: Renmin chubanshe, 2009.

Wang, Richard. "The Cult of *qing*: Romanticism in the Late Ming Period and in the Novel *Jiao hong ji*'." *Ming Studies*, no. 1 (1994): 12–55.

Wang, Shaoxi. *Xiao qie shi* (A history of concubines). Shanghai: Shanghai wenyi chubanshe, 1995.

Wang, Tseng-Tsai. "The Audience Question- Foreign Representatives and the Emperor of China, 1858–1873." *The Historical Journal* 14, no. 3 (1971): 617–26.

Wang, Xiang. "Ru furen de fannao: zhongguo ershi shiji zaoqi youguan naqie de yiji, xushi yu xianshi" (Concubine's troubles: memory, narrative, and reality on taking concubines in early twentieth-century China). MA thesis, Shoudu shifan daxue, Beijing, 2012.

Wang, Zheng. *Women in the Chinese Enlightenment: Oral and Textual Histories*. Berkeley, CA: University of California Press, 1999.

Wang, Zheng. "Wei xuqie wenti zhi Liang Rengong xiansheng" (Questioning Mr. Liang Qichao on the issue of keeping concubines), *Qinghua zhoukan* 24, no. 9 (1925), 9–12.

Wanshi. "Beijing teyue tongxin" (Special correspondence from Beijing). *Shenbao*, June 17, 1923.

Watson, Rubie S. "Wives, Concubines, and Maids, Servitude and Kinship in the Hong Kong Region, 1900–1940." In *Marriage and Inequality in Chinese Society*, edited by Rubie Watson and Patricia Buckley Ebrey, 231–55. Berkeley, CA: University of California Press, 1991.

Widmer, Ellen. "Gentility in Transition: Travels, Novels, and the New Guixiu." In *The Quest for Gentility in China: Negotiations Beyond Gender and Class*, edited by Daria Berg and Chloë F. Starr, 21–44. New York, NY: Routledge, 2007.

Wei, Yi. "Chao yitai zhidu" (Super concubinage). *Nüsheng* 1, no. 1 (1932): 4–5.

Wong, John D. "Fidelity and Sacrifice: The Gender Discourse of Traders in Pre- and Post-Opium War Canton." *Frontiers of History in China* 14, no. 4 (2020): 473–507.

Wong, Max W. L. *Chinese Marriage and Social Change: The Legal Abolition of Concubinage in Hong Kong*. Singapore: Springer, 2020.

Wong, Owen Hong-hin. *A New Profile in Sino-Western Diplomacy: The First Chinese Minister to Great Britain*. Hong Kong: Chung Hwa Book, 1987.

Wong, Shee Ping. *The Poison of Polygamy: A Social Novel*. Translated by Ely Finch. Sydney: Sydney University Press 2019.

Wood, Molly. "Diplomatic Wives: The Politics of Domesticity and the 'Social Game' in the US Foreign Service, 1905–1941." *Journal of Women's History* 17, no. 2 (2015): 142–165.

Wosheng. "Jinshi piping: paiqie" (A critique on recent news: excluding concubines). *Beijing daxue xuesheng zhoukan*, no. 7 (1920): 14.

Wufa. "Wei Wenxiu zajia Wang Kuixuan" (Wei Wenxiu remarried Wang Kuixuan). *Shenbao*, January 21, 1935.

Wu, Shengqing. "Gendering the Nation: The Proliferation of Images of Zhen Fei (1876–1900) and Sai Jinhua (1872–1936) in Late Qing and Republican China." *Nan Nü* 11 (2009): 1–64.

Wu, Yenna. "The Inversion of Marital Hierarchy: Shrewish Wives and Henpecked Husbands in Seventeenth-century Chinese Literature." *Harvard Journal of Asiatic Studies* 48, no. 2 (1988): 363–82.

Wu, Yenna. *The Chinese Virago: A Literary Theme*. Cambridge, MA: Council on East Asian Studies, Harvard University, 1995.

Wu, Yenna. *The Lioness Roars: Shrew Stories from Late Imperial China*. Ithaca, NY: East Asian Program, Cornell University, 1995.

Xiangbeilao. "Zai changchang Chen Hengzhe nüshi de yaowei" (Taste again the medicinal smell of Lady Chen Hengzhe). *Xinxin xinwen*, July 6, 1936.

Xiao, Qing. "Changshi tanhua: oumei shejiao lijie" (A conversation on general knowledge: The social etiquette in Europe and America). *Funü zazhi (Shanghai)* 7, no. 5 (1921): 83.

Xiao, Hongsong and Chen Nana. "Ershi shiji ersanshi niandai Beiping jiaojiwu de sanbo yu shehui fengshang shanbian" (The evolution and spread of ballroom dancing in Beiping during the 1920s-30s). *Hebei daxue xuebao* 40, no. 1 (2015): 96–102.

Xing, Jie. "Dushi, xingbie, biaoyan–yi ershi shiji sanshi niandai zhongguo huaju zhong de jiaojihua wei kaocha duixiang" (City, gender, and performance: A study on the social butterflies in stage plays of 1930s China). *Hangzhou Shifan Daxue Xuebao*, no. 4 (2011): 83–88.

Xiong, Yuezhi. "Daike zhidao: cong waishi huodong kan Shanghai huajie yu zujie guanxi" (The way to receive guests: The relationship between Chinese territory and foreign concessions in modern Shanghai as examined through foreign affairs). *Xueshu yuekan*, no. 7 (2004): 50–55.

Xu, Helin. "Hanghu suxining de funü" (Women from the regions of Shanghai, Hangzhou, Suzhou, Wuxi, and Ningbo). *Funü zazhi (Shanghai)* 13, no. 5 (1927): 5–11.

Xu, Yanwu, Huiying, and Changlin Jiang. "Du xin xing daode hao" (An issue on reading the new sexual morality). *Funü zazhi* 11, no. 4 (1925): 632–640.

Xuedu. "Pian nüxuesheng zuoqie" (Deceiving a female student to be a concubine). *Shijie chenbao*, December 18, 1931.

Yan, Haiping. *Chinese Women Writers and the Feminist Imagination, 1905–1948*. New York, NY: Routledge, 2008.

Yang, Shu. *Untamed Shrews: Negotiating New Womanhood in Modern China.* Ithaca, NY: Cornell University Press, 2023.

Yang, Yuhuan. *Wang Xiulan.* Jinan: Shandong jiaoyu chubanshe, 2001.

Yao, Ming. "Guo Dejie secai xianming" (The colorful Guo Dejie). *Xinwen tiandi,* no. 64 (1949): 19.

Ye, Weili. *Seeking Modernity in China's Name: Chinese Students in the United States, 1900–1927.* Stanford, CA: Stanford University Press, 2001.

Yeh, Catherine Vance. *Shanghai Love: Courtesans, Intellectuals, and Entertainment Culture, 1850–1910.* Seattle, WA: University of Washington Press, 2006.

Yi. "Sanlao xinhun" (Three old men's remarriages). *Shenbao,* March 2, 1935.

Yi, Lü. "Shanxi nüshi zhi ren'ge ziwei" (The self-defense of personhood of Shanxi Women's Normal University). *Minguo ribao.* November 17, 1923.

Ying, Shao. "Jiaojichang zhong de liyi yishu" (The art of etiquette in the sphere of social intercourse). *Funü zazhi* 13, no. 3 (1927): 8–10.

Ying, Qiu. "Qie shi zunao renlei jinhua de zhangai wu" (Concubine is an obstacle to human revolution). In *Fei qie hao* (Abolish Concubinage), edited by Zhu Caizhen, 30.(Hangzhou: Zhejiang shuju, 1922).

Yisheng. "Lun jinri quqie zhe zhi xinli ji suoyi jinzhi zhidao" (An analysis on the psychology of those keeping concubines and ways to ban the custom). *Funü zazhi* 5, no. 7 (1919).

You, Shujun. *Binli dao libin: waishi jinjian yu wanqing shewai tizhi de bianhua* (From guest rituals to courtesies to guests: foreign affairs meetings and institutional changes on foreign affairs in the late Qing). Beijing: Shehui kexue wenxian chubanshe, 2013.

Young Women's Christian Association of China, *First National Convention,* October 19–25, 1923. The YWCA of the U.S.A. Records.

Yu, Hualin. *Nüxing de "chongsu": minguo chengshi funü hunyin wenti yanjiu* (The "reshaping" of women: a study on urban women's marriage issues in Republican China). Beijing: Shangwu yinshuguan, 2009.

Yü. "Oumei shejiao de changshi" (General knowledge on social intercourse in Europe and America). *Guohuo yuekan* (Shanghai), no. 3 (1932): 29.

Zamperini, Paola. "But I Never Learned to Waltz: The 'Real' and Imagined Education of a Courtesan in the Late Qing." *Nan Nü* 1, no. 1 (1999): 107–44.

Zarrow, Peter. "The Origins of Modern Chinese Concepts of Privacy: Notes on Social Structure and Moral Discourse." In *Chinese Concepts of Privacy,* edited by Bonnie McDougall and Anders Hansson, 121–46. Leiden: Brill, 2002.

Zeng, Jize. *Zeng Jize riji* (Journal of Zeng Jize). volume 1. Changsha: Yuelu shushe, 1998.

Zeng, Pu. *Niehai hua* (Flower in a Sea of Retribution). Taibei: Guiguan tushu gongsi, 1983.

Zeng, Yue. "Minguo shiqi nüxuesheng de xingxiang kunjing" (The image dilemma of female students in Republican China). *Shehui kexuejia,* no. 5 (2014): 144–47.

Zhang, Yun. *Engendering the Woman Question: Men, Women, and Writing in China's Early Periodical Press.* Leiden: Brill, 2020.

Zhang, Deyi. *Suishi ying'e ji* (Record of mission to England and Russia). Changsha: Yuelu shushe, 1985.

Zhang, Genghua. *Renlei de xiangrui: Lü Simian zhuan* (Mankind's auspicious sign: a biography of Lü Simian). Shanghai: Huadong shifan daxue chubanshe, 1998.

Zhang, Jing. "Chen Hengzhe zhi sanjin sichuan: jianlun 'Chuanxing suoji shijian.'" (The three entries of Chen Hengzhe to Sichuan: A discussion on the incident of *Chuan Xing Suo Ji*), edited by Zhongguo shehui kexueyuan jindaishi yanjiusuo qingnian xueshu luntan wenji (Young scholar forum of the Modern History Institute of Chinese Academy of Social Sciences), 515–36. Beijing: Shehui kexue wenxian chubanshe, 2007.

Zhang, Rongsheng. "Xianwei renzhi de Li Yuanhong zangli" (The little-known funeral of Li Yuanhong). *Wenshi chunqiu*, no. 3 (1999): 79.

Zhang, Xiaochuan. "Bingdang xuzhang shebian–Cai Jun yu wanqing difang duiwai jiaoshe." (Obstructing Based on Arguments: Cai Jun and the Local Diplomacy in the Late Qing Dynasty). *Zhonghua wenshi luncong* 138, no. 2 (2020): 117–146.

Zhang, Xichen and Zhou Jianren. *Xin xing daode taolun ji* (A collection of discussions on the new sexual morality). Shanghai: Kaiming chubanshe, 1926.

Zhang, Xicheng. "Feiqie lun de qianbo" (The shallowness of anti-concubinage discourse). *Chenbao liu zhounian zengkan*, no. 12 (1924): 59–64.

Zhang, Yaojie. *Hongfen minguo: Zhengxue liangjie de nüquan chuanqi* (The fair sex in Republican China: feminist legends in political and educational circles). Taibei: Xinrui wenchuang, 2013.

Zhang, Yunhe. *Qu zhong ren busan: Zhang Yunhe zi shu wenlu* (The play came to an end, but the audience was not dispersed: A self-account of Zhang Yunhe). Wuhan: Hubei renmin chubanshe, 2009.

Zhang, Yuquan. "Wanqing waijiao shi shang de yidian yiwen: Lun Guo Songtao yu Liu Xihong de guanxi" (A question on the late Qing diplomatic history: A discussion on the relationship of Guo Songtao and Liu Xihong) *Shekewang*, November 2010, 9, accessed December 8, 2022, www.sinoss.net/uploadfile/2010/1130/4913.pdf, 5–10.

Zhao, Xiuli. *Tiaoshi yu Yingdui: Tianzhu jiao hunyin jiating lunli zaihua chujing yanjiu: yi Tianjin "Yishi Bao" wei zhongxin de kaocha (1915–1937)* (Adjustments and Reactions: A study on the situations of Catholic ethics of marriage and family in China: an examination focusing on the newspaper of *Social Welfare* in Tianjin (1915–1937)). Beijing: Zongjiao wenhua chubanshe, 2017.

Zhao, Zichen. "Qiebi zhidu de yinguo he chanchu de fangfa" (The causes and effects of concubinage and servitude). *Jiefang yu gaizao* 1, no. 6 (1919).

Zheng, Leqiang. "Xin zhongguo diyi furen waijiao zhineng tanxi" (An analysis of the functions of First Lady diplomacy of New China). *Caijing zhengfa zixun*, no. 6 (2015): 40–45.

Zhong, Shuhe. "Sai Jinhua zai Bolin" (Sai Jinhua in Berlin). *Luxun yanjiu yuekan*, no. 11 (2002): 76–77.

Zhou, Jiali. "'Diyi furen' waijiao jiazhi yu Peng Liyuan de gonggong waijiao tese" (The value of 'First Lady Diplomacy" and features of Peng Liyuan's public diplomacy). *Chifeng xueyuan xuebao* (Hanwen zhexue shehui kexueban) 37, no. 1 (2016): 144–46.

Zhou, Zheng. "Zhou Ziqi aiqi" (Zhou Ziqi's beloved wife). accessed January 27, 2021, http://blog.sina.com.cn/s/blog_ec5d43bc0102vmwt.html

Zhu, Caizhen. *Fei qie hao* (Abolish Concubinage). Hangzhou: Zhejiang shuju, 1922.

Zurndorfer, Harriet. "Prostitutes and Courtesans in the Confucian Moral Universe of Late Ming China (1550–1644)." *International Review of Social History* 56, no. 19 (2011): 197–216.

Zurndorfer, Harriet. "Wartime Refugee Relief in Chinese Cities and Women's Political Activism, 1937–1940." In *New Narratives of Urban Space in Republican Chinese Cities*, edited by Billy K. L. So and Madeleine Zelin, 65–94. Leiden: Brill, 2013.

Zurndorfer, Harriet. "Polygamy and Masculinity in China: Past and Present." In *Changing Chinese Masculinities: From Imperial Pillars of State to Global Real Men*, edited by Kam Louie, 13–33. Hong Kong: Hong Kong University Press, 2016.

Index

ambassadors, social intercourse, 57
ancestral tablet, respects, 108
Anti-Concubinage Movement (Fei qie yundong), 34, 135
  emergence, 26
  influence, 35
  opposition, 36
  peak, 120
  production, 38
  social/cultural climate generation, 122
  success, 94
anti-concubinage position, 5
anti-imperialism, epistemological framework, 152
Anti-Rightist Campaign, 148
arranged marriages, replacement, 37

backward warlords (defeat), Nationalist (impact), 106
Bai Congxi (Nationalist official), 107
  mother, birthday celebration (public conflict), 112
Bailey, Paul, 14, 97–98
Barlow, Tani, 27
Beijing United Women's Association (Beijing nüjie lianhe hui) (BUWA), 136
Beijing Women's Higher Normal School, opening, 98
Beijing Women's Normal College, 125
Beiyang government, warlord dominance, 72
Beiyang period
  Madame Koo hostess, 82
  presidencies, 78
Bergère, Marie-Claire, 16
Bernhart, Kathryn, 4
betrothal, secrecy, 101

Boxer Indemnity Scholarship, 126
Boyd, Nancy, 130
brothels, tax revenues, 13
Buckingham Palace
  ball (Zeng journal entry), 61
  concert, attendance, 62

Cai Jun
  chahui explanation, 48
  Empress Dowage Cixi ball praise, 66
  guidance, 49
  improvisation, examples, 68
Cai Yuanpei, 6, 34
Cairo Conference, 145
Cao Kun (President of China), 72
  Zhili clique, 78
ceremonial obeisances, absence, 108
chahua hui (social occasions), 21
chahui, 41
  Cai Jun explanation, 48
  concubine attendance, 50
  hosting, 54
  late Qing dynasty hosting, 64
  Liu Xihong description, 47
  London event, 56
  social gatherings, contrast, 49
  term, journal entry, 60
  women, involvement, 47
  Zeng Jize description, 47
Chancellor Otto von Bismarck, Sai Jinhua meeting, 59
Changzhou yuekan (*Changzhou Monthly*), 100
chaste martyrdom (*xunjie*), 89
chastity, double standard (exposure), 5
Chen Bainian (new sexual morality criticism), 36
Chen Hengzhe, 125–27
Chen Yi, 146

INDEX

Chenbao (*Morning News*)
  TCWPA rationale, 131
  Zhang Xichen article, 36
Cheng Liqing, 134
  proposal opposition, 133
Cheng Yu, 26, 29
  argument, corroboration, 30
  trend, observation, 31
Chiang Kai-shek, 21
  Li Yuanhong commemoration, 90
  opposition, 115
  wedding ceremony, 18
Chief of the Guanxi Female Students Northern Expedition Corps, Madame Li Zongren appointment, 114
China
  Communist Party, victories, 116
  Communist takeover, 10
  concubines, classes, 131
  diplomacy, integral ingredients, 69
  educational institutions, opening, 97
  international relations, modernizing, 69
  modernity/backwardness, 79
  modernizing, 98
  Opium Wars defeat, 45
  polygynous, patriarchal hierarchy, 147
Chinese Civil War, 106
Chinese Communist Party, divisions, 141
Chinese concubine, foreign country (presence), 80
Chinese diplomacy, inner circles, 81
Chinese Enlightenment, 68
Chinese feminine sphere, 82
Chinese gender propriety, breach, 42
Chinese Girls' School (Zhongguo nü xuetang), founding, 97
Chinese Legation
  London opening, 51
  reception, 56
Chinese mores, shifts/demands, 42
Chinese social occasions, women (absence), 44
Chinese society, moral depravity, 99
Chinese suffragettes, portrayal, 14
Chinese traditions/customs, improvisations, 68
Chinese womanhood, representation, 82
Chinese women
  invisibility, Macartney disapproval, 44
  public presence, 67
Chinese women/men, separation (Confucian gender codes), 61

Chinese-operated schools, female students (total number), 98
Chow, Shirley T. C., 83
civic organizations, concubine engagement, 41
civil code of 1929–1930, 9–11, 34, 86, 89, 120
civil service examination, women (exclusion), 97
civilized wedding (*wenming jiehun*), 108
class boundaries, transcendence (failure), 135
class loyalties, 130
class status, difference, 140
class struggle, epistemological framework, 152
coeducational reforms, fear (elicitation), 99
cohabiting, 102
college graduates, concubinage (lure), 100
Communist Land Reform Movement, 151
Communist Party
  Fu apology, 149
  victories, 116
concubinage
  abolishment, 131
  abolishment, legal/social efforts, 2
  abolishment efforts, historical forces, 143
  abolition, advocacy, 38
  abolition, question (discussion), 131
  abolition movement, culmination, 34
  "backward" institution, 104
  cessation, Communists (impact), 145
  change, 117
  Chinese custom, criticism, 6
  critique, 120
  curtailing, civil code (impact), 9
  definition, change, 89
  elimination, 95
  Gu Hongming advocacy, 35
  innovations, 73, 105, 143
  institution, corruption, 127
  institution, legal abolition, 142
  institution, manifestation, 137
  late abolition, 11
  lure, 100
  marriage, definition (absence), 9
  outlawing, 12
  prevalence, reasons (identification), 7
  regressive institution, perception, 104
  replacement, advocacy, 5
  shame/barbarism, perception, 7
  social custom, 11
  tongsu hua (popularization), lament, 33

INDEX

trickery, 101
women's press discussion, 41
Concubine is an Obstacle Obstructing Human Evolution article, 28
concubines
  activity (Guangdong Province), 134
  affordability, 7, 32
  auxiliary status, 86
  ban, proposal, 138
  becoming, opportunity, 109
  becoming, practical concerns, 102
  becoming, reasons, 103
  Chinese custom, eradication (efforts), 142
  Chinese history spectrum, 137
  choice, 72
  classes, 131
  concubine servants (*jishi*), 99
  constituency, change, 138
  contaminating influence, fear, 132
  cross-gender mingling skills/social etiquette, learning, 29
  debarring, 130
  degraded women, reference, 132
  degrading influence, 136
  depersonalization, 139
  discrimination, 120
  domestic status, improvement, 25
  domestic status, rise, 25
  domestic/public lives, connections, 41
  economic/social vulnerability, 9
  exclusion, 136
  exclusion, politics, 12
  flourishing, 142
  free love, pursuit, 37
  free will, absence, 136
  hostility, encounter, 38
  illiteracy, 39
  inheritance rights, legal protections (absence), 143
  intervention, Lü Simian proposal, 119
  Japanese household registry removal, 34
  jealousy, 4
  jealousy, topic (media coverage), 139
  killing, mistake (perception), 151
  liberation, 81
  livelihood/status/legal rights, maintenance, 85
  lives, contradictions, 143
  maidservant function, 8
  maintenance, legal entitlement, 86
  members, allowance (problem), 131
  new intellect/new vision, 140
  numbers, allowance, 3
  oppression victims, 137
  pioneering roles, 2
  possession (*xuqie*), 33
  possession, print media depictions, 35
  possession, symbolism, 147
  principal wives, distinctions, 3
  privileges/controversies, 18
  progressive causes, 129
  progressive women's organization exclusion, 43
  progressive women's organizations, 129
  proliferation, caricatures, 105
  public activism, 2
  public activities, 119
  public activities (public reactions), 40
  public appearances, investigation, 143
  public appearances, social protests, 42
  public association, contamination fear, 139
  public engagement, ramifications, 118
  public organization expulsion, 120
  public platform, loss, 143
  public presence, 2
  public presence, controversy, 26
  public presence, sources, 39
  public school exclusion, 43
  public skills, 24
  records, absence, 39
  ren 'ge, loss, 136
  resurfacing, 147
  role, gender difference basis, 24
  role, social wife role (contrast), 22
  service, 118
  social parasites, perception, 28
  social prejudice, protection (absence), 23
  social stigmatization, increase, 12, 25
  social wife role, 50, 119
  social wife role, cessation, 145
  social wife role, rarity, 22
  social/public skills, increase, 142
  status, acceptance, 97
  status, signal, 3
  stereotype, avoidance, 116
  stigmatization, increase, 28
  student, voluntariness, 103
  sympathy, expression (absence), 136
  tainting influence, anxieties, 43
  taking, remedy, 8
  thorough consciousness, 135
  urban public realm, engagement, 41
  widow-concubines, rights/status, 86
  wives, cohabitation, 31

INDEX

concubines of landlords (*dizhu xiao laopo*), 150
concubines of reactionary bureaucrats (*fandong guanliao yitaitai*), 150
concubines of reactionary military officials (*fandong junguan yitaitai*), 150
concubine-taking madness, 33
Confucian gender codes, impact, 61
Confucian gender doctrines, reinterpretation, 138
Confucian gender norms
  rejection, 68
  requirements, 45
Confucian gender separation, principle (upholding), 62
Confucian ideology, foundational principle, 24
Confucian propriety, concern, 71
Cong Xiaoping, 98
conjugal nuclear family
  New Culturalists, impact, 11
courtesans
  competitors/substitutes, 13
  culture, decline, 13, 14
  degraded category, 117
  public appearances, 12
  social/public woman category, 72
cross-gender mingling skills/modern social etiquette, concubine education, 29
cross-gender mingling social culture, 144
cultural differences, basis, 60
Cultural Revolution
  turmoil, escape, 149
  wife diplomacy, 146
culturally-derived misunderstandings, instances, 84

Dagong bao (*L'Impartial*), 101, 121
Daliyuan, monogamy decision, 9
Daoyuan (School of the Way), 138
debased (*jianmin*), social class, 27
degraded women, reference, 132
Deng Yingchao, 146
  communications, 146
Dezhi Middle School, founding, 114
Diana T'sai Lun (Lun Qianru) (concubine), 84
diplomacy, women (advantage), 146
diplomatic socialization process, 69
diplomatic wife, role, 23
Director of the Peiping Field Headquarters (Beiping xingyuan zhuren), Li Zongren appointment, 114
divorce
  avoidance, 101
  freedom, issues, 104
  impossibility, 125
  possibility, 8
  request, 102
doctrinal disagreement, difference, 140
domestic seclusion
  Confucian emphasis, 122
  Confucian gender norms, impact, 12
  Confucian norms, confusion, 60
  Confucian principles, adherence, 22
  marker, change, 11
domestic violence
  incidents, causes, 139
  instances, 4
Dongfang zazhi (*The Eastern Miscellany*)
  editorial, 28
Dream of the Red Chamber (Cao Xueqin), 26
Duli pinglun (*Independent Critic*)
  Chen's husband, response, 128
  co-founding, 126

educated women, white-collar jobs (appropriateness), 102
elite men, courtesan, 73
Embassy Officials Should Not be Allowed to Take Family Members Abroad (court memorial), 55
Embroidery House, invitation, 54
Emperor Wilhelm II, Sai Jinhua meeting, 59
Empress Augusta, Sai Jinhua meeting, 59
Empress Dowager Cixi
  ascension, 45
  birthday ball, Cai Jun (hosting), 65
Empress Dowager Tzu His (Cixi), 84
engagement, lawsuit, 103
excluding concubines (*paiqie*), 134
Exposure of the Official World (Li Baojia), 26

Fei qie hao (*Abolish concubinage*), 28, 100
female sex, refining influence, 44
Female Student Not Tolerated for Having Become a Concubine (*Shibao* article), 123
female students (*nü xuesheng*), 31, 97, 109
  Chinese-operated schools, total number, 98
  concubine occupation, reasons, 42, 95, 105

concubine occupation, visibility, 100
concubine, conflict (focal point), 128
educational institutions, opening, 97
moral deficiencies, 135
public image, change, 99
seduction, 102
visibility (Republican period), 98
feminine social skills/tactics, 72
Feng Yuxiang, 144
Field, Andrew, 13
First Lady of the Republican
   China, 145
First Opium War, 19
   Qing defeat, 64
First World War, economic advantages, 16
Flowers in the Mirror (*Jinghua yuan*) (Li
   Ruzhen), 5
footbinding, defense, 35
foreign country, Chinese concubine
   presence, 80
free companionate marriages, ideal, 8
free love
   marriage (*ziyou jiehun*), 123
   new ideal, 31
   paradigm, issues, 37
   pursuit, 37, 103
   social phenomenon, newness, 103
   trend, 103
free love (*ziyou lian'ai*), experience, 103
free marriage, selection (problems), 104
free social intercourse between men and
   women (*shejiao gongkai*), 15
free women (*ziyou nü*), 137
free-love marriages, usage, 104
friendship, cultivation, 48
Frodsham, J. D., 51, 54
Fu Xiuyun, 151
   interview, 148
Funü gongming (*Women's Resonance*), 92
Funü zazhi (*The Ladies' Journal*), 105
   new sexual morality debates, 36
furen (madam), 26
   social event attendance, 21
   term, usage, 94
   welcoming, idea, 108

Gamble, Sidney, 33
gender differences
   concubine exploitation, 24
   need, 24
   principle, basis, 25
gender equality

espousal, 9
   principles, contradiction, 145
gender hierarchies/stereotypes,
   challenges, 23
gender relations
   Liu Xihong description, 54
   new conceptions, 42
gender separation
   Confucian emphasis, 122
   Confucian gender norms (impact), 12
   Confucian norms, breach, 50
   Confucian norms, transgression, 60
   Confucian principle, legitimacy
      (continuation), 46
   Confucian principles, adherence, 22
   Confucian stricture, breaking, 68
gendered power dynamics,
   transcendence, 25
gender-related etiquette (Western dinner
   parties), 49
gender-segregated groups, 129
girls, sexual behavior control/chastity
   preservation, 99
Glosser, Susan, 21
Gongjin Hui (revolutionary
   organization), 76
good women
   Confucian gender norms,
      requirements, 45
   reputations, 68
Goodman, Bryna, 27, 34, 105, 120, 122
   case study, 122
Grant, Ulysses S. (Shanghai visit), 66
Great Qing Legal Code, basis, 10
Gu Hongming, concubinage advocacy, 35
Gu Weijun (Wellington Koo), 21, 79
   berating, 80
Guan Ruiwu, "Qie zhi yanjiu," 95
Guangdong Province, concubines
   (activity), 134
Guangdong United Women's Association
   (Guangdong nüjie lianhe hui)
   (GUWA)
      founding, 132
      members (gathering), 133
Guangxi Clique, 108
Guangxi Women's Resisting Enemy and
   Assistance Society (Guangxi funü
   kangdi houyuanhui), leadership, 114
Guangzhou Women's Normal School, He
   Zhifen presidential appointment, 121
Guilin Children's Home, establishment, 114

INDEX

Guimao lüxing ji (*My Travels in the Guimao Year*) (Shan Sihili), 64
Guiping (troops, stationing), 108
Guiping Women's Normal School (Guiping nüzi shifan xuexiao), 109
Guiqian Ji (*Writings on Returning to a Life of Seclusion*) (Shan Shili), 64
Guo Dejie, 30
  banquets, attendance, 115
  concubine, role, 106
  concubine status, heightening, 112
  female student, status, 107
  high-profile assistance, 144
  kneeling, insistence, 112
  Madame Li Zongren, title (reference), 113
  Madame Li Zongren title, assumption, 113
  Madame No.2 (*er furen*), 111
  memoir mention, 39
  Nationalist Party congress, election, 115
  public image, establishment, 116
  public profile, enhancement, 115
  public respect, enjoyment, 140
  student turned concubine, 96
Guo Songling, dancing (learning), 18
Guo Songtao
  ambassador appointment, 50
  concubine accompaniment, 42, 46
  concubine role, 58
  Kuo-Ta-jên (Guo daren), 52

Hangzhou (Zhejiang Province), female students (concubinage), 105
Hanyu wailaizi cidian (Chinese dictionary), 27
Harding, Warren (Madame Wellington Koo meeting), 81
Hartini (China visit), 146
He Zhifen
  concubine, 140
  knowledge, 122
  presidential appointment, 121
  resignation letter, 134
Hennessy, John Pope, 61
Hershatter, Gail, 3
Hong Jun
  concubine, accompaniment, 58
  death, 85
Hong Kong, concubinage (outlawing), 10
Hu Shi, 125–26
Hu Ying, 60, 64
Huang Shaohong
  family warmth, providing, 110
  military man, 110
  Nationalist official, 107
  public functions, student accompaniment, 110
Huang Xing, 76
Huayang Women's Association (Huayang funü xiehui), emergency meeting, 127
Hubei Native Place Association in Qingdao (Lüqing hubei tongxianghui), 90
Hubei Women's School of Law and Politics (Hubei nüzi fazheng xuexiao), Yao Wenyu (firing), 1, 121
husbands
  concubines, divorce, 135
  death, concubine existence, 85

Imperial Prince Ch'ing (Qing), 84
independent employment, finding, 123
Inspection Office, public lawsuit filings, 119
international protocol, 45
international relations, modernization, 69
international social intercourse (*guoji shejiao*), 115

Japan, monogamy (legal embracing), 34
Japanese household registries, concubines (removal), 34
Jiang Qing, 146
Jiating zhoukan (*Family Weekly*), 16

kinship structure, 87
Kui Jun (reception hosting), 66

Lady Yu
  challenges, 70
  First Lady of China, 70
  Yuan wife, 70
Land Reform Movement, 150
late Qing dynasty, 64
Li Benwei, 23, 41
  case study, 73
  charity work, 83
  courtesan-turned-concubine, action, 114
  death, 78
  firing, avoidance, 1
  hiding, 78
  legal disputes, 92
  limelight, return, 87
  name, change, 75
  political incident, 78
  privileged concubine, active public life, 77
  public appearance, 76

INDEX

public respect, enjoyment, 140
remarriage, justifications, 88
remarriage, public condemnation, 74
social wife role, 106, 144
social wife role, adaptation/playing, 93
Li Dequan, case study, 144
Li Lian, 134
Li Ruzhen, polygamy critique, 5
Li Xiuwen
  anger, provocation, 112
  banner replacement, Guo demand, 113
  furen, 111
  Li Zongren wife, 107
  Madame No.1 (*da furen*), 111
  memoir, 40
  presence, Guo ignoring, 114
  public appearances, problems, 116
  silence, observation, 109
  son, coexistence (US), 116
  status, security, 111
Li Yinxiang (memoir), 150
  hounding, reason, 151
Li Youlin (birth), 108
Li Yuanhong
  controversy, avoidance, 93
  death, 74
  fate, change, 75
  Li Benwei (social wife), 23
  Li Benwei, concubinage, 1
  main wife, relationship, 74
  President of China, 73
  public events, concubine (absence), 116
  reliance, 114
  travels, 79
Li Zongren, 30, 96
  Madame Li Zongren, title (assumption), 113
  memoir, 39, 107
Li Zongren and I (Tan Ming), 107
Liang Qichao, 5
Liang Shiyi (Beiyang official), 79
Lifan yuan (Board for the Administration of Outlying Regions), replacement, 45
Linfen, PLA attack, 148
Linglong (women's magazine), 16
Link, Perry, 40
Little, Alicia, 67
Liu Bannong, 17
Liu Gong, 76
Liu Shaoqi, 146
Liu Xihong
  chahui description, 47

envoy, 51
  Madame Guo, relationship, 52
  misgivings, sharing, 61
Liu Yi (concubine), 76
Lu Rongting (local ruler, exit), 108
Lü Simian, 100, 119
Lu Xiaoman (*jiaoji hua*), 17
Lu Xun, 125

Macartney, Halliday (Ma Geli)
  family travel advice, 62
  secretary, 51
Macartney, Lord George
  envoy, 44
  women, presence (perception), 44
Madame Chiang Kai-shek, profile, 145
Madame Kuo (Guo), 52
  "oriental" features, media attention, 52
  "Tottering Lily of Fascination," 52
  concubine status, display, 57
  grand reception, 55
  guest reception, 56
  Liu Xihong, relationship, 52
  replacement, 57
Madame Li (Wu Jingjun), 76
  public figure, 92
  public role, 79
Madame Li Zongren
  concubine role, 106
  da furen, public identity (establishment), 113
  Guo role, 144
  Li Zongren *furen*, 96
  name, knowledge, 106
  public knowledge, 117
Madame Liu, disapproval, 72
Madame No. 1 (*da furen*), 111
Madame No. 2 (*er furen*), 111
Madame Wellington Koo
  concubine presence at official parties, resistance, 82
  Harding meeting, 80
  mother, suffering, 82
  Oei Hui-lan, 79
  status/reputation concern, 82
ma-dan (Madame), 49
Majestic Hotel, Chiang Kai-Shek wedding ceremony, 18
Major, Ernest, 56
male-to-female ratio, increase, 13
Manchurian Fengtian clique, 18
Mao Yanwen, 91

Mao Zedong
  jealousy, 146
  movements, upheavals, 152
Margary, Augustus, 51
marriage
  arrangement, 102
  barbaric marriage, nonacknowledgement, 102
  emotional foundation, 101
  free-love marriages, usage, 104
  problems, example, 101
  social mobility, 102
Marriage Law, issuance, 10
Mass Education Movement, 72
masters (relationships), concubines (severing), 10
May Fourth Movement, 80
May Fourth New Culture Movement, 15
  impact, 104
McMahon, Keith, 5, 32
Meiji period, concubinage issue, 34
men, arranged marriages, 103
men/women
  separation, Chinese custom, 55
  state, instability, 104
Merkel-Hess, Kate, 144
military men
  concubines, becoming, 128
  public perception, softening/improvement, 24
  students as concubines, arrangement, 109
Ming dynasty
  concubines, status (elevation), 3
  monogamous marriages, Jesuit insistence, 4
Minguo ribao (*Republican Daily*)
  "Random Thoughts" column, 135
  news reports, 134
  report, 121, 124, 133
  story, 102
Ministry of Rites, replacement, 45
Mistress of Ceremonies, 74
mixed-gender public space, 41
Modern Girls, 99, 137
modernizing conservatives, ambivalence/anxieties, 99
monogamy
  espousal, 9
  legal embracing (Japan), 34
  perfect system, perception, 6
  principle, Daliyuan upholding, 9
  principle, violation, 1
  promotion, 86
moral standing, 139
morality
  cultivation, 136
  pretence, 44

Nanjing Provisional Government of the Republic, establishment, 76
Nanjing Women's Culture Promotion Society (Nanjing shi funü wenhua cujinhui), 92
Nanning, socialization (rounds), 111
National Assembly, formation, 115
national decay, marker, 14
national disgrace (*guoru*), 79
nengli (capabilities), 27
New Culturalists, impact, 11
New Culture Movement, 125, 139
  Chinese Enlightenment, 68
  circa 1915–1923, 7
  impact, 14
  ren 'ge, term (creation), 122
  terms, loftiness/elusiveness, 38
  wife, expectations (changes), 21
New Guangxi Clique, 110
New Life Movement, dancing (crackdown), 17
New Scandal among Women's Circles of Hubei Province, A (*Shenbao* article), 1
new sexual morality (*xin xing daode*), 36
  concept, criticism, 36
  psychological fallout, 37
new women
  activities, symbolic weight, 15
  female students, comparison, 43
  focus, 14
  social reactions, 99
Nie Jigui (reception hosting), 66
Niehai hua (*Flowers in a Sea of Retribution*), 59
ninth sister (*jiu sao*), 112
No. 2 Women's Normal School (Hubei), 77
noble (*gaoshang*) women, 136
North-China Herald, The (ball review), 66
Northern Expedition, 106
  Guangxi/Guangdong provinces, collaboration, 110
  impact, 18
  Madame Li Zongren appointment, 114
  Nationalist Party military campaign, 30
number one concubine of Republican China (*minguo diyi rufuren*), 75

INDEX

Nüsheng (*Women's Voice*)
  editorial, 30
  social intercourse articles, 16

Oei Hui-lan, 21, 79
official parties, concubine presence (Koo resistance), 82
older women, Confucian upbringing, 69
On the Proper Rules of Men and Women Interacting (*Shenbao* editorial), 58
On the Ritual Rule of Separating Men and Women, *Shenbao* editorial, 57
One Hundred Days' Reform, 98
one husband, multiple wives
  institution (*yifu duo qi zhi*), 36
  principle, excuse, 36
Opium Wars, China defeat, 45
oppositional voices, disapproval (expression), 135
oppressed women, suffering (elimination), 132
oral history account, existence, 97
outstanding New Woman, enrollment, 108

Pacification Army, 108
Pan Zihu (struggle sessions), 150
parental authority, individual (triumph), 104
Paris Peace Conference, 80
patriarchal society
  concubine defiance, difficulty, 25
  men/women, inequality, 37
Pearl River Delta, 20
Peking (Beijing), social life, 83
Peking University, women enrollment (allowance), 98
Peng Liyuan, public appearance, 147
People's Court, death sentences, 151
People's Republic of China, founding, 116
People's Liberation Army (PLA), 148–50
personal independence, pursuit, 123
personal realization, 124
personal social connections, importance, 140
physical indisposition, principal wife excuse, 60
poetry societies, 129
Poison of Polygamy, The (*Duo qi du*) (Wong Shee Ping), 6, 85
political consciousness, improvement, 149
political labels, 150
political loyalism, symbols, 22
polygamy
  critiques, 5
  practice, affordability, 32
polygynous households, women (dangers), 4
Prince Henry of Prussia, Shanghai visit, 66
principal wife
  concubines, distinctions, 3
  jealousy, 4
  physical indisposition, public excuse, 60
progressive social organizations, concubine search, 121
progressive women
  anxiety, feeling, 139
  organizations, concubine exclusion, 43
propriety
  cannibalistic rules, 91
  Chinese ideas (contradiction), 55
prostitutes, degraded category, 117
prostitution, commercialization, 13
Pu opera (*puju*), 148
public functions
  concubines/husbands, attendance, 23
public organizations, concubine expulsion, 120
public questions, women (speaking), 132
public schools
  admission, denial, 129
  concubine engagement, 41
  concubine exclusion, 43
purity, importance (overemphasis), 139

qie (concubine)
  term, avoidance, 27
  term, usage, 106
  undifferentiated collective category, 139
qing (passion/love) cult
  attention, 22
  rise, 4
Qing China, defeat, 5
Qing diplomacy, gender/etiquette politics (examination), 143
Qing dynasty
  emperor abdication, 70
  overthrow, 75
  status boundaries, change, 4
Qing Empire
  defeat, 19
  military defeats, impact, 68
  stability, restoration, 58

INDEX

Qing government
    defeat (First Opium War), 64
    defeat (Second Opium War), 65
    international protocol, 45
Qingdao, Wei expulsion, 91
qizhi (temperament), 27
Queen Victoria, Guo (audience), 54

reactionary Nationalist military official (*fandong junguan*), 148
Ren Hongjun, 126
ren'ge (personhood), 38, 89, 99, 128
    absence, 27, 122
    achievement, 123
    consideration, absence, 121
    criteria, meeting, 122
    importance, 124
    possession, absence, 134
    validity, questioning (absence), 138
renchen wu waijiao
    policy (officials in private have no diplomatic power), 64
    principle, death, 65
Rensheng zazhi (*Life Magazine*), concubinage (criticism), 28
Republican bureaucracy, modernizing (increase), 72
Republican China
    concubinage, innovations, 73, 143
    gender politics, 26
    progressive women, differences/divisions, 140
    public sphere, change, 96
    social wife, role, 19
    social women, rise (impact), 12
    urban public realm, concubine engagement, 41
Republican period
    concubine, maintenance (legal entitlement), 86
    concubine constituency, change, 138
    concubine marriage, commonness, 108
    concubines, news reports/articles, 40
    concubines, public activities, 119
    courtesan culture, decline, 13
    female students, visibility, 98
    gender separation, social norm (cessation), 15
    social/ideological flux, 104
revolutionary cause, harm, 110
role model (*mofan*), service (cessation), 1

ru furen (concubine), 26, 114
    term, usage, 21, 93

Sai Jinhua (concubine), 58
Schopenhauer, Arthur, 36
Second Opium War, Qing defeat, 65
Second Sino-Japanese War, 106, 114
secondary wives
    er nai, 147
    membership, refusal, 129
    taking, custom, 33
seduction, 102
self-respect (*zi'ai*), 137
Seton, Grace, 74
    China travels, 120
    China trip, published account, 83
    Madame Koo meeting, 82
    suspicions, 85
sexual services, abstinence, 30
Shaanxi Provincial Assembly, supporters, 124
Shallowness of Abolishing Concubinage, The (Zhang Xichen article), 36
Shan Shili, 63
Shandong Province, transfer, 80
Shanghai
    Prince Henry of Prussia visit, 66
    print media industry, expansion, 40
    Ulysses S. Grant visit, 66
    William Howard Taft visit, 66
Shanghai Daotai (Shanghai Intendant of Circuit), ball (hosting), 65
Shanghai Women's Society (Shanghai *funü hui*) meeting, 135
Shen Congwen, 125
Shen Honglie, 90–91
Shenbao (*Shanghai News*), 56
    lawsuit report, 87
    report, 1, 77
    Wei poem, 91
Shenyang Normal University, 119
Shi Liangcai, assassination, 89
Shibao (*Eastern Times*), 101
    report, 123, 136
Shijie chenbao (*World Morning News*)
    report, 100
shout propaganda (*hanhua*), 148
Sichuan students, concubines (becoming), 127
Sichuan University, 126
Sichuanese, insulting (lawsuit), 128
Sister Guo (*guo sao*), 112

INDEX

social butterfly (*jiaoji hua*), 17
social dancing, 17–18
social degeneration, outcry, 43
social etiquette (*shejiao lijie*), 16
   introduction, 19
social functions (attendance), social wife (requirement), 84
social gathering
   concubine engagement, 41
   format, 47
social interaction, Chinese women (public presence), 67
social intercourse (*shejiao*), *Nüsheng* articles, 16
social mobility, marriage (usage), 102
social occasions, men (attendance), 21
social wife, 12
   appeal, 19
   attendance, requirement, 84
   concubine role, 25, 50
   new role (business world), 20
   novel role, 15
   presence, 46
   requirement, 24
   role, 19
   role, concubine role (contrast), 22
   role, emergence, 24, 46
   role, emergence/rise, 143
social women
   rise, 16
   role/rise, 18
social/cultural climate (generation), Anti-Concubinage Movement (impact), 122
socializing, Western gendered norms (family adjustment), 60
Society to Advance Virtue, The (Jin de hui) (Cai Yuanpei), 34
Song dynasty, status boundaries (change), 4
Song Meiling, 21
   Guo emulation, 115
   Madame Chiang Kai-shek profile, 145
   wedding ceremony, 18
Southern Shanxi Opera Troupe, 148
sphere of socialization (*jiaoji chang*), 17
spiritual teaching, 138
Spring and Autumn period, 57
stand and chat, 48
status boundaries, change, 4
students
   anxiety, 128
   comments, 128

concubinage, trickery, 101
concubine occupation, 99
concubine role, shame, 31
concubine scenarios, 100
Su Fengwen, 51
suicide, report/confirmation, 101
Sukarno (Indonesian President), 146
Sun Ke, Chiang Kai-shek support, 115
Sun Yat-Sen, 77, 115
Super Concubinage (Yiwei editorial), 30
Surrendering Your Heart to the Party (Xiang dang jiaoxin), 148

Taft, William Howard
   gift, student presentation, 67
   Shanghai visit, 66
taidou (leading figure), 77
Taiping Rebellion, suppression, 58
taitai (Mrs.), 26, 127
   name, demand, 30
   need, 111
Taiwan, concubinage (abolition), 10
talisman (*hufu*), excuse, 36
Tan Ming, 107
   Li Xiuwen interviews, publication, 113
Tan Sitong, 5
Tang Kangyu (marriage), 83
Tang Ying (*jiaoji hua*), 17
teacher–student relationship
   impropriety, 124
   public reactions, 125
ten misdeeds (Guo), 55
tezheng (special qualities), 27
Things to Know as an Envoy (*Chushi xuzhi*) (Cai Jun), 48
Tianjin Chinese Women's Patriotic Association (Tianjin nüjie aiguo tongzhihui) (TCWPA), 130
Tianzu hui (Natural Feet Society), founding, 67
Tolstoy, Leo, 36
tongsu hua ("popularization"), lament, 33
Tran, Lisa, 10, 150
Treaty of Nanking (1842), 20
Treaty of Versailles (1919), 80
Tsai Lun (Zai Lun), 84
tu po (old-fashioned woman), 111
Tung Wah Times, 6

uncle's woman (*jiuniang/boniang*), 112
urban literacy rate, increase, 40

INDEX

urban women
  social etiquette, introduction, 19
  social freedoms/mobility, 14
urbanity, public perception, 13

Van, Rachel Tamar, 20
virtue
  importance, overemphasis, 139
  marker, 71
  politics, 120

Wang Guangmei, 146
Wang Kuixuan, 87
Wang Shaoxi, 72
Wang Tao, 5
Wang Xiulan, 148
Washington Naval Conference, 93
  Zhou/concubine attendance, 74
  Zhou/Shunqin attendance, 79
Watson, Rubie, 31
Wei Hongbao (courtesan), 75
Wei Wenxiu, 88
  remarriage, criticism, 88
  remarriage, print media discussion, 89
Western *chahui*, feminine presence (importance), 49
Western dinner parties, gender-related etiquette, 49
Western diplomatic socialization, women (presence), 50
Western gender norms/practices, learning, 81
Western gender-related etiquette, copying, 68
Western powers, Qing court (relationship), 45
white-collar jobs, appropriateness, 102
widow-concubines, rights/status, 86
wife diplomacy (*furen waijiao*), 51, 145–46
wifely virtues, demonstration (continuation), 74
wives
  concubines, cohabitation, 31
  diplomacy (Cultural Revolution), 146
  diplomacy (*furen waijiao*), 51
  divorce, avoidance, 101
  jealousy, topic (media coverage), 139
  New Culture Movement expectations, changes, 22
  older main wives, Confucian education, 29
  secondary wives, taking (custom), 33
  tu po (old-fashioned woman), 111
  violence, sanctioning, 4

wife (*qi*), number (allowance), 3
wife diplomacy (*furen waijiao*), 145
wife-specific responsibilities, 24
xiangxia po (the old woman from the countryside), 111
wives and young ladies' association (*furen xiaojie de lianhehui*), 133
woman question, urgency, 40
Woman's Charitable Society, 83
womanhood, downfall (symbol), 31
womanly skills, study, 97
women
  activists, vulnerability, 132
  collective virtuous reputation, maintenance, 141
  concubines, becoming, 142
  domestic seclusion/segregation, 20
  economic self-reliance, 98
  education, public realm entry, 97
  education/economic independence, 8
  emancipation, 123
  individual autonomy/freedom, absence, 96
  liberation, ability, 135
  liberation, principles (contradiction), 145
  morality, development, 132
  oppressed women, suffering (elimination), 132
  Peking University enrollment, allowance, 98
  public presence, importance, 44
  public visibility, growth, 14
  ren 'ge, loss, 135
  ren 'ge, regaining, 137
  role, importance (increase), 144
  virtue/morality, focus, 124
  virtue/politics, contamination (fear), 28
  virtuous reputations, maintenance, 12
women's circle (*nüjie*), 123
  collaborative work, 76
women's normal school student (*Shifan sheng*), 109
Women's Northern Expeditionary Corps, 76
Women's School of Law and Politics (Nüzi fazheng xuetang), Women's Suffrage Alliance establishment, 77
Women's Suffrage Alliance (Nüzi canzheng tongmenghui), 1, 76
  personnel decision, 1
Wong Shee Ping, 6, 85
Wood, Molly, 23
Wu Jingjun

INDEX

devout Buddhist, role, 74
First Lady of the Land, 74
seclusion, 74
wife, status, 114
Wu Zhimei, 137
GUWA proposal, 133
Wuchang Uprising (1911), 75, 149
victory, government positions, 76
Wuchang, Buddhist temple (coffin placement), 90

Xi Jinping, wife (public appearance), 147
Xi Shangzhen, suicide, 123
Xi'an Women's Normal School (Xi'an nüzi shifan xuexiao), 124–25, 128, 134
Xiandai pinglun (*Modern Review*), new sexual morality debates, 36
xiangxia po (the old woman from the countryside), 111
xingge (disposition), 27
Xinhai Revolution (1911 Revolution), 70, 75
army, women (assistance), 76
initiation, 90
Xinmin bao (*New People*), Chen article reprinting, 126
Xinwen bao (*News Press*) report, 103
Xinwen zazhi (*News Magazine*), 115
Xinxin xinwen (*Latest News*), complaint letters, 126
Xiong Xiling, 71
remarriage, 91
Xu Guangping, 125
Xu Shichang, resignation, 85
Xu Zonghan (concubine), 76

Yao Wenyu (concubine), 140
accountant, 77
firing, 1, 124
job loss, 121
voice, presence, 24
yi niang
aunt mother, 26
term, servant usage, 26
yi taitai (aunt Mrs.), 26
Young Women's Christian Association (YWCA), 129–30
Yu Fengzhi, 21
Yu Hualin, 32
Yu Zhengxie, concubinage critique, 5
Yuan Shikai, 77
death, 77
Presidency, 70

Zeng Guofan, 57
Zeng Jize, 57
Buckingham Palace ball, wife accompaniment, 63
chahui description, 47
chahui organizing, approach, 62
family, 60
family, *chahui* attendance, 63
journal, examination/revision, 63
journal, wife mention (caution), 63
social wife, presence, 46
Western customs, flexibility, 63
Zhang Deyi
guest list preparation, 54
interpreter, 51
Zhang Peilun (attendant reader), 55
Zhang Qian, 146
Zhang Xichen, 36
idealism, 37
Zhang Xueliang, 21
Zhang Zhaohe, 125
Zhang Zhidong (statesman), 75
Zhejiang minbao (*Zhejiang People's Daily*), 37
Zhou Enlai, 146
Zhou Jianren
idealism, 37
new sexual morality debates, 36
Zhou Shunqin, 74
concubine, 79
concubine, case study, 73
concubine, tension/controversy, 106
courtesan-turned-concubine, action, 114
delegation removal, 93
diplomatic mission, 83
"national grace" denunciation, 81
pregnancy, 80
public view, disappearance, 85
social wife role, adaptation/playing, 93
social wife/hostess role, 83
Zhou Ziqi, 73
concubine, accompaniment, 79
concubine, tension/controversy, 106
examination, 79
protests, 93
Zhu Caizhen, 32–33, 100, 104
reputational concern, articulation, 128
Zhejiang minbao (*Zhejiang People's Daily*), 37
Zhu Qihui (Xiong Xiling spouse), 71
Zongli Yamen
creation, 45
memorials, 55

For EU product safety concerns, contact us at Calle de José Abascal, 56–1°, 28003 Madrid, Spain or eugpsr@cambridge.org.

www.ingramcontent.com/pod-product-compliance
Ingram Content Group UK Ltd.
Pitfield, Milton Keynes, MK11 3LW, UK
UKHW022246220326
469255UK00019B/381